Two Studies in the Early Academy

SUNY Series in Ancient Greek Philosophy
Anthony Preus, Editor

Two Studies in the Early Academy

R. M. Dancy

State University of New York Press

Published by
State University of New York Press, Albany

Printed in the United States of America

For information, address State University of New York
Press, State University Plaza, Albany, N.Y., 12246

Production by Dana Foote
Marketing by Fran Keneston

Library of Congress Cataloging-in-Publication Data

Dancy, R. M., 1938–
Two Studies in the Early Academy / R.M. Dancy.
p. cm.—(SUNY Series in Ancient Greek Philosophy)
Includes bibliographical references and indexes.
ISBN 0-7914-0632-6.—ISBN 0-7914-0633-4 (pbk.)
1. Plato—Contributions in concept of Ideas. 2. Plato—Influence.
3. Idea (Philosophy)—History. 4. Eudoxus, of Cnidus, ca. 400-ca.
350 B.C.—Contributions in concept of Ideas. 5. Speusippus—
Contributions in concept of Ideas. 6. Philosophy, Ancient.
I. Title. II. Title: 2 studies in the early Academy. III. Series.
B398.I3D36 1991
111′.0938—dc20 90-40610
CIP

Contents

STUDY II. ANCIENT NON-BEINGS: SPEUSIPPUS AND OTHERS

Preface

These two studies began as journal-length papers.

An earlier draft of Study I, already over that length, was distributed to members of the Society for Ancient Greek Philosophy in the Fall of 1984. There was discussion of it at the December meeting of that society in conjunction with the Annual Meeting of the Eastern Division of the American Philosophical Association. Some parts of the present version correspond to nothing in that one; others bear varying degrees of resemblance.

An earlier version of Study II appeared in *Ancient Philosophy* 9 (1989): 207–243; my thanks to the editor, Ronald Polansky, for permission to reprint. The present version contains considerably more material, and there has been a good deal of revision as well. I hope I have got things straighter by now.

Two things (at least) need explaining. First, I have tried to include very full documentation for the secondary material I cite: I have given page references for every publication of each work available to me. Second, I have included the Greek text for all the passages I translate (and, conversely, I have tried to have a translation for all the Greek: my apologies if I have missed any). Both these features will seem fussy to some.

But the inclusion of multiple references to the several publications of a single article will be of use to anyone who has to work with a library that is not quite up to snuff when it comes to Greek philosophy. There are a great many such libraries, and a great many of us teach at institutions where there are such libraries. Interlibrary loan is a second best, but it takes time. I hope my fussiness on this score will save somebody some time.

And, at least in a book in which space considerations are not paramount, the inclusion of the Greek makes the task easier for any reader who can make use of it. My model here has been Furley's *Two Studies in the Greek Atomists* (Princeton, N.J.: Princeton University Press, 1967), a book that is a delight to use in part because when you get it off the shelf you know that you will not need a half-dozen Greek texts along with it.

The texts used are, for Plato, Burnet [1900/07], for Aristotle, Bekker [1831] (see the Bibliography), and for other authors as indicated when they are referred to. I have indicated any departure from these, except for matters of punctuation, in notes.

The translations are extremely stodgy, even overliteral. I am not trying to present stand-alone translations: they are intended to show as clearly as possible how I have understood (or misunderstood) the Greek. They make slow and sometimes painful reading. So does the Greek.

It is a pleasure to acknowledge some debts; I wish I could acknowledge them all.

John Anton not only got me into this by teaching the first course on Greek philosophy I ever took, directing my undergraduate honors thesis, and so on, he commented on an early draft of Study I at a meeting of the Florida Philosophical Association in the Fall of 1984. I am grateful for his comments on that occasion and for the suggestion he made then that I turn the essay into a monograph.

Tony Preus made the same suggestion when he found that a somewhat later version of Study I was too long for inclusion in *Essays in Ancient Greek Philosophy IV.* His prodding is directly responsible for the existence of this book.

Dan Devereux is mentioned frequently in the notes to Study II. He read a draft of it and gave me written comments that have been invaluable. Also, he and I have spent a good deal of time talking about related issues. His influence is there even where he is not named.

Steve Strange is mentioned frequently as well; I am grateful for his written comments on the whole manuscript. His substantive questions led to a number of reformulations, and his painstaking comparison of the Greek of *Universal Math* iv with my English version of it resulted in many improvements.

My wife Margaret has spent many hours on these studies: checking the English, the Greek, and the sense, organizing the computer files so that a single document emerged, and so on. She has also put up with a good deal of distraction on my part, if not downright bad temper. Her influence, too, is pervasive.

There have been any number of people who have asked pertinent questions, voiced telling objections, and generally helped by being obstreperous. Among those many, I must list at least Merrill Hintikka and George Thomas. But my thanks to all.

INTRODUCTION

The two essays that follow are concerned primarily with the metaphysical ideas of two important figures in Plato's Academy, Eudoxus and Speusippus, respectively.

Here are some dates,[1] for orientation:

Plato:	428/7–348/7
Speusippus:	*ca*. 407–339
Xenocrates:	*ca*. 396–314
Eudoxus:	b. 408/390, d. 356/338
Aristotle:	*ca*. 384–322

It is not known exactly when the Academy was 'founded'; anyway, it was an entity of some sort by 367, when Aristotle arrived as a 'student.' The quotation marks are because we do not even know what sort of an institution it was. It may have started as an informal group of people with common interests that gradually grew into something more. By the time of Plato's death, it had enough of a structure that he could be thought of as its 'head' or 'leader.'

Aristotle stayed for about twenty years. On the death of Plato,[2] Speusippus, Plato's nephew, became the next head of the Academy, and Aristotle and Xenocrates left to do some traveling. There need not have been any animosity on anybody's part in all this, although in later antiquity stories delight in such stuff like tabloid newspapers about celebrities. Sometimes people are amazed that Aristotle was not named head of the Academy after Plato. But, in the first place, we do not know if he applied for the post. And, second, he plainly did not have seniority: Speusippus and Xenocrates were older than he, and had presumably been associates of Plato's for longer.

Eudoxus was a mathematician, astronomer, geographer, and so on, whose connection with the Academy is not entirely clear. His dates are the hardest to fix, as a glance at the list above will illustrate. We need not worry about that here. He apparently was active in the Academy in 367, the year Aristotle arrived.[3]

No complete work by either Eudoxus or Speusippus has survived. Not even a sentence of Eudoxus pertinent to the idea of his we shall be discussing has survived, and if there is anything as long as a whole phrase we are in no position to isolate it (ancient Greek made no use of quotation marks). The situation is a little better with Speusippus, but only a little. What we have to go on is secondhand material in later authors. Aristotle is the first and most important of these. I will be devoting much space to discussion of the sources.

What unifies these essays is a theme. The Academy was not a source of dogma, but of discussion. To explain this, I am going to be dogmatic: I shall make a number of assertions that I believe to be true, but I shall not try here to argue for them. They need argument. Some of that is provided in the studies to follow, but, particularly where Plato is concerned, there will be a great deal left over.

Plato, in the middle of his philosophical career, came to espouse a metaphysical theory, usually called 'the Theory of Forms.' This located the foundation of reality in abstract entities, called *Forms*: the good, the beautiful, the large, the equal, and so on. These alone could be thought of as fully real; everything else was dependent for its existence on them.

The theory was not a complete success. Plato himself participated in exposing its shortcomings, in the dialogue *Parmenides* and no doubt constantly in discussion around the Academy. The reasons for its shortcomings, and what to do with it next, or what to replace it with, were much discussed. Different contributors to the discussion went different ways.

Plato himself, I think, tried to revise the theory by sacrificing some things and embedding what was left in a larger theory according to which the Forms were associated with or even identified with *numbers*, which in turn were derived from a pair of higher-level entities usually referred to as the One and the Indefinite Dyad.

Eudoxus tried out a simpler scheme, treating the Forms as physical things ingredient in the entities they inform. This is the subject of the first of my two studies.

Aristotle took a much more complicated path: he has a Theory of Forms, all right, but his Forms are in some sense in the things they inform—in some sense unlike Eudoxus'. This will be touched on in the first study. But fuller consideration of it requires consideration of the mate to 'Form' in Aristotle: matter. And it also requires consideration of an alternative translation that the word for 'Form' (namely, εἶδος) gets in Aristotle: 'species'. That requires consideration of Aristotle's biology. None of this takes place here.

Speusippus scrapped (what I shall sometimes call) the High Platonic Theory of Forms, as did Aristotle. But he went for the promotion of numbers—at least certain kinds of numbers—and for the idea of deriving them from a pair of first principles. In his case, they were the One and Plurality. And he also took the at first sight outrageous view that the One did not exist. This is the subject of my second study.

Given the extreme shortage of material, I am going to be doing a lot of conjecturing. I do not wish to conceal that fact: to make it sound as if I were proving anything. But I certainly shall be *arguing* for things; the conjecture is not just whistling in the dark. And I find it exciting. I hope others will as well.

STUDY • I

PREDICATION AND IMMANENCE: ANAXAGORAS, PLATO, EUDOXUS, AND ARISTOTLE

1. INTRODUCTION

A theory of predication invokes immanence, as I shall use the word, if it explains why snow is white by introducing something in snow that accounts for its being white.

Aristotle's theory of predication in the *Categories* is partly immanentist: it explains what we may call accidental predications (Aristotle does not use this terminology in the *Categories*) in terms of immanence. A stick is white because white, or, better, whiteness, is in the stick, but Socrates is a man not because of anything in him. In the *Categories*, nothing explains the latter predication: Socrates just is a man. Elsewhere, with the apparatus of matter in place,[1] it is the fact that Socrates is a composite of a form or essence and matter that makes him a man: then there is something that is in him that accounts for his being a man, and the theory is more thoroughly immanentist.

In the *Categories*, Aristotle says (2. 1a24–25): "By 'in a subject' I mean what, belonging in something not as a part, [is] incapable of being separately from that in which it is" (ἐν ὑποκειμένῳ δὲ λέγω ὃ ἔν τινι μὴ ὡς μέρος ὑπάρχον ἀδύνατον χωρὶς εἶναι τοῦ ἐν ᾧ ἐστίν). My object here is to shed some indirect light on this passage. It has aroused considerable controversy;[2] what I have to say does not bear directly on that controversy. The only point touching the controversy that is relevant is this: these lines do not define the 'in' of immanence. To do that, they would have to distinguish being in a subject from being said of a subject; but it is equally true of something that is said of a subject that it is not a part of that subject and is incapable of existing separately from that of which it is said.[3] As Aristotle later tells us (5. 2b5–6b):[4] "So without there being primary substances [it would be] impossible for any of the other [things] to be: for all the others are either said of these as subjects or in these as subjects" (μὴ οὐσῶν οὖν τῶν πρώτων οὐσιῶν ἀδύνατον τῶν ἄλλων τι εἶναι· πάντα γὰρ τὰ ἄλλα ἤτοι καθ' ὑποκειμένων τούτων λέγεται ἢ ἐν ὑποκειμέναις αὐταῖς ἐστίν).

My suggestion is the following. The comment in 1a24–25 is a disclaimer. It responds to an immanentist theory of predication under discussion in the Academy, according to which the something immanent in snow that makes it white is a physical ingredient. This theory was an idea of Eudoxus'. Aristotle was sympathetic to the position, and his own sounded a lot like it. But his was not that position, and so it was important to distance himself from it.

The idea that snow is white because white or whiteness is a constituent of snow has one obvious drawback: it cannot be generalized to cover all the predicates that attach to things. It will not cover the predicates that are not physical ones: we can hardly say that Socrates is ironic because he has irony-stuff in him.[5] Nor will it cover all the physical predicates: we cannot say that Socrates is a small man because he has some smallness-stuff and some man-stuff mixed in with the rest of his properties.

There are really two different types of counterexample to this theory: we cannot say that Socrates is small or ironic because he has some small or ironical stuff in him, because 'small' and 'ironic' do not characterize types of stuff at all; we cannot say he is a man because he has some man-stuff in him, because a man is what he *is*, not something in him. Pursuit of this distinction would head us in the direction of distinguishing *categories* of predicate. I shall not here pursue it; I shall lump all the counterexamples under one head and call the resulting objection the *Drawback*.

I shall initially not pay much attention to the Drawback; it comes in for more detailed treatment at the hands of Plato, and this is discussed in the last section of this study. Until then, we can think of Eudoxianism as a partial theory, intended to explain certain physical predications and elsewhere silent. There will be a few times when we shall have to take note of its incompleteness along the way.

Here is a disclaimer of my own. According to a scholarly tradition still current,[6] when Aristotle arrived and enrolled as a freshman at the Academy, Plato was off in Sicily trying to make a philosopher out of a king and had left Eudoxus in charge. That tradition rests on a single late text, already known to contain inaccuracies, which has been emended, on the basis of a Latin translation, to *make* it say this, and the result of the emendation does not clearly say this anyway.[7] It could, for all anyone knows, be right; perhaps it would even be pretty, given what I am suggesting.[8] But we cannot trust it, and anyway it would make no difference: Eudoxus, at some point or other in the relevant period, hung around the Academy and, apparently, made some contribution relevant to our understanding of what was going on.[9]

To get in on the ground floor of immanentism, we must go back to Anaxagoras. We shall find Aristotle bracketing Anaxagoras and Eudoxus, and

Aristotle's objections against Anaxagoras will be essential background for understanding his objections against Eudoxus, so this is not merely a Sunday excursion.

2. ANAXAGORAS

Anaxagoras does not clearly have a name for what Aristotle would call his *principles* (ἀρχαί; e.g., *Physics* A 1. 184a11, 16, etc.), *underlying bodies* (see σῶμα τὸ ὑποκείμενον, *Physics* A 4. 187a13), or *elements* (στοιχεῖα; e.g., *De caelo* Γ 3. 302a32). He speaks of 'all things' (πάντα χρήματα or just πάντα; e.g., 59B1, DK ii 32.11, 12f.). Aristotle calls them, or some of them, *homoeomers* (ὁμοιομερῆ 187a25, 302a31–32), where a *homoeomer* is something of which any part is of the same type as the whole, as he defines it elsewhere (*De generatione et corruptione* A 1. 314a20), specifically commenting on Anaxagoras' view.[10] But I can neither translate nor pronounce 'homoeomer', and, besides, the term probably does not go back to Anaxagoras.[11] In *De caelo* Γ 3. 302a31–b2 Aristotle suggests, and in *in De caelo* (Heiberg 1893) 603.17–19 Simplicius says, that Anaxagoras called them *seeds* (σπέρματα); this word in fact occurs in Anaxagoras fr. 4, and I think what Aristotle suggests and Simplicius states is the truth. But this is controversial,[12] and the controversy is not of much relevance here. So let us just speak of 'ingredients'.

Anaxagoras' views about these ingredients and the mixtures they compose were relevant to the concerns of Plato's Academy,[13] for Anaxagoras accounts for the truth of "snow is white" by making white present in snow as a part of it; he even says that snow 'partakes of' white.[14] But, in addition, the white cannot be separated from the snow.

Aristotle interprets this as an immanentist theory of predication. He thereby interprets Anaxagoras in terms that were unavailable to Anaxagoras. There is no more wrong with that than there is with our stating the views of Anaxagoras in English rather than Greek: it does not mean that Aristotle's interpretation is incorrect.[15] You might take the present section as an effort, not to understand Anaxagoras, but to understand how Aristotle understood Anaxagoras; this is all we really need to get at the positions we are ultimately after, those of Eudoxus and Aristotle, anyway. That way it does not matter as much as it might whether Aristotle has read Anaxagoras rightly. In fact, I think Aristotle's interpretation is correct, and I should suppose that the burden of proof is on anyone who would deny that it is. But I do not insist on this.

Anaxagoras says, in 59B6 (DK 35.13–20, from Simplicius *in Physica* 164.26–165.1):

> And since the portions of the great and the small are equal in plurality, so also all [things] would be in[16] everything; and they cannot be separately,[17] but all things

partake of a portion of everything. Since there cannot be a least, it is not possible [for anything] to be separated,[17] or to come-to-be by itself, but just as in the beginning also now all things are together. In all things there are present[16] many things, equal in plurality in the greater and in the smaller of the things being disjoined.[18].

καὶ ὅτε δὲ ἴσαι μοῖραί εἰσι τοῦ τε μεγάλου καὶ τοῦ σμικροῦ πλῆθος, καὶ οὕτως ἂν εἴη ἐν παντὶ πάντα· οὐδὲ χωρὶς ἔστιν εἶναι, ἀλλὰ πάντα παντὸς μοῖραν μετέχει. ὅτε τοὐλάχιστον μὴ ἔστιν εἶναι, οὐκ ἂν δύναιτο χωρισθῆναι, οὐδ' ἂν ἐφ' ἑαυτοῦ γενέσθαι, ἀλλ' ὅπωσπερ ἀρχὴν εἶναι καὶ νῦν πάντα ὁμοῦ. ἐν πᾶσι δὲ πολλὰ ἔνεστι καὶ τῶν ἀποκρινομένων ἴσα πλῆθος ἐν τοῖς μείζοσί τε καὶ ἐλάσσοσι.

In 59B8 (DK ii 36.14–16, from Simplicius *in Physica* 176.29 with 175.12–14), he says: "The things in the one cosmos are not separated,[17] not cut off from each other with an ax, neither the hot from the cold nor the cold from the hot" (οὐ κεχώρισται ἀλλήλων τὰ ἐν τῷ ἑνὶ κόσμῳ οὐδὲ ἀποκέκοπται πελέκει οὔτε τὸ θερμὸν ἀπὸ τοῦ ψυχροῦ οὔτε τὸ ψυχρὸν ἀπὸ τοῦ θερμοῦ).

In B12 (at DK ii 39.2–4 = Simplicius *in Physica* 157.1–2), he says: "But nothing is totally disjoined[18] and disconnected[19] from anything else except mind" (παντάπασι δὲ οὐδὲν ἀποκρίνεται οὐδὲ διακρίνεται ἕτερον ἀπὸ τοῦ ἑτέρου πλὴν νοῦ).

"Just as in the beginning also now all things are together": he thinks there once was a Cosmic Soup[20] in which everything was mixed. In that Cosmic Soup, "when all [things] were together, nothing was manifest" (B1, 32.12–13 = Simplicius *in Physica* 155.28: καὶ πάντων ὁμοῦ ἐόντων οὐδὲν ἔνδηλον ἦν); specifically, "no color was manifest" (B4, 34.17–18 = Simplicius *in Physica* 156.4–5, 34.21–22: οὐδὲ χροιὴ ἔνδηλος ἦν οὐδεμία). But we want him to tell us why snow is white. So we can pass up the Soup course, except for one point.

The ingredients that were all together in the Cosmic Soup and still are all together are "unlimited in plurality" (ἄπειρα . . . πλῆθος B1, 34.11 = Simplicius *in Physica* 155.27); Aristotle says that Anaxagoras made the ἀρχαί unlimitedly many (*Metaphysics* A 3. 984a11–13; *Physics* A 4. 187a25, 26–27, Γ 3. 203a19–20, etc.).[21] So there is no end (or beginning, or middle) to the list of features covered by Anaxagoras' theory of predication; as Aristotle will tell us, the accidents of a thing are unlimited (ἄπειρα γὰρ ἂν τῷ ἑνὶ συμβαίη, *Physics* B 5. 196b28–29). Even so, it is only a partial theory. For the Cosmic Soup, which had all the ingredients in it, had no horses or men or turnips.[22]

Here we first encounter the Drawback mentioned at the outset. And, because Anaxagoras' position is a response to Parmenides' denial of the possibility of anything's coming-to-be, the problem is acute, for that denial is completely general.

But this is the norm for the fifth-century cosmologists: Empedocles and the atomists also respond only partially to Parmenides' challenge. So, for the present, let us ignore the Drawback.

"Since there cannot be a least, it is not possible [for anything] to be separated, or to come-to-be by itself": if there were atoms of white or cold, one could imagine detaching one. He thinks there are not: there is no least quantity of any ingredient. But this does not show the impossibility of isolating some pure white or pure cold; it merely denies one of the conditions under which that would be possible.[23] Anaxagoras' argument for the inseparability of white must be sought elsewhere.

"All" things are "in everything"; "all things partake of a portion of everything": snow has white in it, along with everything else; everything else has snow, and white, and everything else in it. This, the "Principle of Universal Mixture,"[24] is the proximate explanation for the inseparability of Anaxagoras' ingredients: there is no getting the white out of the snow because then there would be white that had nothing else in it and snow that had no white in it.

So the question is, Why does Anaxagoras accept Universal Mixture? Or rather, why does Aristotle think Anaxagoras accepted it?[25]

After commenting, in *Physics* A 4, that Anaxagoras employs unlimitedly many principles, Aristotle gives an explanation (187a26-b2):

> Anaxagoras seems to have thought them unlimited in that way because of his taking the opinion common to the physicists to be true, that nothing comes-to-be out of what is not (for because of this they[26] say 'all things were together', and 'the coming-to-be of any sort of thing consists in being altered',[27] while the others[28] [make it] combination and disconnection[19]); and again, from the fact that the contraries come-to-be from each other; therefore they were present in[29] [it before]; for if everything that comes-to-be necessarily comes-to-be either from things that are or things that are not, and of these [alternatives], that it comes-to-be from things that are not is impossible (for about this all those concerned with nature thought the same), they thought that the remaining [alternative] followed of necessity, and it comes-to-be from things that are and are present in[29] [it before], but imperceptible to us because of the smallness of their bulks. Which is why they[26] say that everything is mixed into everything, because they see everything coming-to-be from everything.

> ἔοικε δὲ 'Αναξαγόρας ἄπειρα οὕτως οἰηθῆναι διὰ τὸ ὑπολαμβάνειν τὴν κοινὴν δόξαν τῶν φυσικῶν εἶναι ἀληθῆ, ὡς οὐ γινομένου οὐδένος ἐκ τοῦ μὴ ὄντος (διὰ τοῦτο γὰρ οὕτω λέγουσιν, ἦν ὁμοῦ [τὰ] πάντα, καὶ τὸ γίνεσθαι τοιόνδε καθέστηκεν ἀλλοιοῦσθαι, οἱ δὲ σύγκρισιν καὶ διάκρισιν)· ἔτι δ' ἐκ τοῦ γίνεσθαι ἐξ ἀλλήλων τἀναντία· ἐνυπῆρχεν ἄρα· εἰ γὰρ πᾶν μὲν τὸ γι-

> νόμενον ἀνάγκη γίγνεσθαι ἢ ἐξ ὄντων ἢ ἐκ μὴ ὄντων, τούτων δὲ τὸ μὲν ἐκ μὴ ὄντων γίνεσθαι ἀδύνατον (περὶ γὰρ ταύτης ὁμογνωμονοῦσι τῆς δόξης ἅπαντες οἱ περὶ φύσεως), τὸ λοιπὸν ἤδη συμβαίνειν ἐξ ἀνάγκης ἐνόμισαν, ἐξ ὄντων μὲν καὶ ἐνυπαρχόντων γίνεσθαι, διὰ μικρότητα δὲ τῶν ὄγκων ἐξ
> **187b** ἀναισθήτων ἡμῖν. διό φασι πᾶν ἐν παντὶ μεμῖχθαι, διότι πᾶν ἐκ παντὸς ἑώρων γινόμενον.

Aristotle's presentation of the argument is not orderly, but it is clear. The overarching premise is the one 'common to the physicists', which Aristotle formulates twice in this passage (a28–29, 33–34):

> (1) Nothing can come-to-be from what it is not already.[30]

Aristotle elsewhere (*Physics* Γ 4. 203a28–29) puts Anaxagoras' view as "τὸ γιγνόμενον ἐκ τοῦ τοιούτου γίνεται σώματος"; this might be translated 'what comes-to-be comes-to-be from the sort of body [it is]';[31] it is another version of (1).

In our text, Aristotle adds to (1) (187b1–2):

> (2) Everything comes-to-be from everything,

or perhaps, referring again to Aristotle's account elsewhere (203a24):

> (2*) Anything comes-to-be from anything,

no doubt, as Simplicius explains, "even if not immediately, still, in due course" (εἰ καὶ μὴ ἀμέσως, ἀλλὰ κατὰ τάξιν, *in Physica* 460.13). Aristotle concludes:

> (3) Everything (or anything) already is everything (or anything).

But nothing *seems* as if it were everything: there is a difference between being something and manifestly being something, between being something and both being and seeming to be something. Aristotle next says (*Physics* A 4. 187b2–7):

> but [they say things] show up and are named differently from each other on the basis of that which most exceeds in plurality in the mixture of the unlimited things; for [they say] there is no whole purely white or black or flesh or bone, but whatever each thing has most of, that the nature of the thing is taken to be.

> φαίνεσθαι δὲ διαφέροντα καὶ προσαγορεύεσθαι ἕτερα ἀλλήλων ἐκ τοῦ μάλισθ' ὑπερέχοντος διὰ πλῆθος ἐν τῇ μίξει τῶν ἀπείρων· εἰλικρινῶς μὲν γὰρ ὅλον λευκὸν ἢ μέλαν ἢ γλυκὺ ἢ σάρκα ἢ ὀστοῦν οὐκ εἶναι, ὅτου δὲ πλεῖστον ἕκαστον ἔχει, τοῦτο δοκεῖν εἶναι τὴν φύσιν τοῦ πράγματος.

Here he is accurately representing Anaxagoras; in 59B12 (at DK ii 39.6–7 = Simplicius *in Physica* (157.4) we read: "but whatever [things] there is most of in [anything], these [things] each one thing is and was" (ἀλλ' ὅτων πλεῖστα ἔνι, ταῦτα ἐνδηλότατα ἓν ἕκαστόν ἐστι καὶ ἦν). This principle[32] needs a bit of commentary:[33] snow is white because white predominates in the mixture that is snow, but that does not mean every feature apart from white is blanked out, for snow is also cold. It must be that, in the mixture that is snow, white predominates over black, and cold over hot.

At this rate, the features the theory is to account for must come in contrary pairs: for a feature to predominate, it must have something to predominate over.[34] It is not obvious how this could be made to apply to some of the features most popularly associated with Anaxagoras' doctrine: flesh, bone, hair, bread, and so on (see, for these examples, *De caelo* Γ 3. 302a32–b1, *De generatione animalium* A 18. 723a10–11, Simplicius *in Physica* 460.15–17 = DK ii 18.14–16, 'Aëtius' i.3.5 at DK ii 18.34–36). But if the scholiast on Gregory of Nazianzus is not lying,[35] Anaxagoras said (59B10, DK ii 37.6–7):

"For how could hair come-to-be from not hair and flesh from not flesh?" (πῶς γὰρ ἂν ἐκ μὴ τρίχος γένοιτο θρὶξ καὶ σὰρξ ἐκ μὴ σαρκός;). And then he was in possession of a cheap device for manufacturing contraries ad lib.

3. PLATO

Plato had some things to say about forms. And some of the things he said sound immanentist.[36]

3.1. Immanentist Language in the Early Dialogues

There is a group of immanentist passages in the early dialogues. They sometimes have been taken as showing that Plato once held an immanentist theory of forms.[37] They do not show that. In these early passages, Plato is arguing about matters other than metaphysics (namely, ethics or something like ethics)[38] and drawing such distinctions as he thinks he needs to make points about these. His arguments require no backing by any metaphysical system, whether immanentist or separatist.[39]

For example, in the initial conversation in the *Hippias Major*, the word καλόν and its cognates are used with great freedom. It occurs to Socrates to ask Hippias what he thinks it means, or, if you prefer, what the beautiful is. He sets up this question by first asking Hippias whether he thinks there is such a thing as the beautiful (287c4, c6–8, d1–2). This does not require anyone to reflect on the ontological status of the beautiful: it simply nails down the topic for discussion.[40]

But philosophers sometimes do fall to reflecting about ontology. They ask, What is the status of meanings, or essences, or universals, or intentions, or forms, or ideas, or the general, or whatever? Are such things to be identified with, or distinguished from, any of the ordinary things we encounter here on the ground? And so on. And when they do, their starting point for understanding is likely to be just such conversations as the one between Socrates and Hippias, or those we are about to notice. The question takes the form: What precisely is the *status* of this thing whose existence Socrates and Hippias are agreeing on? And, when Socrates and one or another of his interlocutors agree that it is because courage, say, is in someone that that person is courageous, what weight is to be attached to the word *in*? This is the sort of question Plato must at some point have asked himself: How seriously should I take Socrates', or my own, language in places like these?

The occurrences of ἐν in *Laches* 191e5, e6, e10, 192a2, a3, a5, a9, b6, b7 are sometimes cited.[41] We cannot count all of these: at 191e5, e6, 192b6, b7 what courage, cowardice and quickness are *in* are not the people or even the actions that are courageous, cowardly, or quick, but the circumstances and conditions in which people do courageous, cowardly, or quick things. Still, in 192a1–6 Socrates says:

> But I mean it like this: just as if I were to ask what is quickness, which we happen on in running, in zither-playing, in speaking, in learning, and in many other things, and we possess something of it worth mentioning in the actions of our hands, legs, mouth, voice, or understanding.
>
> 'Αλλ' ὧδε λέγω, ὥσπερ ἂν εἰ τάχος ἠρώτων τί ποτ' ἐστίν, ὃ καὶ ἐν τῷ τρέχειν τυγχάνει ὂν ἡμῖν καὶ ἐν τῷ κιθαρίζειν καὶ ἐν τῷ λέγειν καὶ ἐν τῷ μανθάνειν καὶ ἐν ἄλλοις πολλοῖς, καὶ σχεδόν τι αὐτὸ κεκτήμεθα, οὗ καὶ πέρι ἄξιον λέγειν, ἢ ἐν ταῖς τῶν χειρῶν πράξεσιν ἢ σκελῶν ἢ στόματός τε καὶ φωνῆς ἢ διανοίας.

And a little later we get talk of 'partaking of' courage and wisdom (μετέχειν, 193e3, 197e2).[42]

At *Euthyphro* 5d1, the pious is the same *in* every action; in 5d3 things are said to *have* a single ἰδέα in as much as they are impious.

When he wrote the *Hippias Major*, Plato[43] seems to have been stuck on the word προσγίγνεσθαι[44], 'to become added to'; at 289d2–4 he refers to what he wants defined as "the beautiful itself, by which all other [things] are adorned and show themselves as beautiful when that form becomes added to them" (αὐτὸ τὸ καλόν, ᾧ καὶ τἆλλα πάντα κοσμεῖται καὶ καλὰ φαίνεται, ἐπειδὰν προσγένηται ἐκεῖνο τὸ εἶδος), and the use of this verb in this connection is picked up by Hippias (d8, e5) and reverted to by Socrates (290b7, 292d1). Put up against talk of adding flesh to flesh by eating (*Phaedo*

96d1, d3; cf. *Timaeus* 82b4, *Laws* vii 789a5), this sounds immanentist and even Anaxagorean.

In *Charmides* 157a Socrates discusses an alleged Thracian treatment of the soul with beautiful words; at 157a5–7 he says: "From such words self-control comes-to-be in our souls, which, when it has come-to-be-in and is-present-to [them], [makes] it easy to provide health for the head and the rest of the body" (ἐκ δὲ τῶν τοιούτων λόγων ἐν ταῖς ψυχαῖς σωφροσύνην ἐγγίγνεσθαι, ἧς ἐγγενομένης καὶ παρούσης ῥᾴδιον ἤδη εἶναι τὴν ὑγίειαν καὶ τῇ κεφαλῇ καὶ τῷ ἄλλῳ σώματι πορίζειν).

In 158b5–6, he says to Charmides, by way of raising a question: "If self-control is already present-to you and you are adequately self-controlled" (εἰ μέν σοι ἤδη πάρεστιν . . . σωφροσύνη καὶ εἶ σώφρων ἱκανῶς . . .). And when he raises it it has the form (158c2–4): "so do you yourself say that you already adequately partake of self-control . . . ? (αὐτὸς οὖν . . . καὶ φῂς ἱκανῶς ἤδη σωφροσύνης μετέχειν . . . ;)[45] And there is more immanentist language to come: self-control is something to be possessed (κέκτησαι 158d8), something that is present-to (παρεῖναι 158e7, 160d7, 161a9, 175e2) or present-in (ἐνεῖναι 159a1, a2, a9) someone.

In the *Gorgias*, Socrates gives a more general formulation involving the expression 'presence-to' (497e1–3): "don't you call good men good by the presence-to [them] of goods, just as you call those beautiful whom beauty is present-to?" (τοὺς ἀγαθοὺς οὐχὶ ἀγαθῶν παρουσίᾳ ἀγαθοὺς καλεῖς, ὥσπερ τοὺς καλοὺς οἷς ἂν κάλλος παρῇ;). This is echoed at 498d2–3, and the formula is recast in terms of 'coming-to-be-present-in' (παραγίγνεσθαι, ἐγγίγνεσθαι) in 506de. No one wishes to see in this any heavy ontology.[46] But suppose we lean on it anyway. It is an odd formulation; in fact, it incorporates two formulations: one, generalized, would be that things are F when F's are present-to them, and the other, generalized, would be that things are F when F-ness is present-to them. As far as I can tell, this point is completely irrelevant to understanding the *Gorgias*.

But the formulation is one about which Plato was reflective, even before he was asking expressly metaphysical questions.

In the *Euthydemus*, it is parodied:[47] Socrates is trying to say that there are beautiful things (cf. καλὸν πρᾶγμα 300e3) that are not the same as the beautiful (301a1–4); "but," he says, "there is some beauty present-to each of them" (301a4: πάρεστιν μέντοι ἑκάστῳ αὐτῶν κάλλος τι).[48] This is ambiguous between the two formulations we found in the *Gorgias*, because 'some beauty' has the same idiomatic range in Greek as it does in English. In any case, Dionysodorus skewers him with this (301a5–6): "So if an ox became present-to you, you would be an ox, and because I am present-to you, you are Dionysodorus?" ('Εὰν οὖν . . . παραγένηταί σοι βοῦς, βοῦς εἶ, καὶ ὅτι νῦν ἐγώ σοι πάρειμι, Διονυσόδωρος εἶ;) to which Socrates responds 'don't even say it!' No doubt drawing a philosophical moral from slapstick shows failure to grasp the genre, but surely what Socrates should say to Dionysodorus is that not just any and every sort of 'presence-to' makes for character. That would raise the question of when it is that something's presence makes a difference (301a8–9).

That, slapstick or no, is precisely Dionysodorus' next question (301a8–9): "But in what way, he [*sc.* Dionysodorus] said, when one [thing] is present-to another, could the one be other?" (ἀλλὰ τίνα τρόπον, ἔφη, ἑτέρου ἑτέρῳ παραγενομένου τὸ ἕτερον ἕτερον ἂν εἴη;). This is tricky. Socrates has said that the beautiful is other than the many beautiful things he has seen, although there is some beauty present-to each of them. Dionysodorus construes this as tantamount to saying that the beautiful is present to those beautiful things; and Socrates registers no objection to this reading. There is no great difficulty so far. But just what is Dionysodorus asking? There are two possibilities. (1) The beautiful, by Socrates' admissions (as construed by Dionysodorus) makes something different from it, and not already beautiful, beautiful: it makes it different from what it was. How, in general, can that be?[49] (2) Dionysodorus is using 'other' as a predicate variable: how can one thing, the F, by being present to another, make that other thing F?[50] Either way, he is asking a generalized version of the preceding question: when does the presence of the F make something F?

Socrates does not say, there (where he goes on to duck the question by perpetrating some fallacies of his own) or anywhere else. But at *Lysis* 217c3–e4 we find this:

> For I say that, for some things, where what is present-to them is such-and-such, they themselves are such-and-such; for others, not. Just as if someone plastered something with some color, I suppose what was plastered on would be present-to what was plastered [with it].
>
> Very much so.
>
> Then is that which is plastered also therefore at that time of such a color as that which is-on [it]?
>
> d I don't understand, he said.
>
> But [it's] as follows, I said. If someone plastered your hair, which is yellow, with lead,[51] would it then *be* white, or *seem* white?
>
> It would seem white, he said.
>
> And whiteness would be present-to it.
>
> Yes.
>
> But nevertheless it wouldn't yet *be* any more white, but while whiteness is present-to it it is neither at all white nor black.
>
> True.
>
> But when, my friend, old age brings on it this same color, then it has come-
> e to-be such as what is present-to [it]: white, by the presence-to [it] of white.
>
> How else?
>
> This, then, I am asking now: whether, where something is present-to a thing, that which has it will be such as that which is present-to [it]; or [is it that] if it is

present-to [it] in a certain way, it will be, and if not, not?

Rather the latter, he said.

217c
λέγω γὰρ ὅτι ἔνια μέν, οἷον ἂν ᾖ
τὸ παρόν, τοιαῦτά ἐστι καὶ αὐτά, ἔνια δὲ οὔ. ὥσπερ εἰ
ἐθέλοι τις χρώματί τῳ ὁτιοῦν [τι] ἀλεῖψαι, πάρεστίν που
τῷ ἀλειφθέντι τὸ ἐπαλειφθέν.—Πάνυ γε.—Ἆρ᾽ οὖν καὶ
ἔστιν τότε τοιοῦτον τὴν χρόαν τὸ ἀλειφθέν, οἷον τὸ ἐπόν;
d —Οὐ μανθάνω, ἦ δ᾽ ὅς.—᾽Αλλ᾽ ὧδε, ἦν δ᾽ ἐγώ. εἴ τίς
σου ξανθὰς οὔσας τὰς τρίχας ψιμυθίῳ ἀλείψειεν, πότερον
τότε λευκαὶ εἶεν ἢ φαίνοιντ᾽ ἄν;—Φαίνοιντ᾽ ἄν, ἦ δ᾽ ὅς.—
Καὶ μὴν παρείη γ᾽ ἂν αὐταῖς λευκότης.—Ναί.—᾽Αλλ᾽ ὅμως
οὐδέν τι μᾶλλον ἂν εἶεν λευκαί πω, ἀλλὰ παρούσης λευκό-
τητος οὔτε τι λευκαὶ οὔτε μέλαιναί εἰσιν.—᾽Αληθῆ.—᾽Αλλ᾽
ὅταν δή, ὦ φίλε, τὸ γῆρας αὐταῖς ταὐτὸν τοῦτο χρῶμα ἐπα-
γάγῃ, τότε ἐγένοντο οἷόνπερ τὸ παρόν, λευκοῦ παρουσίᾳ
e λευκαί.—Πῶς γὰρ οὔ;—Τοῦτο τοίνυν ἐρωτῶ νῦν δή, εἰ ᾧ
ἄν τι παρῇ, τοιοῦτον ἔσται τὸ ἔχον οἷον τὸ παρόν· ἢ ἐὰν
μὲν κατά τινα τρόπον παρῇ, ἔσται, ἐὰν δὲ μή, οὔ;—Οὕτω
μᾶλλον, ἔφη.

This is certainly fledgling metaphysics, and if it ever flew, it might be Eudoxianism.[52] It would account for the fact that something, which I shall call the host entity, is (say) white by the presence in it of an intermediary which is also white.

In the *Lysis*, it is not worked out.[53] In the case of white, there is no candidate named for the intermediary entity: it cannot be old age, which is the only thing mentioned (d7) as explaining why the hair is white, since, as Socrates states it (c3–4, 6–7, d8–e1), the intermediary itself possesses the imported property, and old age is not white. If the intermediary were something like a pigment, like the white lead mentioned, that, in old age, was present-to the hair in a special way, as Socrates says, and not just plastered on to the outside, and if this special presence-to were a matter of the pigment's being physically a part of the hair itself, the whole thing might be Eudoxianism.

But it would be an error to charge Plato with Eudoxianism or with any other metaphysical theory here. The passage is a part of an attempt to characterize the paradigm situation in which x is *friendly toward* or *loves* y as follows: "y is good, and there is present in x something that is bad, but x is not thereby himself bad" (see 217e–218a). For example, there are people who have (οἱ ἔχοντες 218a6) ignorance, which is bad, but are not yet witless or stupid, and so their possession of ignorance has not yet rendered them bad. These, according to the line Socrates is trying out, are the lovers of wisdom. So he distinguishes cases in which something F (something bad, or white) by its presence in something else makes that something else also F, from cases in which it does not. There is no hint that the notion of 'presence-in,' which has to cover physical presence as well as whatever the relationship is between my ignorance and me, is embedded in any general account of why things are what they are.[54]

Socrates once (*Charmides* 161a4) quotes[55] and once (*Laches* 201b2–3) alludes to *Odyssey* xvii 347: "Modesty is not [a] good [thing] to be-present-to a man in need" (αἰδὼς δ' οὐκ ἀγαθὴ κεχρημένῳ ἀνδρὶ παρεῖναι). We do not want to put Homer on the list of immanentists.[56] In the *Lysis*, we have very little better reason for putting Plato on that list. But we shall encounter the relation of presence-to again. And then it will be metaphysics.

3.2. The Phaedo

Immanentist language is not abandoned when Socrates has been launched into the orbit of the Theory of Forms: there are many passages in dialogues from the period of high theory to consider. Here I confine myself to the *Phaedo*. In that dialogue, Plato speaks the language of immanence. Mostly the language is metaphorical, but occasionally it can be taken literally, as we shall see.

Sometimes a rather elaborate theory involving immanence is ascribed to Plato in this dialogue. Toward the end (102d7 and ff.), Socrates uses the phrase 'the tallness in us'; so it is thought that he has in his universe not only forms and ordinary things (or, better: forms, ordinary things, and souls) but also 'form-copies,'[57] 'immanent characters,'[58] or 'immanent forms';[59] indeed, to some, the passage is explicit about these.[60] I think there are no such animals as 'immanent characters' or 'form-copies.' What immanence there is is of an entirely different kind.

3.2.1. The Safe Theory. A little earlier Socrates had been discussing theories that explain the truth of true predications. He has his own. It requires, first (100b5–7): "hypothesizing that there is a beautiful itself by itself and a good and a tall and all the others" (ὑποθέμενος εἶναί τι καλὸν αὐτὸ καθ' αὑτὸ καὶ ἀγαθὸν καὶ μέγα καὶ τἆλλα πάντα). Socrates asks Cebes to grant that there are such things (b7: εἶναι ταῦτα).

This existential admission is no longer innocent: we have already had (in 74a–c) the generalized argument (generalized from one in *Hippias Major* 287e–289d) that puts the forms on a different level from ordinary things.

Next (100c4–6): "It seems to me that, if there is anything else beautiful except the beautiful-itself, it is not beautiful because of any other one [thing] than because it partakes of that beautiful" (φαίνεται γάρ μοι, εἴ τί ἐστιν ἄλλο καλὸν πλὴν αὐτὸ τὸ καλόν, οὐδὲ δι' ἓν ἄλλο καλὸν εἶναι ἢ διότι μετέχει ἐκείνου τοῦ καλοῦ). In fact, he cannot understand other causes

(100c9–10): if somebody says that anything is beautiful because of its color or shape, he gets confused (c10–d3); he says (100d3–8):

> but simply, artlessly, and perhaps foolishly I hold on to this, that nothing else makes it beautiful other than the presence of that beautiful to [things] or its communion [with them] or however and in whatever way it becomes added to [them];[61] for I don't make any further claims about that, but [I do claim] that [it is] by the beautiful that all beautiful [things are] beautiful.

> τοῦτο δὲ ἁπλῶς καὶ ἀτεχνῶς καὶ ἴσως εὐήθως ἔχω παρ' ἐμαυτῷ, ὅτι οὐκ ἄλλο τι ποιεῖ αὐτὸ καλὸν ἢ ἡ ἐκείνου τοῦ καλοῦ εἴτε παρουσία εἴτε κοινωνία εἴτε ὅπῃ δὴ καὶ ὅπως προσγενομένη· οὐ γὰρ ἔτι τοῦτο διισχυρίζομαι, ἀλλ' ὅτι τῷ καλῷ πάντα τὰ καλὰ [γίγνεται] καλά.

This theory tells us that:

(1) There are the F-itself, the G-itself, etc.

(2) If anything is F besides the F itself, it is F because it partakes of the F itself.[62]

(3) It is not by anything other than the F itself that anything is F.[63]

But also, there is something about which the theory is explicitly silent: the relationship between the F itself and the things that are F because of it. Socrates mentions as possibilities 'presence-to,' 'communion,' and treats 'becoming added to'[64] as a general label for the relation; on the next page he uses various idioms of 'participation' (μετέχειν, μετάσχεσις, μεταλαμβάνειν 100c5, 101c3, c4, c5, c6, 102b2). All of these are immanentist formulations, and only the second (used in this connection for the first time here) is new to us. But he is emphatic that he is committed to nothing whatever. He most often talks of participation: but this is now only a place holder. The nature of the relation is up for grabs, as Aristotle tells us it was.[65]

So we have no right to take Socrates' immanentist language seriously:[66] it is at best metaphorical, and he is telling us that he is not sure what it is metaphorical for. And in the *Symposium* Diotima denies immanence and speaks of participation in the same sentence; she says of the beautiful itself that it will not appear to its contemplator as anything bodily (211a6–7)

> b nor as being somewhere in something else, e.g., in an animal, in the earth, in heaven, or in anything else, but itself by itself with itself, always being singular in form, while all the other beautiful [things] are partakers of that [beautiful] in such a way that, while the others are coming-to-be and passing-away, that [beautiful] in no way comes-to-be any larger or smaller or undergoes anything (211a8–b5).[67]

> οὐδέ που ὂν ἐν ἑτέρῳ τινι, οἷον ἐν ζώῳ ἢ ἐν γῇ ἢ ἐν οὐρανῷ
> b ἢ ἐν ἄλλῳ, ἀλλ' αὐτὸ καθ' αὑτὸ μεθ' αὑτοῦ μονοειδὲς ἀεὶ ὄν, τὰ δὲ ἄλλα πάντα καλὰ ἐκείνου μετέχοντα τρόπον τινὰ τοιοῦτον, οἷον γιγνομένων τε τῶν ἄλλων καὶ ἀπολλυμένων μηδὲν ἐκεῖνο μήτε τι πλέον μήτε ἔλαττον γίγνεσθαι μηδὲ πάσχειν μηδέν.

At 102b1–2, Phaedo reminds us of what has been so far agreed on: that "each of the forms is something, and the other things by participating in them get named after these themselves" (102b1–2: εἶναί τι ἕκαστον τῶν εἰδῶν καὶ τούτων τἆλλα μεταλαμβάνοντα αὐτῶν τούτων τὴν ἐπωνυμίαν ἴσχειν). The next words are (102b3–6):

> Then if, he said, you say these things like that, won't it be that, whenever you say that Simmias is taller than Socrates, but shorter than Phaedo, you are saying that then both are in Simmias, both tallness and shortness?

> Εἰ δή, ἦ δ' ὅς, ταῦτα οὕτως λέγεις, ἆρ' ούχ, ὅταν Σιμμίαν Σωκράτους φῇς μείζω εἶναι, Φαίδωνος δὲ ἐλάττω, λέγεις τότ' εἶναι ἐν τῷ Σιμμίᾳ ἀμφότερα, καὶ μέγεθος καὶ σμικρότητα?

Here we first run into a form 'in' Simmias. Suppose there were immanent forms or form-copies here. Socrates' question would be this: "Consider, Cebes, the sentence 'Simmias is taller than Socrates but shorter than Phaedo'. Our theory tells us that for this we must have, to begin with, Socrates, Simmias, and Phaedo; then tallness and shortness themselves; and, third, another tallness and another shortness that are in Simmias, that mediate between the forms and Simmias. Not so?"

And Cebes, a sharp customer, would have replied, "But, O Socrates, where did this third group come from? You spoke only of ourselves and of forms; you said you knew nothing about the relationship between forms and their mundane participants. When did you learn of these go-betweens?"

That is not Socrates' question. The theory has given us only one tallness: tallness itself. And here he says it is 'in' Simmias, where earlier he had said it was 'present-to' him. There is no new theory in that: Socrates would be as noncommittal about this locution as he was about the preceding ones.

He continues with 'in' in 102d5 and following. It is this passage that the advocates of immanent forms rely on most. Socrates says (102d5–103a2):

102d

> I'm saying [this] for this reason, that I want it to seem to you just as it does to me. For it seems to me that not only tallness itself is never willing to be at the same time both tall and short, but also tallness[68] in us never admits the short and is not willing to be exceeded, but one or the other of two [things comes about]:
> e either it flees and withdraws when its contrary, the short, approaches, or when

that [contrary] comes toward it it perishes; but it is not willing, abiding and accepting shortness, to be other than just what it was. Just so I, having accepted and abided shortness, while still also being just what I am, this same [person], am short; but that, while being tall, hasn't submitted to being short; and in the same way the short in us is not willing ever to come-to-be or to be tall, nor [is] any other of the contraries, while being what it was, [willing] to come-to-be and
103 to be the contrary, but it either goes away or perishes in this undergoing.

102d
Λέγω δὴ τοῦδ' ἕνεκα, βουλόμενος δόξαι σοὶ ὅπερ ἐμοί.
ἐμοὶ γὰρ φαίνεται οὐ μόνον αὐτὸ τὸ μέγεθος οὐδέποτ' ἐθέλειν
ἅμα μέγα καὶ σμικρὸν εἶναι, ἀλλὰ καὶ τὸ ἐν ἡμῖν μέγεθος
οὐδέποτε προσδέχεσθαι τὸ σμικρὸν οὐδ' ἐθέλειν ὑπερέχεσθαι,
ἀλλὰ δυοῖν τὸ ἕτερον, ἢ φεύγειν καὶ ὑπεκχωρεῖν ὅταν αὐτῷ
e προσίῃ τὸ ἐναντίον, τὸ σμικρόν, ἢ προσελθόντος ἐκείνου
ἀπολωλέναι· ὑπομένον δὲ καὶ δεξάμενον τὴν σμικρότητα
οὐκ ἐθέλειν εἶναι ἕτερον ἢ ὅπερ ἦν. ὥσπερ ἐγὼ δεξάμενος
καὶ ὑπομείνας τὴν σμικρότητα, καὶ ἔτι ὢν ὅσπερ εἰμί, οὗτος
ὁ αὐτὸς σμικρός εἰμι· ἐκεῖνο δὲ οὐ τετόλμηκεν μέγα ὂν
σμικρὸν εἶναι· ὡς δ' αὔτως καὶ τὸ σμικρὸν τὸ ἐν ἡμῖν οὐκ
ἐθέλει ποτὲ μέγα γίγνεσθαι οὐδὲ εἶναι, οὐδ' ἄλλο οὐδὲν τῶν
ἐναντίων, ἔτι ὂν ὅπερ ἦν, ἅμα τοὐναντίον γίγνεσθαί τε
103 καὶ εἶναι, ἀλλ' ἤτοι ἀπέρχεται ἢ ἀπόλλυται ἐν τούτῳ τῷ
παθήματι.

There has been no mention of immanent forms in the build-up to this. Tallness, Socrates tells us, cannot be both tall and short. This is familiar ground: it was part of the underpinning for the argument of 74a–c that showed us that the forms were radically distinct from mundane things. But he now adds that the situation has not changed when we turn from consideration of tallness just by itself (αὐτὸ τὸ μέγεθος 102d6), which cannot admit the short (τὸ σμικρόν 102e1), to tallness as it turns up in us: here, too, it cannot admit the short (102d5–103a2). And again, we are not getting any new theory. There are tallness and Simmias, and tallness when it is in Simmias still would not be short.

But 102d9–e2 and 103a1–2 speak of tallness in us going away or *perishing* at the approach of the short, and surely there can be no question of a form perishing: so, some think,[69] we must have a new entity, one that can perish.

But Socrates is speaking abstractly here: these are the two logical possibilities. One of them is irrelevant when we are talking about forms. But it will *not* be irrelevant when the theory is expanded later: it will be at the center of our attention when we turn to proving the immortality of the soul, and Socrates plants the option here for later use.

In fact, as the dialogue continues, it becomes clear not only that Socrates has failed to introduce immanent forms and has no need for them, but that he has no room for them.

Consider Socrates' reply to the anonymous interlocutor who thinks Socrates is now saying 'just the opposite'[70] of something he had said earlier (103a5–10). Socrates draws a distinction (103b2–c2):

103b

For then it was being said that the contrary *thing*[71] comes-to-be from the contrary *thing*, but now, that the contrary itself[72] can't come-to-be contrary to itself, neither that in us nor that in nature. For then, my friend, we were speaking about the things that have the contraries, derivatively naming them after those, but now [we are speaking] about those things themselves [from] which, when they are in [them], the things named get their derived names; and these themselves,
c we are saying, will never admit each other's coming-to-be.

b2 τότε μὲν γὰρ ἐλέγετο ἐκ τοῦ ἐναντίου πράγματος τὸ ἐναντίον πρᾶγμα γίγνεσθαι, νῦν δέ, ὅτι αὐτὸ τὸ ἐναντίον ἑαυτῷ ἐναντίον οὐκ ἄν ποτε γένοιτο, οὔτε τὸ ἐν ἡμῖν οὔτε τὸ ἐν τῇ φύσει. τότε μὲν γάρ, ὦ φίλε, περὶ τῶν ἐχόντων τὰ ἐναντία ἐλέγομεν, ἐπονομάζοντες αὐτὰ τῇ ἐκείνων ἐπωνυμίᾳ, νῦν δὲ περὶ ἐκείνων αὐτῶν ὧν ἐνόντων ἔχει τὴν ἐπωνυμίαν τὰ ὀνομαζό-
c μενα· αὐτὰ δ' ἐκεῖνα οὐκ ἄν ποτέ φαμεν ἐθελῆσαι γένεσιν ἀλλήλων δέξασθαι.

When he says that the F can't be non-F, "neither that in us nor that in nature" (b5), he is not speaking of *two* things, the F in us, the form-copy, immanent form, or character, and the F in the sky, the Form, the F itself, for he goes on (b7–8), "now we are speaking about the things themselves which, *when they are in*" things here below, account for predications about them.

There are no immanent forms here. But, for immanence, that is not the end of the story.

3.2.2. The Extended Theory. In 103cd, Socrates asks us to concede the existence of the hot and the cold and distinguish them from fire and snow, respectively. He then tells us that, despite the difference between fire and the hot, fire is in one respect like the hot: at the approach of heat's opposite, it must withdraw or perish (103d5–e1).

He thinks that there are many cases like this, in which (e2–6) "not only is the form itself entitled to the same name for all time, but also something else that is not that, but always, whenever it is, has the shape of that" (μὴ μόνον αὐτὸ τὸ εἶδος ἀξιοῦσθαι τοῦ αὐτοῦ ὀνόματος εἰς τὸν ἀεὶ χρόνον, ἀλλὰ καὶ ἄλλο τι ὃ ἔστι μὲν οὐκ ἐκεῖνο, ἔχει δὲ τὴν ἐκείνου μορφὴν ἀεί, ὅτανπερ ᾖ; cf. 104c7–9).

He gives four sets of examples. First, we have fire and snow, which always carry hot and cold with them. Second, there are the numbers 1, 3, 5, and so on, which always carry the form of the odd, and the numbers 2, 4, 6, and so on, which always carry the form of the even (103e5–104b5, 104c1–3, d5–e6, e8–105a1, 105a5–b1; see also the somewhat curious cases in 105b1–3). Third, very much in passing, Socrates mentions fever (πυρετός), which imports disease into a body (105c2–4). And last there will be the soul, which always carries with it the form of life (105c9 ff.).

Here, by contrast with the safe theory, perishing is not just an abstract possibility but a live option: not for the numbers, but for fire, snow, fever, and perhaps even for the soul. Socrates' project is going to be to show that it is not, in fact, an option for the soul.

He determines or defines (ὁρισώμεθα 104c11, ὁρίσασθαι e7, ὁρίζῃ 105a2) these things as ones "which force whatever they occupy[73] to have not only its own [i.e., the occupier's][74] idea, but also always [the idea] of some contrary" (104d1–3: ἃ ὅτι ἂν κατάσχῃ μὴ μόνον ἀναγκάζει τὴν αὑτοῦ ἰδέαν αὐτὸ ἴσχειν, ἀλλὰ καὶ ἐναντίου [αὐτῷ] ἀεί τινος).[75] For example, what the idea of three occupies it forces to become odd (104d5–7); what fire occupies it forces to become hot; what the soul occupies it forces to be alive.

But that means, says Socrates (105b5–8), that there's another safe answer besides the one that says something is F because it bears some unspecified relation to the form for F, namely (105b8-c6):

> For if you ask me what it is that, when it comes-to-be in a body, that body is hot, I
> c shall not state to you that safe but unlearned reply, that it is heat, but one more
> clever, based on what's just been said, that it is fire; nor, if you ask what it is that,
> when it comes-to-be in a body, that body will be sick, should I say that it is
> sickness, but fever; nor, [if you ask] what it is that, when it comes-to-be in a
> number, the number is odd, should I say oddness, but unit, and other things
> similarly.

> εἰ γὰρ ἔροιό με
> ᾧ ἂν τί ἐν τῷ σώματι ἐγγένηται θερμὸν ἔσται, οὐ τὴν
> c ἀσφαλῆ σοι ἐρῶ ἀπόκρισιν ἐκείνην τὴν ἀμαθῆ, ὅτι ᾧ ἂν
> θερμότης, ἀλλὰ κομψοτέραν ἐκ τῶν νῦν, ὅτι ᾧ ἂν πῦρ· οὐδὲ
> ἂν ἔρῃ ᾧ ἂν σώματι τί ἐγγένηται νοσήσει, οὐκ ἐρῶ ὅτι
> ᾧ ἂν νόσος, ἀλλ' ᾧ ἂν πυρετός· οὐδ' ᾧ ἂν ἀριθμῷ τί
> ἐγγένηται περιττὸς ἔσται, οὐκ ἐρῶ ᾧ ἂν περιττότης, ἀλλ'
> ᾧ ἂν μονάς, καὶ τἆλλα οὕτως.

The mechanism is this: there are certain intermediate entities, that always have one of a pair of opposite properties. These intermediates, when they come to be present in something, carry their properties with them, and their presence explains why the host entity in which they are present has those properties.

This is the theory suggested by the *Lysis*, having come out of its closet as unabashed immanentist metaphysics.

It is not that forms are immanent in things: the intermediates are, and the intermediates need not be forms.

The earlier safe explanation for x's being F was that x bears an unknown relation, 'participation,' to the form for F. Now we are to say instead, sometimes, that x has in it y, and y partakes of the form F. The entities imported by the intermediates are, and are referred to as, forms (103e5 [quoted earlier], 104b9, d9–10).

In some cases, so are the intermediates: three, five, and so on are called forms (104d5–6). But no such thing is said about snow and fire.[76] And the soul is treated as a non-form throughout the *Phaedo* (see esp. 79de).[77] The present argument is simple: the soul is an intermediate which imports the form life and so cannot admit the opposite, death; so it is deathless; so it is imperishable. Nothing here demands that the soul be a form.[78]

Consider the examples once more.

1. The presence of fire in something explains why it is hot. On the face of it, the host entity and the intermediate are both physical.

2. The presence of three or five in some number explains why it is odd. Neither host nor intermediate is physical; the intermediate is a form.

3. The presence of fever in a body explains why it is sick. The host entity is unambiguously physical; the intermediate is not unambiguously anything. It sounds to me slightly odd, in this dialogue, to say it is a form, but that does not count for much.

4. The presence of soul in a body explains why that body is alive. Here the host entity is physical, the intermediate not, but still, not a form.

In the first case, we are close to Eudoxianism. We are not all the way there: what the intermediates import are still forms that are radically distinct from the intermediate entities and the host entities.

3.2.3. The *Parmenides* and the Academy. Suppose you were a working member of the Academy, and what you were working on was the question what to do with the theory of forms in the face of objections that focus on the relation between forms and ordinary things. You would reconsider the ways in which that relationship had been explained. And in the course of that reconsideration, you would run into some passages that sound in one way or another Eudoxian or at least immanentist. And you might well ask, Can the troublesome relationship be explained by taking this 'immanentist' way of speaking seriously?

My suggestion is that both Eudoxus and Aristotle did just that, that Eudoxus came up with one version and Aristotle with another, that Aristotle did not think Eudoxus was right, and that this is what he is saying in 1a24–25.

The 'objections that focus on the relation between forms and ordinary things,' or, at any rate, some of them, are canvassed in Plato's *Parmenides*. But we need not assume any particular chronological relationship between the promulgation of the *Parmenides* and that of Eudoxus' immanentism,[79] for there is no reason to suppose that the objections were news when the *Par-*

menides was 'published': it is not as if the members of the Academy communicated with each other by publishing position papers.[80]

Then the *Parmenides* could perfectly well be recording objections current in the Academy. If it is, Eudoxus' proposal could either have preceded the writing of the *Parmenides* or followed it. Either way, there are passages in the *Parmenides* that have a bearing on that proposal. Let us consider three.

Parmenides 130e–131e objects that participation in a form requires either the whole form or a part of it to be in each of its participants, and that each alternative leads to absurdity: if the whole form is in each participant, it is going to be separate from itself; if only a part of it is, then the form is divisible (and there are additional absurdities). It is worth noting that Plato took this argument seriously enough to echo it in the *Philebus* (15b).[81] It constitutes a problem for any view that construes the relation between a form and its participants as involving the immanence of the form or some part of it in those participants: any view that says this stick is white because there is in it a form, or part of a form. And so it constitutes a problem for Eudoxus' view. If Eudoxus had already made his suggestion, Plato could not have written this passage without thinking of Eudoxus.[82] If Eudoxus' suggestion came later, he could not have made it without supposing he had a way around this objection.[83] But there is nothing so far to tell us how to choose.

We shall encounter this objection again later, in Alexander's list of objections against Eudoxus, and that will require a reconsideration of this point. For now, let us stay within the *Parmenides*.

Socrates' admissions in the *Parmenides* actually commit him to the denial of immanence. As he propounds his theory of forms in 128e–130a, the claim that each form is 'itself by itself' (αὐτὸ καθ' αὑτό) is built into it (128e6–129a1, 129d7–8; cf. 130b8).[84] In 133c3–6, we encounter the following exchange:

> Socrates, I think that you and anyone else who posits that there is some substance of each [thing] itself by itself would agree, first, that none of them can be in us.[85] [Yes], for how could it still be itself by itself? said Socrates.
>
> ὦ Σώκρατες, οἶμαι ἂν καὶ σὲ καὶ ἄλλον, ὅστις αὐτήν τινα καθ' αὑτὴν ἑκάστου οὐσίαν τίθεται εἶναι, ὁμολογῆσαι ἂν πρῶτον μὲν μηδεμίαν αὐτῶν εἶναι ἐν ἡμῖν.
> Πῶς γὰρ αὐτὴ καθ' αὑτὴν ἔτι εἴη; φάναι τὸν Σωκράτη.

There is some friction between this and the immanentist trend of 130–131; it is as well to remember that Socrates is in some logical trouble in this dialogue, precisely over the question of the relationship between forms and their participants.[86]

Eudoxus' suggestion is that forms are literally *in* their participants. The text at 133c obviously bears on that: Parmenides is arguing that, if you retain the Platonic thesis that forms are 'themselves by themselves,' then the suggestion will not do. But, once more, there is nothing here to show whether the suggestion is one Eudoxus had already made or had yet to make.

Finally, in the dialectic of the second part of the *Parmenides*, in the course of an argument to the effect that the One is equal to itself and to the Others, we encounter (149d–150d) a curious (but this does not distinguish it from many others in this part of the *Parmenides*) subargument[87] purporting to show that the One cannot be larger or smaller than the Others, nor they than it. It runs as follows. If the One were small, the form (see εἴδη, 149e9) smallness would be in it, and if it were in it, it would be in either a part of it or the whole of it. But if it were in the whole of it, it would be either equal to the One or larger than the One. But smallness cannot be either equal or large, so if it is in the One, it must be in a part of the One. But then it cannot be in the whole of that part, or we are back where we started. Parmenides concludes that it cannot be in anything (150b5–6): he expects us to fill in the regress toward which the argument was headed. His conclusion is that nothing is small except smallness (150b6–7), and a parallel argument purports to show that nothing is large except largeness itself (150bc).[88]

The upshot here is quite general: if there were anything to this argument, it would show that we can never explain why anything is small by appealing to the physical presence in it of something that is small. This pattern of explanation is indeed that of Eudoxianism, so the argument would tell against that. And it is certainly true that 'small' is one of the predicates that illustrates our initial Drawback: the idea that something is small because it literally has in it something small is weird. Perhaps Eudoxus would be particularly vulnerable here:[89] he is responsible for a theory of magnitudes and their comparative sizes that finds expression in Euclid, *Elements* v[90] (see esp. def. 5).[91]

But Parmenides' argument is another story: it does not bring out what is weird about the idea that small things are so because they have something small in them. A defender of that idea could easily reply that what is present in the One making it small is something that is equal in size relative to the One, but small relative to something else. This leads to further questions, and we should end up very far afield if we tried to deal with them now. For present purposes, we have enough to see that the argument does not plainly tell against anyone, and that includes Eudoxus. So, as far as this argument goes, Eudoxus might either have been its target, or have been inspired by its very weakness to defend the cause of immanentism.

Immanentism is plainly an option under consideration in the *Parmenides*. But whether Eudoxus had already espoused it or had yet to when Plato wrote the *Parmenides* is not at all clear. Indeed, it is not at all clear that the phrase "when Plato wrote the *Parmenides*" nails down a date specific enough to lend meaning to the question: he might have written it over some time.[92] And, as we shall see, it is also not clear what we mean when we speak of Eudoxus 'espousing' this position. If, as will appear possible if not likely, it is a position he would defend in discussions of difficulties about relating forms to ordinary things, and the *Parmenides* was being written while such discussions were taking place, there is really no question which came first: neither did.

That is the way I am inclined to think things were. But it does not matter a great deal whether my inclination is in the right direction.

4. EUDOXUS AND ARISTOTLE

The two texts that tell us about Eudoxus' theory of forms are a passage in *Metaphysics* A 9 and Alexander's commentary on that passage.

4.1. *Aristotle,* Metaphysics *A 9. 991a14–19 and Its Context*

In the course of his polemic against the Theory of Forms and related theories in A 9, Aristotle says (991a8–22, broken up for ease of reference):[93]

991a8/9 Most of all, one might raise the problem what the forms contribute either to the eternal among the perceptibles or to the ones that come-to-be and pass-away;

a11 for they are causes neither of motion nor of any change for them.

a12 But then, they are of no help in connection with the knowledge of the other things, either (for they are not the substance of these; for then they would be in them[94]),

a13/14 nor as far as their being goes, since they are not present in[94] their participants;

a14/15 for then they might perhaps be thought to be causes in the way that[95] the white is, by being mixed into the white [thing],[96]

a16 but this account, which first Anaxagoras and later Eudoxus and certain others[97] used to state, is very easily overthrown (for it is easy to collect[98] many quite impossible [things] against such a view);

a19 but surely the other [things] are not composed of forms in any of the customary ways of speaking.[99]

a19/20 But to say that they are paradigms and the other [things] partake of them is to talk emptily and to use poetic metaphors. . . . [There follow objections to the paradigm-conception of forms.]

πάντων δὲ μάλιστα διαπορήσειεν ἄν τις τί ποτε συμβάλλεται τὰ εἴδη τοῖς ἀϊδίοις τῶν αἰσθητῶν ἢ τοῖς γιγνομένοις καὶ φθειρομένοις· οὔτε γὰρ κινήσεως οὔτε μεταβολῆς οὐδεμιᾶς ἐστὶν αἴτια αὐτοῖς. ἀλλὰ μὴν οὔτε πρὸς τὴν ἐπιστήμην οὐθὲν βοηθεῖ τὴν τῶν ἄλλων (οὐδὲ γὰρ οὐσία ἐκεῖνα τούτων· ἐν τούτοις γὰρ ἂν ἦν), οὔτε εἰς τὸ εἶναι, μὴ ἐνυπάρχοντά γε τοῖς μετέχουσιν· οὕτω μὲν γὰρ ἂν ἴσως αἴτια δόξειεν εἶναι ὡς τὸ λευκὸν μεμιγμένον τῷ λευκῷ, ἀλλ' οὗτος μὲν ὁ λόγος λίαν εὐκίνητος, ὃν 'Αναξαγόρας μὲν πρῶτος Εὔδοξος δ' ὕστερον καὶ ἄλλοι τινὲς ἔλεγον (ῥᾴδιον γὰρ συναγαγεῖν πολλὰ καὶ ἀδύνατα πρὸς τὴν τοιαύτην δόξαν)· ἀλλὰ μὴν οὐδ' ἐκ τῶν εἰδῶν ἐστὶ τἆλλα κατ' οὐθένα τρόπον τῶν εἰωθότων λέγεσθαι. τὸ δὲ λέγειν παραδείγματα αὐτὰ εἶναι καὶ μετέχειν αὐτῶν τἆλλα κενολογεῖν ἐστὶ καὶ μεταφορὰς λέγειν ποιητικάς.

The connections are not very tight here, but we should begin by getting a fix on the structure of this passage.

Aristotle begins by raising three objections against the forms: they do not bring about (1) the motion (991a11), (2) the knowledge (a12–13),[100] or (3) the being (a13–14) of mundane objects. In the course of making the objections, he suggests that (2) and (3) find a foothold because Platonic Forms are not *in* their participants, are not immanent. And then he suggests a way of conceiving immanence he thinks is wrong: that of Anaxagoras and Eudoxus (a14–19). But, he goes on (a19–20), really things are not composed of forms "in any of the customary ways of speaking." This is ambiguous (see n. 99). But if things worked the Anaxagorean-Eudoxian way, perceptibles would be composed of forms. Aristotle has just denied that things work that way. It sounds as if he is saying that we cannot think of perceptibles as composed of forms along those lines or along any other of the ways we might suppose things to be composed of things: he is generalizing his rejection of Eudoxianism. And then (a20–22) he turns to a new way of conceiving Forms, as paradigms.

The last point will be helpful later, when we look at Alexander's list of objections against Eudoxus. Let us now go back to the immediately crucial part of this text.

The three objections Aristotle raises against the Forms, (1)–(3) above, are ones he may have supposed to be closely related. To put it briefly, by his lights, to know something is to know its substance or essence, and its substance or essence is its being, and knowing this involves knowing what causes its being. And when it comes to perceptible things, their being depends on their being subject to motion (see *Metaphysics* Z 11. 1036b28–30). The claim that the forms do not cause the motion of the things that are not forms is, then, tantamount to the claim that they do not cause them to be, and that, in turn, means that there's no knowing them. This account of the matter is plainly impressionistic, but the important point for the present is that Aristotle quite likely supposed that a way around any one of these difficulties would be internally connected with ways around the other two.

He provides no reason at this point for the first claim, that the forms do not bring about motion. He does this elsewhere, most clearly in *De generatione et corruptione* B 9. 335b9–24, in the course of which he asks the perfectly straightforward question (b18–20): "For if the forms are causes, why are they not always generating, continuously, rather than sometimes and sometimes not, since both the forms and their participants always exist?" (εἰ μὲν γάρ ἐστιν αἴτια τὰ εἴδη, διὰ τί οὐκ ἀεὶ γεννᾷ συνεχῶς, ἀλλὰ ποτὲ μὲν ποτὲ δ' οὔ, ὄντων καὶ τῶν εἰδῶν ἀεὶ καὶ τῶν μεθεκτικῶν;). (The last clause plainly only means that at any given time there is, for example, a body that can come to be healthy as well as the form of Health.)[101] This criticism is echoed in the *Metaphysics* shortly below our passage (A 9. 991b4–5 = M 5. 1080a3–4) and elsewhere (cf. A 7. 988b2–4, Λ 6. 1071b14–17, 10. 1075b27–28).[102] It certainly looks cogent. Plato's defenders[103] generally challenge its relevance: Plato, they say, never intended the forms to be Aristotelian efficient causes. But in *De generatione et corruptione* B 9 and *Metaphysics* A 9, Aristotle (see 335b10 and 991b3) is commenting on the *Phaedo*. There Socrates says (95e9–96a1) that his defence against Cebes' last objection requires a general consideration of "the cause of coming-to-be and passing-away" (περὶ γενέσεως καὶ φθορᾶς τὴν αἰτίαν 95e9), and he duly turns to "the causes for each [thing], why each comes-to-be and perishes and why it is" (τὰς αἰτίας ἑκάστου, διὰ τί γίγνεται ἕκαστον καὶ διὰ τί ἀπόλλυται καὶ διὰ τί ἔστι 96a9–10; cf. also, e.g., 97b5–6, c6–7). It then emerges that he thinks forms are the best, and the only super-safe, causes of that kind (100b3 ff., esp. c2–7).[104] So the charge looks not only cogent but relevant.[105]

The remaining two claims against Plato's forms in our passage are ones for which Aristotle gives some justification. The justification is pretty sketchy.

On behalf of (2), that the forms are no help in getting to know the other things (perceptibles), he says: "for they are not the substance of these; for then they would be in them" (991a13). If the form F were of any use in knowing f, because to know f is to know its substance, the form F would have to be the substance of f.[106] But it is not, because if it were, it would have to be in f (for the inference, see 991b1–3: the substance of something cannot be separate [χωρίς] from it).[107] And Aristotle is plainly assuming that it is not.

This argument is not airtight, but it is there. Aristotle is at this point attacking what we might call the High Theory of Forms, and he is attacking it on the ground that it does not make its forms immanent in things.[108]

He offers a reason for (3), the claim that the Forms do nothing for the being of perceptible things: "they are not present in their participants" (991a14). This is the same as the reason for (2). It is even harder to be clear about the argument here than it was in the case of (2): we need to be told *why* the Form F could only provide for the being of f by being in it, and Aristotle does not tell us (cf., perhaps, 992a26–29, but it is not much help).

But, again, that is what he says. He thinks that if a Platonist could see his Forms as being *in* things, as Aristotle conceives *his* forms, he would not have these troubles about knowledge and being.

Aristotle is a committed immanentist. But now he mentions an immanentist position he rejects: you might think, he says, that once we have the form for white situated in the white thing, it makes the white thing white by being mixed into it, like a pigment.[109] And he ascribes this view to Anaxagoras and Eudoxus.

So Eudoxus is presented as having what he supposed was a solution to the problems Aristotle has been raising for forms, one very like Aristotle's own, but which is for some reason inadequate.

It has been argued that Eudoxus had nothing to do with theories of forms.[110] It is true that Aristotle mentions Anaxagoras as stating the same view: Anaxagoras was not trying to respond to difficulties for the theory of forms, so the view is not inherently a response to such difficulties. But this is of no significance whatever. Anaxagoras' theory of ingredients has, we saw, a structural similarity to views of Plato's, and a participant in Academic discussions would be bound to wonder whether a revival and revision of Anaxagoreanism would help to clarify the problematic relation which even Plato refers to as *participation*. And that is precisely the way it is presented in Aristotle.[111] So even in the absence of the passage in Alexander's commentary to which we shall shortly turn, it seems clear that Eudoxus was trying out this line.

But that commentary clinches the case: there were objections lodged against the view in Aristotle's Περὶ ἰδεῶν, and these treat the theory as a theory of forms. (This does not mean that one should accept Alexander's commentary as a report of the content of *On Ideas*: see later.)

Another misguided consideration operates here. The Theory of Forms, that is, the High Platonic Theory, sits so badly with the idea that a form might be a physical thing—there is even an explicit contradiction between Eudoxus' idea the the forms are mixed into things and Plato's characterizing the form as 'unmixed' (ἄμεικτον) in *Symposium* 211e1[112]—that Eudoxus' enterprise looks like throwing out the baby with the bath water. And, indeed, it would be, if the object were saving The High Platonic Theory of Forms. But who wanted to do that? Not Speusippus, who rejected the theory and yet became the next head of the Academy. Not Aristotle, who has a theory of forms that stands in opposition to the High Platonic Theory. Not even (at least, so I think) the later Plato, who had a theory that abandoned certain key tenets of the High Theory.[113] Xenocrates sounds like the bastion of orthodoxy; Proclus (*in Parmenidem* [Cousin [1864]] col. 888.1–15) tells us that Plato took his forms to be both complete or perfect and causally effective, and adds (888.15–19):[114]

> Whence, having run up to these principles, he made the whole of coming-to-be depend on them, as Xenocrates says, who had posited the idea to be the paradigmatic cause of the [things] that are ever constituted by nature . . .

> ὅθεν ἐπὶ ταύτας ἀναδραμὼν τὰς ἀρχάς, τούτων ἀνήρτησε τὴν σύμπασαν γένεσιν, καθά φησιν ὁ Ξενοκράτης, εἶναι τὴν ἰδέαν θέμενος αἰτίαν παραδειγματικὴν τῶν κατὰ φύσιν ἀεὶ συνεστώτων . . .

This certainly has the ring of the High Theory.[115] But Aristotle tells us that "some say that forms and numbers have the same nature" (ἔνιοι δὲ τὰ μὲν εἴδη καὶ τοὺς ἀριθμοὺς τὴν αὐτὴν ἔχειν φασὶ φύσιν, *Metaphysics* Z 2. 1028b24–25), and Asclepius (*in Metaphysica* [Hayduck [1888]] 379.17) tells us that this refers to Xenocrates.[116] This is hardly the theory of the *Phaedo*.

The important thing, for perhaps all but Speusippus (but see note 115), was the concept of a form: whatever it is that makes a thing F and is definable. The question was, What do forms have to be like? There is a partial answer to that question in the *Phaedo* and *Republic*; clearly no one at the time thought that those mighty dialogues contained the final word.[117]

We have it from both Plato and Aristotle that it was open to argument what the relationship between forms and their 'participants' was (see above pp. 15–16), and different determinations of that relationship will give drastically different theories. Eudoxus presents us with a determination of that relationship as physical immanence. That will make a large difference to the kind of thing a form is.

So I shall speak of Eudoxus' theory of forms. There is, however, reason for dissatisfaction with the theory as it is usually presented: the contradictions between the theory of physical immanence and the High Platonic Theory are made to survive within Eudoxus' theory to account for certain objections Aristotle may have raised against it. But I think the usual presentation is wrong, and that our texts can be accounted for differently.

The tradition tells us very little about this theory: even less than it does about the metaphysics of Speusippus and Xenocrates. It is customary to suppose[118] that this, and our failure to hear of works of Eudoxus' in which the theory was exposed, are indications that Aristotle's report is not based on a written text but on what he had heard in the halls of the Academy. That sounds likely.

It is also sometimes said,[119] as if it were the same point, that the position was not a fully developed theory but something Eudoxus tried on for size by way of handling problems about the participation-relation. It is not the same point. That an ancient Greek did not write a book about something is hardly an indication that he had no detailed theorizing to offer. The fact that Aristotle apparently never wrote a book on the material discussed in *Metaphysics* ZHΘ shows that. But still, even if it is not the same point, it seems to me likely to be right. I should like to add the following.[120]

There is one difference between the version of Aristotle's report in A and its doublet in M: the latter speaks, in 1079b20–22, of the account that "first Anaxagoras and later Eudoxus used to state *in the course of discussing difficulties* (διαπορῶν),[121] and certain others as well."[122] It will not do to lean too hard on a word, and 'διαπορεῖν' is a vague one.[123] The translation I have given is as strong as I can make it. Weaker ones would make Eudoxus even less committed to the view: he stated it 'to make trouble', for example.[124]

But the fact that the view was not propounded in a treatise in fourteen books, and perhaps was one that Eudoxus raised only in the course of dialectical discussion, is not a reason for not taking it seriously. Dialectical discussion was philosophical discussion for those people. And Aristotle took the view seriously enough to say that it was wrong.

What did he think was wrong with it? He does not say here. For this, we must turn to Alexander.

4.2. *Alexander* in Metaphysica *97.2–19: The Position*

Alexander, in commenting on this passage, expands a little. His expansions may be of great importance. For when he lists objections to which Aristotle might be referring, he makes it plain that he has something more to go on than we do: at the end of his list he says (98.21–22): "and [there are] the rest of the absurdities that he [*sc*. Aristotle] showed this view to contain when he examined it in the second [book] of *On Ideas*" (καὶ ὅσα ἄλλα ἐν τῷ δευτέρῳ Περὶ ἰδεῶν τὴν δόξαν ταύτην ἐξετάζων ἔδειξεν ἄτοπα ἔχουσαν). So let us look more closely at what he has to say about immanence.

He gives an initial paraphrase (97.2–8):

> For if it were by being mixed into these [things] [*sc*. things here below] that they [*sc*. the forms] were causes for their being, it would be as if the white were said to be a cause for the white body of its being white, through being mixed into it as a certain nature capable of being by itself; for in that way the white, by being mixed in, would be a cause of the things' being white into which it is mixed. So the ideas too, if they had been mixed into the things that are by nature, would be capable of being causes for them of their being such as they are: [the idea would be] that the man is a man through the mixture [in it] of the idea of man-itself.

> εἰ γὰρ ἦν τῷ μεμῖχθαι τούτοις αἴτια αὐτοῖς τοῦ εἶναι, οὕτως ἂν ἦν ὡς εἰ τὸ λευκὸν λέγοιτο αἴτιον εἶναι τῷ λευκῷ σώματι τοῦ λευκῷ εἶναι διὰ τὸ μεμῖχθαι αὐτῷ ὥς τις φύσις καθ' αὑτὴν εἶναι δυναμένη· οὕτω γὰρ ἂν ἦν τὸ λευκὸν τῷ μεμῖχθαι αἴτιον τοῦ λευκοῖς εἶναι οἷς μέμικται. ὥστε καὶ αἱ ἰδέαι, εἰ ἦσαν μεμιγμέναι τοῖς φύσει οὖσιν, αἰτίαι ἂν αὐτοῖς ἠδύναντο εἶναι τοῦ εἶναι ὁποῖά ἐστιν, ὡς εἶναι τὸν ἄνθρωπον ἄνθρωπον διὰ τὴν τῆς ἰδέας τοῦ αὐτοανθρώπου μῖξιν.

It is not immediately obvious what this is a paraphrase of. It has been seen[125] simply as a paraphrase of the position of "Eudoxus and certain others." Fortunately, Alexander does not say this. For the position Aristotle ascribes to "Eudoxus and certain others" in *Metaphysics* A 9 he also ascribes to Anaxagoras, and, as we have seen, it is a major part of Anaxagoras' position that the white that is mixed into something by virtue of which it is white is *not* capable of existing on its own. It may be a partial description of the argument Aristotle is about to give against the position. Where Alexander is getting it is an open question: he may be looking at *On Ideas* or only at the text of the *Metaphysics*.[126]

After a few lines (97.8–12) of unexciting paraphrase of Aristotle's *Metaphysics*, Alexander goes on (97.12–19):

> And he even sets out whose view it was that states that each of the things that are is what it is by something's being mixed into it because of which it is that which it is.
>
> 14 For Anaxagoras used to say that each of the things that are is mixed from all the homoeomers;[127] and that of which [there was] most mixed in it, from this the substance of the thing seemed to be;[128] so that each of them was what it was by certain other [things] being mixed into it.
>
> 17/18 And Eudoxus, among Plato's associates, thought that each [thing] existed by a mixture of the ideas in the [things] that have their being relative to them, and certain others [thought so as well], as he [*sc.* Aristotle] was saying [in 991a17–18].

> καὶ παρατίθεταί γε τίνων ἦν δόξα ἡ λέγουσα ἕκαστον τῶν ὄντων εἶναι τοῦτο ὅ ἐστι τῷ μεμῖχθαί τι αὐτῷ δι' ὅ ἐστι τοῦτο ὅ ἐστιν. Ἀναξαγόρας τε γὰρ ἕκαστον τῶν ὄντων ἔλεγε μὲν ἐκ πάντων μεμῖχθαι τῶν ὁμοιομερῶν· οὗ δὲ πλεῖστον ἐν αὐτῷ μέμικται, ἐξ αὐτοῦ τούτου δοκεῖν εἶναι τὴν ουσίαν τοῦ πράγματος· ὥστε ἕκαστον αὐτῶν ἦν τοῦτο ὃ ἦν τῷ μεμῖχθαι αὐτῷ τινα ἄλλα. καὶ Εὔδοξος τῶν Πλάτωνος γνωρίμων μίξει τῶν ἰδεῶν ἐν τοῖς πρὸς αὐτὰς τὸ εἶναι ἔχουσιν ἡγεῖτο ἕκαστον εἶναι, καὶ ἄλλοι δέ τινες, ὡς ἔλεγε.

Alexander makes two claims about Anaxagoras: in 97.14–15 that he thought each being was a mixture from all the 'homoeomers,' and in 15–16 that what each of them was depended on what there was most of in it. Each of these two claims is accurate, and each can be found in Aristotle's *Physics* A 4 (see notes 127 and 128).

Alexander goes on to the position of Eudoxus, and we have for this no independent check on his accuracy. The sentence at 97.17–18,[129] in speaking of "the things that have their being relative to the forms," gives a formulation of the position more precise and more abstract than that in 991a14–18. The things in question are of course what we have been referring to as the forms' *participants*: those things that exist by virtue of whatever relationship they have to forms.[130] It would be nice to know whether this formulation goes back to Aristotle and the Academy. But phrases like the one in question occur elsewhere in Alexander[131] when he is merely paraphrasing Aristotle and not, apparently, looking at *On Ideas*. Unfortunately, there is nothing to indicate that 97.17–19 is based on anything more than the text being commented on.

We do not learn much from this part of Alexander's commentary. He is accurate so far where we are in a position to check up on him, but he does not add much, except for an occasional phrase, and those phrases may be his own.

We can summarize the position, Immanence, that is about to be attacked, as follows:

> (I1) There are certain basic ingredients: 'Ideas' or 'Forms.'
>
> (I2) The things that exist are mixtures of these Ideas (and so depend for their existence on, are what they are because of, the Ideas in them).
>
> (I3) Each true predication about something that exists lists one of the Ideas that is mixed in the thing.
>
> (I4) Each Idea, the F, is itself F.

Alexander also supposed that these ingredients were taken to be capable of existing on their own; we are not making this a part of the theory.

4.3. *Alexander* in Metaphysica *97.19–98.24: The Objections*

Alexander now turns to refutation; his opening comment is intended to cover both Anaxagoras and Eudoxus (97.19–21): "But he [Aristotle] says this account, which states that each of the things that are has its being a certain this by participation in something, is very easily refuted" (τοῦτον δὲ τὸν λόγον λίαν φησὶν εὐέλεγκτον εἶναι τὸν μεθέξει τινὸς ἕκαστον τῶν ὄντων τὸ εἶναι τόδε τι ἔχειν λέγοντα).

This sentence, like that in 97.17–19, is of interest. This one mentions participation, and if it could be taken as going back to Aristotle, it might support the idea that Eudoxus' use of the notion of mixture was sparked by Plato's talk of participation. But, as with 97.17–19, the text can bear no weight: in this case not only is there the general worry that Alexander might be going on nothing more than the text of the *Metaphysics*, but the clause τὸν μεθέξει τινὸς . . . λέγοντα ("which states that . . . by participation in something") is missing in two manuscripts:[132] it could easily be a gloss.

The objections Alexander lists against Anaxagoras are independent of those he lists against Eudoxus. We shall have to consider those against Anaxagoras, so here they are, for future reference (97.21–27):

> And that the nature of things that are is not generally like that, he has shown in what he has said against Anaxagoras.[133]

22/23 (1) For neither is everything of a nature to be mixed with everything;[134] for mixture is of things separate and capable of subsisting in their own right, but the accidents are not like that. But if that which is mixed in can be separated, the affects of substances would be separable.[135]

25/26 (2) And coming-to-be and passing-away are destroyed by those who say this,

26/27 and [there are] as many other things as he has stated in the first book of the *Physics* lectures[136] against this view.

καὶ ὅτι μὲν οὐχ οὕτως ἔχει καθόλου ἡ τῶν ὄντων φύσις, ἔδειξεν ἐν οἷς πρὸς Ἀναξαγόραν εἶπεν. οὔτε γὰρ πᾶν παντὶ μεμῖχθαι πέφυκε· τῶν γὰρ κεχωρισμένων καὶ καθ' αὐτὸ ὑφίστασθαι δυναμένων ἡ μῖξις, οὐ τοιαῦτα δὲ τὰ συμβεβηκότα. εἰ δὲ τὸ μεμιγμένον οἷόν τε χωρισθῆναι, χωριστὰ ἂν εἴη τὰ πάθη τῶν οὐσιῶν. ἀναιρεῖταί τε καὶ γένεσις καὶ φθορὰ κατὰ τοὺς οὕτω λέγοντας, καὶ ὅσα ἄλλα εἶπεν ἐν τῷ πρώτῳ τῆς Φυσικῆς ἀκροάσεως πρὸς τήνδε τὴν δόξαν.

Then we must look to the objections against Eudoxus, where the reference to *On Ideas* occurs. Here they are (97.27–98.24):[137]

And [to show] that other things [do] not, as Eudoxus and certain others thought, [exist] by mixture of the ideas [in them],[138] he says it is easy to collect many impossible consequences of this view. They would be such as these:

30 If the ideas are mixed with the other things,

30/**98**.1 (1) first, they would be bodies, for mixture is of bodies.

98.1 (2) Again, they would have contrariety toward each other; for mixture is in accordance with contrariety.

2 (3)[139] Again, they will be mixed either as a whole in each of the things in which they are mixed or as a part.

(a) But if as a whole, what is one in number will be in many [things];[140] for the idea is one in number;

4/5 (b1) but if as a part, that which partakes of a part[141] of the man-itself, not that which partakes of the whole of the man-itself, will be a man.

(b2) Again, they will be divisible and partible,[142] although they are impassible.

(b3) And next they will be homoeomers, if all the things that have any part of one are like each other; but how can the forms be homoeomers? For the part of a man can't be a man, as the part of gold is gold.[143]

9/10 (4) Again, as he too says a little farther on,[144] in each thing there will be not one idea mixed but many; for if there is one idea of animal and another of man, and the man is both [an] animal and [a] man,[145] he would partake of both ideas.

12/13 And man-itself, an idea, inasmuch as it is also [an] animal, would itself partake of the animal; but then the ideas would no longer be simple, but composed of many [things], and some of them would be first and others second.

15/16 But if it is not animal, how could it fail to be absurd that a man is not an animal?[146]

16/17 (5) And again, if they are mixed into the things that are relative to them, how would they still be paradigms, as they say? For paradigms are not thus causes of the likeness of their images to them, by being mixed into them.

19 (6) And again, they would be co-destroyed with the things in which they are, when these are destroyed. But they would not exist as separable, by themselves, but [would exist] in the things that participate in them.[147]

21 (7) And in addition to these, they would no longer be immovable;

21/22 and there are as many other absurdities as he showed this view to involve in examining it in the second book of *On Ideas*. For this is why he said "for it is easy to collect many impossible things against this view": they are collected there.[148]

97

ὅτι δὲ μὴ ὡς Εὔδοξος ἡγεῖτο καὶ ἄλλοι τινὲς μίξει τῶν ἰδεῶν τὰ ἄλλα, ῥᾴδιόν φησιν εἶναι συναγαγεῖν πολλὰ καὶ ἀδύνατα ἑπόμενα τῇ δόξῃ τῇδε. εἴη δ' ἂν τοιαῦτα. εἰ μίγνυνται αἱ ἰδέαι τοῖς ἄλλοις, πρῶτον μὲν σώματα ἂν εἶεν·

98 σωμάτων γὰρ ἡ μῖξις. ἔτι ἕξουσιν ἐναντίωσιν πρὸς ἀλλήλας· ἡ γὰρ μῖξις κατ' ἐναντίωσίν ἐστιν. ἔτι οὕτως μιχθήσεται ὡς ἢ ὅλην ἐν ἑκάστῳ τῶν οἷς μίγνυται εἶναι ἢ μέρος. ἀλλ' εἰ μὲν ὅλη, ἔσται ἐν πλείοσι τὸ ἓν κατὰ τὸν ἀριθμόν· ἓν γὰρ κατὰ τὸν ἀριθμὸν ἡ ἰδέα· εἰ δὲ πρὸς μέρος, τὸ μέρος τοῦ αὐτοανθρώπου μετέχον, οὐ τὸ ὅλου τοῦ αὐτοανθρώπου ἔσται ἄνθρωπος. ἔτι διαιρεταὶ ἂν εἶεν αἱ ἰδέαι καὶ μερισταί, οὖσαι ἀπαθεῖς. ἔπειτα ἔσται μὲν ὁμοιομερῆ, εἴ γε πάντα τὰ ἔχοντά τι μέρος ἐξ αὐτοῦ ὅμοιά ἐστιν ἀλλήλοις· πῶς δὲ οἷόν τε τὰ εἴδη ὁμοιομερῆ εἶναι; οὐ γὰρ οἷόν τε τὸ μέρος τοῦ ἀνθρώπου ἄνθρωπον εἶναι, ὡς τὸ τοῦ χρυσοῦ μέρος χρυσόν. ἔτι, ὡς καὶ αὐτὸς ὀλίγον προελθὼν λέγει, ἐν ἑκάστῳ οὐ μία ἔσται ἰδέα μεμιγμένη ἀλλὰ πολλαί· εἰ γὰρ ἄλλη μὲν ζῴου ἰδέα ἄλλη δὲ ἀνθρώπου, ὁ δὲ ἄνθρωπος καὶ ζῷόν ἐστι καὶ ἄνθρωπος, ἀμφοτέρων ἂν μετέχοι τῶν ἰδεῶν. καὶ ὁ αὐτοάνθρωπος δὲ ἰδέα, ᾗ μὲν καὶ ζῷόν ἐστι, μετέχοι ἂν καὶ αὐτὸ τοῦ ζῴου· οὕτως δὲ οὐκέτι ἂν ἁπλαῖ αἱ ἰδέαι εἶεν, ἀλλ' ἐκ πολλῶν συγκείμεναι, καὶ αἱ μὲν αὐτῶν πρῶται αἱ δὲ δεύτεραι. εἰ δὲ μὴ ἔστι ζῷον, πῶς οὐκ ἄτοπον ἄνθρωπον λέγειν μὴ εἶναι ζῷον; ἔτι δέ, εἰ μίγνυνται τοῖς πρὸς αὐτὰ οὖσι, πῶς ἂν ἔτι εἶεν παραδείγματα, ὡς λέγουσιν; οὐδὲ γὰρ οὕτως τὰ παραδείγματα ταῖς εἰκόσι τῆς ὁμοιότητος τῆς πρὸς αὐτὰ αἴτια τῷ μεμῖχθαι. ἔτι τε καὶ συμφθείροιντο ἂν τοῖς ἐν οἷς εἰσι φθειρομένοις. ἀλλ' οὐδὲ χωρισταὶ ἂν εἶεν αὐταὶ καθ' αὑτάς, ἀλλ' ἐν τοῖς μετέχουσιν αὐτῶν. πρὸς δὲ τούτοις οὐδὲ ἀκίνητοι ἔτι ἔσονται, καὶ ὅσα ἄλλα ἐν τῷ δευτέρῳ Περὶ ἰδεῶν τὴν δόξαν ταύτην ἐξετάζων ἔδειξεν ἄτοπα ἔχουσαν. διὰ τοῦτο γὰρ εἶπε τὸ ῥᾴδιον γὰρ συναγαγεῖν πολλὰ καὶ ἀδύνατα πρὸς τὴν δόξαν ταύτην. ἐκεῖ γὰρ συνῆκται.

We must first deal with the question, How much of this can we take as Alexander reporting objections of Aristotle's from the lost Περὶ ἰδεῶν?

Scholars have resorted to some strange devices to reassure themselves here. Von Fritz[149] undertook a comparison between Alexander's immediately preceding objections against Anaxagoras and those of Aristotle in *Physics* A 4 in order to test Alexander's reliability as a reporter. Let us consider this.

Aristotle in that chapter gives eight objections against Anaxagoras (187b7–188a18). Alexander gives two objections. One of them, (2) (97.25–26), is that Anaxagoras does away with coming-to-be. This is not an *objection* of Aristotle's, but part of Aristotle's statement of Anaxagoras' position (*Physics* 187a28–29, 34–35). The other of Alexander's objections, (1) (97.22–25), is that, as the components of a mixture must be separable, Anaxagoras makes white, an accident or affect of a substance, separable from it; but that (on Aristotelian grounds) is impossible. There is nothing in *Physics* A 4 that this points straight at. But Aristotle's sixth objection (188a5–13: discussed later, pp. 51–53) is to the effect that Anaxagoras does not understand why the components of his mixture are not separable: it is not because of the argument we considered earlier (pp. 7–9, based on the claim that you can, eventually, get anything out of anything), but because the affects of a substance are not separable. This and Alexander's argument are related, but different: Alexander's employs the Aristotelian premise that the components of a mixture can be separated out of it, but that plays no role at all in *Physics* A 4.

Plainly, if Aristotle's *Physics* had not survived, we would not have had the faintest idea what happened in the fourth chapter of its first book.

Yet von Fritz managed to persuade himself, and, apparently, Cherniss,[150] that Alexander had got *Physics* A 4 essentially right. He simply failed to notice that what Alexander was paraphrasing was, *not Physics* A 4, but a passage three columns earlier in the *Metaphysics* (A 8. 989a33-b4):

> For while to say that in the beginning all [things] were mixed is absurd otherwise, but also because it follows that they had to pre-exist unmixed and because one chance thing is not of a type to mix with any other chance [thing], and in addition to these [reasons], because the affects and accidents would be separated from their substances (for there is mixture of the same [things] as [there is] separation) . . .

> ἀτόπου γὰρ ὄντος καὶ
> ἄλλως τοῦ φάσκειν μεμῖχθαι τὴν ἀρχὴν πάντα, καὶ διὰ
> **989b** τὸ συμβαίνειν ἄμικτα δεῖν προϋπάρχειν καὶ διὰ τὸ μὴ
> πεφυκέναι τῷ τυχόντι μίγνυσθαι τὸ τυχόν, πρὸς δὲ τούτοις
> ὅτι τὰ πάθη καὶ τὰ συμβεβηκότα χωρίζοιτ' ἂν τῶν οὐσιῶν
> (τῶν γὰρ αὐτῶν μῖξίς ἐστι καὶ χωρισμός) . . .

Here Aristotle *does* state the first of Alexander's objections, although Alexander manages to run two objections into one (see 989b1–2, b2–3, with *in Metaphysica* 97.22–25).[151]

So, *pace* von Fritz and Cherniss, Alexander is making no attempt to paraphrase from the *Physics*. And yet he does close his objections to Anaxagoras with the words "and there are as many other things as he [that is, Aristotle] has stated in the first book of the *Physics* against this view" (καὶ ὅσα ἄλλα εἶπεν ἐν τῷ πρώτῳ τῆς Φυσικῆς ἀκροάσεως πρὸς τήνδε τὴν δόξαν, 97.26–27).

The Eudoxus passage closes with the words "and there are as many other absurdities as he showed this view to involve in examining it in the second book of *On Ideas*." The received opinion (see note 148) is that these words indicate that Alexander's list of objections against Eudoxus are drawn from *On Ideas*. The case of the reference to the *Physics* shows that this is completely false. There is no assurance that *any* of the objections come from *On Ideas*.

And the words with which Alexander opens the objection I have listed as (4) are ominous: "Again, as he also says himself a little farther on" (ἔτι, ὡς καὶ αὐτὸς ὀλίγον προελθὼν λέγει, 98.9–10); the reference is forward in the *Metaphysics* to a passage, quoted later, in which Aristotle gives something like objection (4) as an objection against Platonizing positions in general: there is no specific reference to Eudoxus. If we had only that passage, there would not be the slightest reason to think that the objection it registers could be applied to the position Aristotle ascribes to Eudoxus.

The words "as he too says a little farther on" are ambiguous between 'as he, too [i.e., in addition to me, Alexander] says later' and 'as he also says later in the *Metaphysics* as well as here in *On Ideas*.' Taken the latter way,[152] we are on safe ground in ascribing the material to *On Ideas*; taken the former way, as Karpp did, Alexander is winging it, and comparing what he comes up with with what Aristotle says later in the *Metaphysics*.[153] We must confront this issue.[154]

There is a general point to be made here: adducing Aristotelian parallels for objections on Alexander's list will not silence Karpping critics (see note 153). For the parallels do nothing whatever to guarantee that Aristotle himself thought that these objections were applicable against Eudoxus' position, and a fortiori do nothing to guarantee that he applied those objections against that position in the lost work *On Ideas*.

And there is a specific point to be made as well. The ominous words just adverted to are, granted, not a proof that Aristotle has not been speaking all along. But they are echoed two pages later.[155] Alexander is listing the ways in which, as he sees it, the Platonists tried to make participation work. He says (100.27–33):

> For, investigating in what way the partaking of the forms [might work], either they say it is such that in each of the particulars the idea is present, e.g. in each of the particular men [there is] the man-itself, or [they say that] in each [there is a] part of the idea, or the form is a paradigm for its participants. Of which the first two ways

of partaking are impossible, as we showed a little way back, and he too said when he had mentioned Eudoxus that "it is easy to collect many impossible things against such a view."

> ζητοῦντες γὰρ τίνα τρόπον ἡ μετοχὴ ἡ τῶν εἰδῶν, ἢ οὕτως φασὶν ὡς ἐν ἑκάστῳ τῶν κατὰ μέρος ἐνυπάρχειν τὴν ἰδέαν, οἷον ἐν ἑκάστῳ τῶν τινῶν ἀνθρώπων τὸν αὐτοάνθρωπον, ἢ ἐν ἑκάστῳ μέρος τῆς ἰδέας, ἢ παράδειγμα τὸ εἶδός ἐστι τοῖς μετέχουσιν. ὧν οἱ μὲν πρῶτοι δύο τρόποι τῆς μετοχῆς ἀδύνατοι, ὡς ἡμεῖς τε ἐδείξαμεν πρὸ ὀλίγου, καὶ αὐτὸς εἶπεν Εὐδόξου μνημονεύσας ὅτι "ῥᾴδιον συναγαγεῖν πολλὰ καὶ ἀδύνατα πρὸς τὴν τοιαύτην δόξαν".

The proof that "the first two ways of partaking are impossible" is the long dilemma I have numbered (3) (98.2–9). Alexander here refers to this argument when he says "as we showed"; when he adds "and he too said," and cites the *Metaphysics* (not the *On Ideas*), he is fairly plainly referring this argument to himself, not Aristotle. The first "he too said" was ominous. This one, with its contrasted "we showed", seems to me funereal. Objection (3) is a construction of Alexander's.

So Alexander did not, when he came to the reference to Eudoxus, dutifully go to the stacks, pull down the roll containing *On Ideas* ii, scroll his way laboriously to the objections against Eudoxus, and transcribe them into his commentary, any more than he went to the *Physics* when he encountered the reference to Anaxagoras.

We cannot use Alexander unconfirmed, and it is not enough to confirm him to find an Aristotelian parallel. But if we can find the right kind of parallel, we may have something we can use. For Alexander is working, as always, with Aristotelian materials, and has read, as we have not, *On Ideas*, and does say that there are objections against Eudoxianism in that work. What does that leave us with?

Almost precisely the list that Karpp pronounced genuine,[156] I think, although not precisely for his reasons. He believed that the words "as he himself says a little farther on" meant that all the objections up to and including my (4) came from Alexander. This is too sweeping: those words only cast doubt on (4) itself. The words that recall them a page later carry (3) into the same limbo.[157]

The objections require individual consideration. I take them up in order of increasing interest. In each case, I begin by speaking as if Alexander were the author of the objection. This is not meant to prejudice the case: it is just that Alexander wrote the commentary in which the objections are found.

4.3.1. Objection (3), 98.2–9. As I have already said, I think this is a construction of Alexander's. But it is of interest, since it revives an argument in the *Parmenides* we have already considered.

As I read it,[158] it is a dilemma with each horn leading to absurdity, and several consequences tacked on to the second horn.[159] The dilemma is set up, as at *Parmenides* 131a4–6, with the premise (98.2–3; from here on, *P* indicates a premise, *S*, a supposition for the purpose of reduction to absurdity, and *C*, a conclusion):

(P1) Either the whole of each Idea will be in each mixture in which it figures, or a part of it will be.

The first horn is handled in a way reminiscent of *Parmenides* 131a8-b2[160] (98.3–4):

(S1) The whole of each Idea is in each mixture.
(P2) Each Idea is one in number.
(P3) There are many mixtures for each Idea.
∴ (C1) What is one in number is in many things.[161]
[(P4) It is impossible for what is one in number to be in many things (or, in many places).]

The square brackets around (P4) indicate that it is not something Alexander says outright. He must have assumed something like this, as Parmenides and Socrates do in *Parmenides* 131bc, for this horn of the dilemma goes no further, and yet he tells us (as we have seen) in 100.30–31 that he has proven this alternative wrong. He could have supposed that he had the authority of Aristotle for (P4), see *Metaphysics* Z 14. 1039a33-b2 (and possibly B 6. 1003a7–12).

In fact, an Immanentist would have no interest in this horn, and no anxiety over its being shown absurd: on his position, for each ingredient the F, there is some of it in each thing that is F, and the case in which some mixture has all the F there is is very rare if not impossible; if it occurred, of course nothing but that thing could be F. The dilemma in the *Parmenides* was constructed with another target in view: Socrates' theory makes the forms separate, but then tries to explain their relation to ordinary things by cashing in metaphors that sound immanentist, like 'partaking.'

The absurdities that count, then, we expect to be those that occur on the second horn of the dilemma. Here we conceive the Theory of Immanence as holding that, where x is distinct from the F but is F, x has some of the Idea, the F, in it; in general or even always, x will not have all of the F in it, but only a part of the F. Let us assume, as Alexander plainly does, that x will always have only a part of the F:

(S2) x $\neq$ the F $\rightarrow$ (x is F $\leftrightarrow$ x has a (proper) part of the Idea, the F).

Alexander first tells us that (98.4–5):[162]

∴ (C2) x has a (proper) part of the man-itself $\rightarrow$ x is a man.

Some articulations of these objections (see note 139) count this as an absurdity all on its own. It is difficult to see why:[163] this is just repeating part of the supposition that is to be shown absurd, as Parmenides does in *Parmenides* 131c6–7.

Alexander now produces an absurdity (98.6):

∴ (C3) Each Idea is divisible and partible, but
(P5) Each Idea is impassible,

where to be 'impassible' (ἀπαθής) is to be incapable of being affected in any way, and to be 'divisible' (διαιρετός) or 'partible' (μεριστός) is to be capable of being divided or partitioned, so that (C3) and (P5) are in contradiction.

But what entitles Alexander to (P5)? Aristotle says "the ideas are thought to be impassible . . . by those who say there are ideas" (*Topics* Z 10. 148a20–21: ἀπαθεῖς . . . δοκοῦσιν ⟨εἶναι⟩ αἱ ἰδέαι τοῖς λέγουσιν ἰδέας εἶναι). And when Parmenides draws the conclusion that the forms are partible in the corresponding part of the *Parmenides* (131c5 μεριστὰ . . . ἔστιν αὐτὰ τὰ εἴδη), there is an aura of paradox, and Socrates seems reluctant to accept the conclusion (131c8). But, first, Aristotle is thinking mostly of Plato in *Topics* Z 10 (see 148a15, where he is named), and nothing whatever shows that he intended Eudoxus as one of 'those who say there are ideas' there. Second, in the *Parmenides*, Socrates' hesitation has a real basis: his position as he stated it in 129b6–c1, c4–8, d2–6 required the form, the one, and perhaps each of the other forms as well (see 129d6-e4) to be unitary in a way that excluded the possibility of its having parts, and any reluctance he has at 131c8 is due to his awareness of where Parmenides is going next (131c9–11):

> Then, Socrates, will you be willing to say that the one form is in truth partitioned among us, and will it still be one?
>
> In no way, he said.

> Ἦ οὖν ἐθελήσεις, ὦ Σώκρατες, φάναι τὸ ἓν εἶδος ἡμῖν τῇ ἀληθείᾳ μερίζεσθαι, καὶ ἔτι ἓν ἔσται;
>
> Οὐδαμῶς, εἰπεῖν.

Eudoxus need not have the same commitments.

Recall Anaxagoras, the Immanentist whose position Eudoxus is reviving. One item in his universe was not part of any mixture: mind (νοῦς); "it is mixed with no thing, but it alone is by itself" (μέμικται οὐδενὶ χρήματι, ἀλλὰ μόνος αὐτὸς ἐφ' ἑαυτοῦ ἐστιν, Simplicius *in Physica* 156.14–15).[164] As Aristotle paraphrases this position, "mind is impassible and unmixed" (τὸν νοῦν ἀπαθῆ . . . καὶ ἀμιγῆ εἶναι, *Physics* Θ 5. 256b25; cf. *De anima* A 2. 405b19–21).[165] To stay 'impassible', mind has to keep out of the mixture.

When Eudoxus tries blending Immanentism with the Theory of Forms, some things in the latter have to go. He can hardly have failed to see that what is mixed into something has something done to it. One of the things that will have to go is the Forms' 'impassibility.'

It is fortunate, then, that we do not have to ascribe this argument to Aristotle.

In fact, the only part of the entire dilemma that looks as if it might have touched Eudoxus is the last. Alexander finishes by arguing that

∴ (C4) Each Idea is a homoeomer;[166]

that is, for the F, not only is it F, every part of it is F as well. Alexander gives as his reason for this: "all the things that have any part of one [*sc*. an Idea] are like each other."[167] That is, by (S2), any part of the F will do to make a mixture F: any such part of the F must then still be F. Alexander is here harking back to the still more general assumption of Plato's and Eudoxus' theories from which (I4) descends: explaining why something is F requires something that is itself F.[168] In Eudoxus' theory, it is the presence of some (pure) white in something white that explains why the latter is white, and, in general, of something that is purely F in an x that is F that explains why x is F. So if any part of an Idea, the F, will serve to make something F, each such part must itself be F, and the F is a homoeomer.

But, by (I4):

∴ (C5) The Idea of a man is a man,

and because

(P6) A part of a man is not a man,
∴ (C6) A man is not a homoeomer,

and

∴ (C7) The Idea of a man is not a homoeomer.

It is plain that what we have here is an elaborate version of the Drawback: Immanentism cannot be made to apply to every predication, because some predicates, like 'man', cannot be construed as naming a part of that of which they are true.

When we first considered the dilemma in the *Parmenides*, we reflected that if Eudoxus' Immanentism postdated the *Parmenides*, he would have supposed he had a way around it. We have just encountered a revised version of that dilemma in Alexander, used against Eudoxus. And it is plain that Eudoxus could easily have supposed he had a way around the dilemma, for the only part of it that could be construed as a good objection to his position, the last, was no part of the original. This of course does not prove that the *Parmenides* preceded Eudoxus' adoption of Immanentism; it only confirms the sad conclusion we reached before: we are not in a position to tell which preceded which.

4.3.2. Objection (4), 98.10–16. Alexander first (98.10–12) argues that each thing that exists will have mixed in it not just one but many Ideas; this is straightforward:

(P1) There is one Idea of an animal.
(P2) There is another Idea of a man.
(P3) Socrates is both a man and an animal.
∴ (C1) There are two Ideas in Socrates.

At (P3), Alexander's claim (98.11–12) that "the man is both [an] animal and [a] man" is taken to be about an individual man (see note 145).

(C1) follows from its premises and the assumptions of the theory (p. 30), especially (I3). But so far, there is nothing objectionable at all: it is not in the faintest absurd that there should be more than one Idea in Socrates. So it is best not to count this much as a separate objection (see note 146).

It is, of course, strange that Socrates' being a man and his being an animal should be due to two separate ingredients, but the argument so far does not point to that oddity. That is where it is going.

Alexander next (98.12–13) uses as a premise the claim that the Idea of a man is an animal; at the end of the argument (98.15–16), he blusters that it would be absurd if the Idea of a man were not an animal. We can make this follow from the theory:

(P4) The Idea of a man is a man. (I4)
(P5) Every man is an animal.
∴ (C2) The Idea of a man is an animal.

But then it follows that (98.13–14):

∴ (C3) The Idea of an animal is in that of a man.

This comes from (C2) and (I3). Alexander extracts from this the conclusion that the Idea of a man is itself composite, and that some Ideas are prior to others (98.14–15):

∴ (C4) The Idea of man is a mixture.
∴ (C5) The Idea of a man depends for its existence on the Idea of an animal.[169]

(C4) comes from (C3) and (I2): the Idea of man has that of an animal mixed into it, so it is a mixture. But (C4) is at least close to being absurd: the Idea of man was supposed to be a basic ingredient. And we can see, although Alexander does not tell us this, that it would not help to demote the Idea of man to the status of a mixture. For the argument is easily generalized: wherever we have one predicate more inclusive than another, we would then be forced to demote the Idea corresponding to the included one to the status of a mixture, so that in the end the only unmixed ingredients left would be those corresponding to the terms that encompass all the rest: perhaps just the single term *being* or *one* (cf. *Metaphysics* Z 11. 1036b19–20).

(C5) similarly follows from the theory, assuming that the priorities in question are the standard ones among the Academics: one thing is prior to another where the second depends on the first for its existence (cf. *Metaphysics* Δ 11. 1019a2–4); for (I2) tells us that ordinary things depend for their existence on their ingredients. And it, too, points to an absurdity: the theory told us that each predicate true of a thing listed one of its constituent Ideas, a basic ingredient, but now it turns out that Socrates has in him one ingredient that depends for its existence on, has as a constituent, another. Once more, the futility of going along with this and demoting 'the man-itself' to the status of a mixture is plain.

Is this objection likely to have come from Aristotle? We have seen reason to be mistrustful. But, oddly, when Alexander at 98.9–10 refers forward in the *Metaphysics* to 991a27–b1, he errs.

There Aristotle is arguing against the conception of forms as paradigms. On the face of it, he takes this to be a distinct way of thinking of forms, as we saw (see earlier, p. 24), and different objections would be appropriate to it. The two he gives there are these (991a27–b1, paralleled, with slight differences as noted, by M 5. 1079b31–35):

991

a27 And there will be many paradigms of the same thing, and so also forms, e.g. of the man, the animal and the two-footed, and at the same time the man-itself.

a29/30 Again, not only [will] the forms [be] paradigms of the perceptibles but also of [the ideas][170] themselves, e.g. the kind, as a kind of forms;[171] so that the same [thing] [will be] paradigm and image.

ἔσται τε πλείω παραδείγματα τοῦ αὐτοῦ,
ὥστε καὶ εἴδη, οἷον τοῦ ἀνθρώπου τὸ ζῷον καὶ τὸ δίπουν, ἅμα
δὲ καὶ τὸ αὐτοάνθρωπος. ἔτι οὐ μόνον τῶν αἰσθητῶν παρα-
a30 δείγματα τὰ εἴδη ἀλλὰ καὶ αὐτῶν [τῶν ἰδεῶν], οἷον τὸ γέ-
νος, ὡς γένος εἰδῶν· ὥστε τὸ αὐτὸ ἔσται παράδειγμα καὶ
b1 εἰκών.

The objection of a27–29 is that, under the paradigm-conception, there will be multiple models, forms, for the same thing: for *man*, both the animal and the two-footed will be models, as well as the man-itself. This looks somewhat different from the corresponding part of Alexander's Objection (4) against Eudoxus, the argument for (C1): that focused on the individual Socrates, and there was really no absurdity in (C1). Here in Aristotle, the emphasis is not on there being multiple forms for the same individual; that, again would not be odd. Rather, the point is that multiple forms will explain the application of the same *predicate*: the form man-itself will explain the truth of "Socrates is a man," but so will the conjunction of the animal and the biped.

The objection of a29–b1 is to the effect that the forms are not just models for perceptible things, but for themselves as well: a *kind-* or *genus-* Idea (form) will be a model for the *form-* or *species-*Ideas that fall under it. So the same thing will be both a model and a copy. For example, the form man-itself is itself an animal, so to explain the truth of that on this conception we must invoke the form animal-itself as a model for the man-itself. Then the man-itself is a model for Socrates, but a copy from the animal-itself.

So far, it is not easy to see what the absurdity is. But Aristotle is plainly picturing the paradigm-conception as one in which the universe divides into two strata: that of models, the forms, and that of their copies, the perceptibles. Then there should be no copies among the forms: they should all be on a par as far as this goes.

The attempt to recast the argument Alexander gives leading to (C4) so that it parallels this does not work right. We begin by trying to take the theory of Immanence as dividing the world into (unmixed) Ingredients and Mixtures. Then the Idea of man, which we invoke as an Ingredient in explaining Socrates' being a man, is treated as a Mixture, because it is an animal and so has to have the Idea of animal mixed into it. But this is not by itself absurd at all: of course, some Ingredients are themselves Mixtures; they just are not pure or unmixed Ingredients.

There is an obvious similarity between the way Aristotle's arguments against the paradigm-conception work and the way Objection (4) against Eudoxus works: many of the premises are common. But the absurdities are quite different. Aristotle's complaints against the paradigm-conception are specific to the attempt to generalize the copy-paradigm relation to cover all subject-predicate relations. The complaints against Eudoxus are specific to the attempt to cover the mixture-ingredient relation to cover all subject-predicate relations. The premises are similar, but the absurdity in each case turns on the specific relation being generalized.

What Alexander says is: "as he himself says a little farther on, in each thing there will be not one idea mixed but many." Aristotle does not say this a little farther on, and the similarity between what he does say and the objection Alexander gives is fairly superficial. Alexander, in his commentary on 991a27, makes the similarity greater by adding conclusions corresponding to (C4) and (C5); Aristotle mentions no such conclusions. At least one of them looks quite inappropriate. In his discussion of the first of the two arguments against the paradigm-conception (that of a27–29), Alexander gets man participating in the man-itself, the animal-itself, and the two-footed-itself, all different (105.2–5); this much is merely expanding on Aristotle. But then he says (105.5–8):

> But if [things] differing from each other exist at the same time in the man-itself, the idea will not be simple, but composed of ideas; and if each of them is an idea, an idea will be prior to an idea (for the animal-itself will be first over the man-itself; for the animal is [a] kind over the man-itself) . . .
>
> ἀλλ' εἰ μὲν ἅμα ἔστιν ἐν τῷ αὐτοανθρώπῳ διαφέροντα ἀλλήλων, οὐχ ἁπλοῦν ἡ ἰδέα, ἀλλ' ἔσται ἐξ ἰδεῶν συγκειμένη· εἰ δὲ ἔστιν ἰδέα ἕκαστον αὐτῶν, προτέρα ἔσται ἰδέα ἰδέας (τὸ γὰρ αὐτοζῷον πρῶτον τοῦ αὐτοανθρώπου· γένος γὰρ τὸ ζῷον τοῦ αὐτοανθρώπου) . . .

This of course assimilates the argument here to that for (C4) and (C5), but it does so at the cost of running together Immanence and the paradigm-conception. A defender of the paradigm-conception would have no reason to concede that the participation of the Idea of man in that of animal and in that of two-footed meant that the latter two Ideas were in the Idea of man: for him, the relation of participation is spelled out as that of copy to original. So he would have no reason to see the Idea of man as 'composed of Ideas.'

This does not show anything about the question whether Objection (4) stems from *On Ideas*. It is quite possible that Alexander had Objection (4) from *On Ideas* before him, spotted the superficial resemblance between it and 991a27–b1, and so was led to say what he does and to try to tighten up the resemblance. It is also, unfortunately, possible that Alexander saw a way of exploiting the premises that drive the arguments at 991a27–b1 in an argument against Immanence, and penned Objection (4) all by himself. I can see no way of choosing.

4.3.3. Objection (2), 98.1–2. This is an obscure one. Alexander unambiguously employs the premise (98.1–2):

(P1) Mixture is between contraries.

(I2) has the Ideas mixed with each other, and (I3) has them mixed into everyday objects. As the argument is standardly read,[172] Alexander is focusing on the latter in 98.1: he infers

∴ (C1) The Ideas are contrary to the particulars.

But, on the face of it, the conclusion should be

∴ (C2) The Ideas are contrary to each other;

the subject of the immediately preceding sentence was plainly the Ideas, and the feminine in πρὸς ἀλλήλας ("toward each other," 98.1) picks up the feminine αἱ ἰδέαι ("the ideas", 97.30).[173] The argument seriously misfires if it is supposed to show that the Ideas are contrary to the particulars: the particulars are not themselves ingredients in the mixtures; they *are* the mixtures.

And (C2) might be construed to give an objection: it means that any two Ideas that mix are contrary to each other. If there is some of the white in Socrates and some of the hot, the Idea of white must be contrary to that of hot.[174]

But there is trouble. The premise, that mixture is between contraries, is one of the more arcane points[175] in Aristotle's doctrine of mixture proper (μῖξις), or 'chemical combination' as it is sometimes called, as opposed to blending (κρᾶσις).[176] It is apparently mentioned just once in all of Aristotle;[177] in *De generatione et corruptione* A 10. 328a31–33 he says: "So it is plain that, of things that act, those that have contrariety are mixable; for these are indeed passible by each other (φανερὸν οὖν ὅτι ταῦτ' ἐστὶ μικτὰ ὅσα ἐναντίωσιν ἔχει τῶν ποιούντων· ταῦτα γὰρ δὴ ὑπ' ἀλλήλων ἐστὶ παθητικά). This "so it is plain" is one of Aristotle's particularly frustrating ones. Without getting into the details of this passage, we can see that the claim it makes descends from A 7. 323b28–29, 29–324a9, 324a11–12; 323b29–33 states the general thesis:

> But since not any chance [thing] is of a nature to be affected and to act, but those that either are contraries or have contrariety, necessarily both what acts and what is affected are alike and the same in kind (or: in genus), but unlike and contrary in form (or, in species)
>
> ἀλλ' ἐπεὶ οὐ τὸ τυχὸν πέφυκε πάσχειν καὶ ποιεῖν, ἀλλ' ὅσα ἢ ἐναντία ἐστὶν ἢ ἐναντίωσιν ἔχει, ἀνάγκη καὶ τὸ ποιοῦν καὶ τὸ πάσχον τῷ γένει μὲν ὅμοιον εἶναι καὶ ταὐτό, τῷ δ' εἴδει ἀνόμοιον καὶ ἐναντίον.

Incautious formulations such as that in (P1) could lead to severe trouble: it is one of Aristotle's considered doctrines that "it is impossible for contraries to be affected by each other (ὑπ' ἀλλήλων γὰρ πάσχειν τἀναντία ἀδύνατον *Physics* A 7. 190b33).[178] Aristotle allows himself such an incautious formulation in *De generatione et corruptione* 324a2–3: "contraries act on and are affected by each other" (ποιεῖ δὲ καὶ πάσχει τἀναντία ὑπ' ἀλλήλων). The way out of this contradiction is plainly the same as that taken by Socrates in *Phaedo* 103a–c (p. 18 earlier): the claim in *Physics* A 7 pertains to the contraries *themselves*; that in *De generatione et corruptione* A 7 to the contrary *things*. The premise really should read (where 'conF' is the predicate contrary to F):

(P1*) x mixes with y → (∃F)(Fx & conFy & x mixes qua F with y qua conF).

The *quas* in this formulation are intended to ensure that the requirement is not met by something white mixing with something hot where the white thing is big and the hot thing little. The paradigm cases are ones in which, say, something hot is mixed with something cold to produce something lukewarm, or something wet is mixed with something dry to produce something damp, and so on. The cases to be ruled out are cases in which, say, something white is mixed with something hot to produce something in between, or something sweet is mixed with something dark to produce something in between.

Or, anyway, these are the kinds of cases Alexander lists when he lays out the requirement in his treatise *On Mixture* (Bruns [1892], 13. 229.19–25).

But the resulting more cautious formulation makes the argument more complicated. Suppose Socrates is white and hot. Then Immanence tells us that in the mixture that is Socrates there are two ingredients: (some of) the white and (some of) the hot. These are mixed together. We want to get to (C2): in this case, to the conclusion that the white and the hot are contrary to each other. (P1*) will not do it by itself: it will get us only to the conclusion that for some F the white is F and the hot conF, and the white mixes with the hot inasmuch as the white and the hot are F and conF respectively.

Perhaps we could fill in steps to make this work, but it is not going to be easy. The whole argument leans very hard on a very precise notion of mixture, one that incorporates the contrariety requirement. That requirement does not play a very large role in Aristotle's theory of mixture. But it figures much more largely, as Karpp notes, in Alexander's theory of mixture.[179] So there is no particularly good reason to suppose that Aristotle used this argument against Eudoxus, in *On Ideas* or anywhere else.

4.3.4. Objection (5), 98.16–19. This is quite simple; on the Theory, by (I2),

> ∴ (C1) The Ideas are mixed into the things whose features they explain.

But

> (P2) The Ideas are paradigms,

and

> (P3) Paradigms are not mixed into the things whose features they explain,

which yields a contradiction.

There is reason to be suspicious of it.[180] The criticism of the Ideas as paradigms, in Aristotle's *Metaphysics*, occurs immediately after the criticism of Eudoxus (991a20–22): "But to say that [the forms] are paradigms and that the other things partake of them is to speak emptily and to speak in poetic metaphors" (τὸ δὲ λέγειν παραδείγματα αὐτὰ εἶναι καὶ μετέχειν αὐτῶν τἆλλα κενολογεῖν ἐστὶ καὶ μεταφορὰς λέγειν ποιητικάς). The contrast introduced by the *but* (δέ) at the beginning of this is with the position announced as that of Anaxagoras and Eudoxus (the μέν in 991a14).[181] That is, the way the grammar makes it go, Aristotle is saying that, on the one hand, there is the position that regards the form as a physical ingredient in its participants, and, on the other, there is the claim that it is a paradigm; there are lots of objections to the first, and the second is senseless. He seems to think of the ingredient picture as an alternative to the paradigm picture. If Alexander is remembering something from *On Ideas* here, it is all too likely to be on a par with his 'remembering' that Aristotle criticized Anaxagoras for ruling out coming-to-be: Aristotle might merely have said that Eudoxus suggested that the relation of form to instance was not that of a paradigm to its image, but physical ingredience. Anyway, it would be strange if one of the objections he has to the physical ingredient picture is that it rules out the talk of paradigms.

4.3.5. Objection (1), 97.30–98.1. Objection (1) tells us that, on this view, the forms would be bodies, because mixture is only between bodies. There is material in Aristotle that shows he thought the argument sound. In *Topics* Z 12. 149a38–b3 he says:

> Again, [see] if that of which [your opponent] has rendered an account is among the things that are, while what [falls] under the account is among the things that are not, e.g. if the white is defined as color mixed with fire; for it is impossible for the bodiless to be mixed with a body, so that there can't be color mixed with fire; but there is white.

> Πάλιν εἰ οὗ μὲν τὸν λόγον ἀποδίδωσι τῶν ὄντων ἐστί,
> τὸ δ' ὑπὸ τὸν λόγον μὴ τῶν ὄντων, οἷον εἰ τὸ λευκὸν ὡρί-
> 149b σατο χρῶμα πυρὶ μεμειγμένον· ἀδύνατον γὰρ τὸ ἀσώμα-
> τον σώματι μεμῖχθαι, ὥστ' οὐκ ἂν εἴη χρῶμα πυρὶ μεμι-
> γμένον· λευκὸν δ' ἔστιν.

Aristotle himself is prepared to relax the strictures:[182] in *De caelo* A 9. 277b33–34 he says "the shape itself by itself and mixed with the matter are different" (ἕτερόν ἐστιν αὐτὴ καθ' αὑτὴν ἡ μορφὴ καὶ μεμιγμένη μετὰ τῆς ὕλης), and at 278a13–15 he concludes an argument by saying: "Therefore the heavens here [*i.e.*, this particular system of earth, stars, etc.] and heavens [taken] simply [*i.e.*, the universal *heavens*, of which this particular system is an instance] are different, and the one [exists] as form and shape, the other as mixed with the matter" (ἕτερον ἄρα ὅδε ὁ οὐρανὸς καὶ οὐρανὸς ἁπλῶς, καὶ τὸ μὲν ὡς εἶδος καὶ μορφή, τὸ δ' ὡς τῇ ὕλῃ μεμιγμένον). And in *Meteorology* A 5. 342b8–9, red and purple are said "to appear from the fiery and white when they are mixed by superposition" (ἐκ τοῦ πυρώδους καὶ λευκοῦ φαίνεσθαι μιγνυμένων κατὰ τὰς ἐπιπροσθήσεις; see also Γ 2. 372b6–9). But this latter is presumably to be explained as elliptical expression: what is really involved is a mixture of fiery and white bodies, as in *De sensu* 3. 440a31-b23:[183] cf. *Meteorology* Γ 4. 374a6–7, 23–25. The strategy here is the same as that employed earlier in rescuing Aristotle from his own words in *Physics* A 7 and *De generatione et corruptione* A 7 (see p. 43 earlier).

At any rate, his official line is that what can be mixed can be separated (*De generatione et corruptione* A 10. 327b20–22), and he roundly condemns his own words in the *De caelo* when he says, at *De generatione et corruptione* A 10. 327b14–15, "nor [do we say that] the shape, by being mixed with the wax, shapes the mass" (οὔτε τὸ σχῆμα τῷ κηρῷ μιγνύμενον σχηματίζειν τὸν ὄγκον). Physical objects mix only with other physical objects.

In an obscure passage in *Metaphysics* N 5, he may be employing this principle against some Platonists. There the question is "in what way number is composed of its principles" (τίνα τρόπον ὁ ἀριθμός ἐστιν ἐκ τῶν ἀρχῶν, 1092a23–24); the principles are the One and the Indefinite Dyad. Aristotle says (1092a24–26): "Is it by mixture? But not everything is mixable, and what comes-to-be is different, and then one will not be separable or a different nature, but they want [it to be] (πότερον μίξει; ἀλλ' οὔτε πᾶν μικτόν, τό τε γιγνόμενον ἕτερον, οὐκ ἔσται τε χωριστὸν τὸ ἓν οὐδ' ἑτέρα φύσις· οἱ δὲ βούλονται). As this passage is standardly understood,[184] the first objection is to the effect that only bodies are capable of mixing with each other, so the One and the Indefinite Dyad cannot mix.[185]

Suppose this is right, and Aristotle was prepared to use the claim that mixture is only between bodies against Platonists. It does not follow[186] that he used it against Eudoxus. First off, the positions attacked are quite different. The Platonists under scrutiny in N 5 are not saying that the number 5 (say) is one and also indefinitely dyadic due to the presence of the One and the Indefinite Dyad as ingredients in it. And what is more important, these Platonists would presumably have quailed at the idea that the One and the Indefinite Dyad were bodies. But if Eudoxus was trying out the idea that the forms were physical ingredients in things, the comment that physical ingredients are themselves physical is less an objection to the idea than a clarification of it.

This latter is a feature of many of Alexander's objections: we have already encountered it in connection with Objection (3), here it is again, and it will recur. Put generally, the difficulty is this. The objections are reductiones ad absurdum. But for a reduction to absurdity to come off, the alleged absurdity must be either admittedly or arguably a real absurdity. Cherniss apparently supposed the former: that Eudoxus would have admitted that it was absurd that forms should be bodies, or divisible, or whatever. This is, at least in part, because Cherniss thinks that these things just *are* absurdities. But the effect is to saddle Eudoxus with a position that is simply contradictory. And this Cherniss admits.[187]

My own inclination is to think that, if Eudoxus is suggesting that the forms are physical ingredients of things, it cannot be to him obviously absurd to suppose that they are themselves physical. The spectre this raises is that we may be left with nothing: could not Eudoxus simply have accepted all of the supposed absurdities as part of his position?

This free-wheeling attitude ignores the other way a reductio can be made to work: if the alleged absurdity is something that is arguably an absurdity, and in particular something that we know Aristotle would have argued to be an absurdity, we may be able to keep going.

We are close to this situation with Objection (1). Eudoxus' theory is the extended theory of the *Phaedo*, with the intermediates of that theory taking over the role of the forms: that is, on that theory fire imported the hot into the host body; on this one, the hot is just a physical constituent of the host body. But this makes for a difficulty. The theory is a theory of predication, albeit a restricted theory, as it stands, accounting only for physical predications, and not even for all of those. The extended theory of the *Phaedo* used an intermediate entity, fire, that was itself hot; this was used to explain why a certain glowing piece of wood (say) was hot: fire is in it. When it comes to the question why fire is hot, the *Phaedo* theory told us that that was due to the unexplained relation labeled *participation* between fire and the form, The Hot. On the theory we are handing Eudoxus, the reason the stove is hot is that it has something in it that is itself hot, but this is not an intermediate; it *is* the form, The Hot. But, because we are allowing that this ingredient, The Hot, is a body, a physical ingredient, there is now a physical predication that the theory must leave unexplained: the one that predicates hot of this ingredient body. One might well feel that a theory that ascribes the fact that a body is hot to the presence in it of another hot body is either empty or headed for a regress.

There is here an echo of some of the difficulties that Academics raised against the High Platonic Theory. But we can hardly read all of this into (1), so I shall persist in scrapping (1).

That leaves us with (6) and (7). Is there any reason to think that Aristotle might have used them against Eudoxus?

4.3.6. Objection (7), 98.21. This again is quite simple; Alexander uses (I2) to infer

(P1) Things move
∴ (C1) The Ideas move

and juxtaposes this and

(P2) The Ideas are immovable.

This argument certainly goes back to Aristotle, whether it appeared in *On Ideas* or not. In *Topics* B 7. 113a24–32 he says:[188]

Or [see] if something has been said of something such that when it is so necessarily contrary things belong; e.g. if he has said that the ideas are in us; for it will follow that they move and rest, and again are perceptible and intelligible. For the ideas are thought to rest and to be intelligible by those who posit that there are ideas; but being in us it is impossible for them to be unmoved; for when we move, necessarily also all the things that are in us move along. And it is clear that they are perceptible as well, if they are in us; for by means of the perception that pertains to sight we know the shape in each thing.

ἢ εἴ τι τοιοῦτον εἴρηται κατά τινος, οὗ ὄντος ἀνάγκη τὰ ἐναντία ὑπάρχειν· οἷον εἰ τὰς ἰδέας ἐν ὑμῖν ἔφησεν εἶναι· κινεῖσθαί τε γὰρ καὶ ἠρεμεῖν αὐτὰς συμβήσεται, ἔτι δὲ αἰθητὰς καὶ νοητὰς εἶναι. δοκοῦσι γὰρ αἱ ἰδέαι ἠρεμεῖν καὶ νοηταὶ εἶναι τοῖς τιθεμένοις ἰδέας εἶναι· ἐν ἡμῖν δὲ οὔσας ἀδύνατον ἀκινήτους εἶναι· κινουμένων γὰρ ἡμῶν ἀναγκαῖον καὶ τὰ ἐν ἡμῖν πάντα συγκινεῖσθαι. δῆλον δ' ὅτι καὶ αἰσθηταί, εἴπερ ἐν ἡμῖν εἰσι· διὰ γὰρ τῆς περὶ τὴν ὄψιν αἰσθήσεως τὴν ἐν ἑκάστῳ μορφὴν γνωρίζομεν.

Still, we might think: well, why not? If we are prepared to allow that the form might be physical, why should we not allow it to be movable?

But, forms, if they are anything, are objects of definition. The account Aristotle gives us[189] of Plato's development of the theory of Ideas or forms has him separating the forms from ordinary things on precisely this ground: ordinary things are constantly changing, but definitions have to nail down something stable. And the stability of forms is something Aristotle requires of his own theory of forms: when the wood gets hot "the motion is plainly in the wood, not in the form [that is, the hot], for the form . . . neither moves nor is moved" (*Physics* E 1. 224b4–5: ἡ δὴ κίνησις δῆλον ὅτι ἐν τῷ ξύλῳ, οὐκ ἐν τῷ εἴδει· οὔτε γὰρ κινεῖ οὔτε κινεῖται τὸ εἶδος).[190] And when it turns white it is not the white that comes-to-be but the wood comes-to-be white (*Metaphysics* H 5. 1044b23–24: οὐ γὰρ τὸ λευκὸν γίγνεται ἀλλὰ τὸ ξύλον λευκόν), where white is given as an example of a form (see τὰ εἴδη καὶ αἱ μορφαί b22–23).

So here the parallel in *Topics* B 7 (above) can be taken seriously: Aristotle did think that a physical ingredient in something was subject to motion when the thing itself was. And this is a response to Eudoxianism, if not to Eudoxus himself.

It raises an obvious question about pots calling kettles black: does it not apply to Aristotle's own theory, according to which certain attributes are *in* their possessors? The best answer to this I know of is the only one I know of. Owen[191] pointed out that Aristotle can distinguish between something moving in its own right and moving *per accidens*; his attributes do not move in their own rights, "and if they are said to move *per accidens* this is in a sense still weaker than that in which any physical part of the moving body does so."

Owen cites *Physics* Δ 4. 211a17–23: there Aristotle says that whiteness and knowledge (ἡ λευκότης καὶ ἡ ἐπιστήμη a22), by contrast with the nail in the ship, are *always* moved accidentally: "this is how they change place, because what they are present in changes place" (a22–23: ταῦτα γὰρ οὕτω μεταβέβληκε τὸν τόπον, ὅτι ἐν ᾧ ὑπάρχουσι μεταβάλλει).

Then why does Aristotle not allow Eudoxus this distinction? According to Owen, because it is Aristotle's.[192] Perhaps here we can go a little farther. If the whiteness in the stick is a physical ingredient in it, it is more like the nail than the knowledge. It makes sense to think of it as moving on its own. That goes with calling it a physical part of the thing. And when, in *Categories* 2. 1a24–25, Aristotle insists that by speaking of white(ness) as 'in' the stick he does not mean it is a part of the stick, he at least would be announcing that his position is not open to such objections.

4.3.7. Objection (6), 98.19–20. This reads (98.19–20): "Again, [the ideas] would be co-destroyed with the things in which they are, when these are destroyed. But they would not exist as separable, by virtue of themselves, but [would exist] in the things that participate in them." And it appears to tell us the following.

It follows from (I2) and (I3) that (where *E* stands for *Eudoxianism*)

(E) The form F is mixed into things that are F.

We need two ancillary premises:

(P1) What is mixed into things is co-destroyed with them.
(P2) What is co-destroyed with certain things is not separable from them.

And then, from (P1) and (E), it follows that

∴ (C1) The form F is destroyed when the Fs are.

And from this and (P2) we can derive

∴ (C2) The form F is not separable from Fs.

If this analysis were correct, we should have to reject objection (6) as well as most of the others.

(P2) tells us that, if you have x and y and there is no way of getting rid of y that does not carry x along with it, then x is not separable from y. The author of objection (6), I take it, thought that true by definition (of 'separable'). This could be Aristotelian, although the term *co-destroyed* is unusual (I shall return to this).

But (P1) is not, in general or in Aristotle, true: a thing can be destroyed by being broken down into its components, and then they survive it. We find Aristotle saying (*Met.* B 4. 1000b25–26): "All things are destroyed into the things of which they are composed" (πάντα γὰρ φθείρεται εἰς ταῦτ' ἐξ ὧν ἔστιν). And the objection to Eudoxus here, understood as above, would simply contradict Aristotle's objection to Anaxagoras elsewhere. As Alexander records the latter objection, it is to the effect that the ingredients of a mixture are 'separate and capable of being in their own rights' (τῶν γὰρ κεχωρισμένων καὶ καθ' αὑτὸ ὑφίστασθαι δυναμένων ἡ μῖξις 97.23–24). This is a formulation that improves on its original (*Metaphysics* A 8. 989a33–b4). But it also brings out the contradiction quite clearly.

Anyway, why should Eudoxus have thought (C2) an absurdity? If he was prepared to give up as much of the High Platonic Theory as he has already, why should he not give up the famous separateness of the forms as well, and go over to the Aristotelian camp, at least on this score? At this rate, he might even be in a position to evade Objection (7).

And then we might find in the unusual term *co-destroyed* fuel for our doubts. The word is absent from Bonitz's *Index*. It is used by the Stoics in connection with their conception of mixture, and it plays a central role in Alexander's attack on that conception. For example, he says (*De mixtione* 221.20–25):

> But if, according to what is said by them [*sc*. the Stoics], it is necessary that the things blended be inseparable from each other (for [they say] that the total blend cannot come-to-be apart from co-destruction, and they say that things co-destroyed are inseparable), but we see them separated in some cases, it is clear that the blending cannot come-to-be in the way it is said to by them.
>
> εἰ δὲ κατὰ μὲν τὰ λεγόμενα ὑπ' αὐτῶν ἀχώριστα ἀλλήλων ἀναγκαῖον εἶναι τὰ κεκραμένα (οὐ γὰρ δὴ οἷόν τε τὴν δι' ὅλων κρᾶσιν γενέσθαι χωρὶς συμφθάρσεως, ἀχώριστα δέ φασιν εἶναι τὰ συνεφθαρμένα), ὁρῶμεν δὲ ἐπ' ἐνίων χωριζόμενα, δῆλον ὡς οὐκ ἂν ἡ κρᾶσις γένοιτο κατὰ τὸν ὑπ' αὐτῶν εἰρημένον τρόπον.

So, it may seem, the terminology itself is post-Aristotelian.

This case against (6) is my own. I propose to destroy it anyway.

Start at the last point, which is a red herring. The term *co-destroyed* is not used by the Stoics, or by Alexander discussing them, in the way Objection (6) uses it. The ingredients in a Stoic 'total mixture' are 'co-destroyed' *into* the mixture: their total mixture entails their mutual annihilation.[193] In Objection (6), the question is whether the ingredients in a mixture are co-destroyed *with* the mixture, that is, when the mixture is.

And the word is in Aristotle. In *Topics* Z 13 he discusses various things to look for when you are trying to defeat an opponent's definition, where the definition is one that treats its object as having parts. In 150a33–36 he says:

Again, [see] if the parts are co-destroyed with the whole; for, on the contrary, it ought to turn out that when the parts are destroyed the whole is destroyed, but when the whole is destroyed it is not necessary that the parts be destroyed.

πάλιν εἰ τῷ ὅλῳ συμφθείρεται τὰ μέρη· ἀνάπαλιν γὰρ δεῖ συμβαίνειν, τῶν μερῶν φθαρέντων φθείρεσθαι τὸ ὅλον, τοῦ δ' ὅλου φθαρέντος οὐκ ἀναγκαῖον καὶ τὰ μέρη ἐφθάρθαι.

From this we can see Aristotle's response to a Eudoxian who proposes simply to bite the bullet and concede that the forms, thought of as physical parts of things, are not separable. He would argue that they must be separable: not because we are discussing Platonic forms, which must be separate, but because we are talking about physical mixtures, and parts or ingredients of such a mixture are separable from it. This was his complaint against Anaxagoras in *Metaphysics* A 8: if Anaxagoras were right (989b3–4), "the affects and accidents of substances would be separable (for there is mixture of just those things of which there is separation)" [τὰ πάθη καὶ τὰ συμβεβηκότα χωρίζοιτ' ἂν τῶν οὐσιῶν (τῶν γὰρ αὐτῶν μῖξίς ἐστι καὶ χωρισμός)].

But all of this makes it obvious that we cannot have (P1). To see what we must replace it with, let us take a closer look at Aristotle's attack on Anaxagoras in *Physics* A 4. 188a5–13:[194]

That [they] will never be disjoined[195] is not said with reason, but it is said truly; for the affects are inseparable;[196] so if colors and states are mixed, if they are disjoined, there will be something white and healthy that is not something else or [said] of a subject. So that [Anaxagoras'] mind is absurd, attempting things that are impossible, if it wants to disjoin [them],[197] and it is impossible to do this, both in quantity and in quality: in quantity because there is no least magnitude, and in quality because attributes are inseparable.[196]

τὸ δὲ μηδέποτε διακριθήσεσθαι οὐκ εἰδότως μὲν λέγεται, ὀρθῶς δὲ λέγεται· τὰ γὰρ πάθη ἀχώριστα· εἰ οὖν μέμικται τὰ χρώματα καὶ αἱ ἕξεις, ἐὰν διακριθῶσιν, ἔσται τι λευκὸν καὶ ὑγιείνον οὐχ ἕτερόν τι ὂν οὐδὲ καθ' ὑποκειμένου. ὥστε ἄτοπος τὰ ἀδύνατα ζητῶν ὁ νοῦς, εἴπερ βούλεται μὲν διακρῖναι, τοῦτο δὲ ποιῆσαι ἀδύνατον καὶ κατὰ τὸ ποσὸν καὶ κατὰ τὸ ποιόν, κατὰ μὲν τὸ ποσὸν ὅτι οὐκ ἔστιν ἐλάχιστον μέγεθος, κατὰ δὲ τὸ ποιὸν ὅτι ἀχώριστα τὰ πάθη.

This is a complex objection; I shall not try to explain all of it. The part of it relevant here is this.

On the face of it, things that are mixed together need not be mixed together. Anaxagoras has given us an argument to show that the ingredients cannot be extracted pure: if they were, then you would have some pure white, and then you could not get any blood out of it; but you can get anything from anything, sooner or later. Yet this does not, in fact, explain *why* you cannot extract the white, and the theory provides nothing further that explains what stops you from getting the white out.[198]

This much we had before, but there is more. Anaxagoras' idea that white and healthy are ingredients of a thing does not mean that there is something, say blood, that is healthy and is an ingredient in the mixture, and something else, say the thing's surface, that is white, and so on. These ingredients are identified as white and healthy, and there is no further question as to what it is that is white or healthy.

To Aristotle, this is an impossibility: something white is always something specifiable—snow, a stick—that is colored white. Anaxagoras thinks that the white is inseparable from his mixture; he is right that it is inseparable, but it is so because of this impossibility, not because of the alleged impossibility of there being anything from which any of the ingredients is absent. If it *were* a mixture, the elements would, in fact, be separable.

This charge transfers to Eudoxus. Aristotle would be asking Eudoxus: just *what* is this physical ingredient whose presence in something makes it white? In the extended theory of the *Phaedo*, it was fire whose presence in something made it hot. But in your theory, the only answer to the question 'what makes white things white?' is 'it is white'. But, as I explained in *On length and shortness of life* (*Long*. 3. 465b12–14): "for while it is possible for the hot or the straight to be in the whole [of something],[199] it is impossible that all it is is hot or straight or white; for then its properties would be separable (παντὶ μὲν γὰρ ἐνεῖναι τὸ θερμὸν ἢ τὸ εὐθὺ ενδέχεται, πᾶν δ' εἶναι ἀδύνατον ἢ θερμὸν ἢ εὐθὺ ἢ λευκόν· ἔσται γὰρ τὰ πάθη κεχωρισμένα). Or, as I put it in the *Posterior Analytics* (A 22. 83a30–32): "Things that don't signify a substance have to be predicated of a subject, and there's nothing white that isn't something else that is white: the forms can be dismissed, for they're nonsense" (ὅσα δὲ μὴ οὐσίαν σημαίνει, δεῖ κατά τινος ὑποκειμένου κατηγορεῖσθαι, καὶ μὴ εἶναί τι λευκὸν ὃ οὐχ ἕτερόν τι ὂν λευκόν ἐστιν. τὰ γὰρ εἴδη χαιρέτω· τερετίσματά τε γάρ ἐστι . . .). And that's just as much true of your theory of forms as of the original.

Then the premise we need for Objection (6) is not (P1): it is not the fact that white is an *ingredient* in the mixtures that are white things that makes it co-destroyed with, and hence inseparable from, the white things, but the fact that it is *white*. When you erase the white things, you cannot do it in such a way that the white is left behind. So what we need is this:

> (P1*) The F that is (allegedly) mixed in Fs is co-destroyed with them.

This now means that there is no way of getting rid of the white things or the hot things that leaves behind entities that are just white, or just hot. And then, by the definition of *separable,* it follows that

∴ (C1*) The F is not separable from Fs.

But now, if the F were literally mixed with Fs, we could employ the following by now well-known fact about mixtures:

(P2*) An ingredient in a mixture is separable from it.

And that would, with (E), give us

∴ (C2*) The F is separable from Fs.

And that is a contradiction. So Eudoxus is wrong.

What Alexander says in (6) is only the first half of this, down to (C1*). But that much, by itself, is no objection. My suggestion is that the principle of the separability of physical ingredients, (P2*), that Aristotle uses against Anaxagoras, tells us how Aristotle would have shown (C1*) objectionable: that forms are inseparable is only what Aristotle himself would like to say, but it does not comport with the idea that they are physical ingredients.

And this argument may, I think, have stood in *On Ideas*, but Alexander garbled it, just as we have found him garbling other things. Plainly this is a speculative suggestion. But it has one advantage.

On this reading, the objections Aristotle raised in *On Ideas* against Eudoxus are possibly a rewritten version of (5), (7), and a rewritten version of (6). And they do not attack a position that is simply outright contradictory, such as "the forms are immovable, impassible, bodiless, physical ingredients of things that exist in separation from those things." In particular, in (6), Eudoxus has simply fallen in the path of one of Aristotle's favorite anti-Platonic tanks; his position retains a feature of the High Platonic Theory that Aristotle quite reasonably thinks absurd. And so, if I am right, Aristotle takes care, in *Categories* 2, to distinguish his own immanentism from that of Eudoxus.

5. PLATO AGAIN

Let us, finally, reconsider the drawback to Eudoxian immanentism mentioned at the outset: the theory cannot in any obvious way be generalized to cover such predicates as 'wise,' 'just,' 'good,' and so on. This objection to the theory is so obvious that it is mildly surprising to find that it plays so minor a role in Alexander's list.

But someone in the tradition did register this objection against this kind of theory: Plato himself did, in the *Sophist*. There the Eleatic Stranger speaks of a war over being, between some gods and some giants (246a4–5);[200] the giants among them (246a7-b3)

> drag all things to earth out of the heavens and the invisible, crudely grasping stone and oak[201] in their hands. For seizing on all such things they insist that that only *is* which offers some contact and touch, defining body and being as the same, and if any of the others should say that anything that does not have body *is*, they despise him altogether and wish to hear nothing else.

> εἰς γῆν ἐξ οὐρανοῦ καὶ τοῦ ἀοράτου πάντα ἕλκουσι, ταῖς χερσὶν ἀτεχνῶς πέτρας καὶ δρῦς περιλαμβάνοντες. τῶν γὰρ τοιούτων ἐφαπτόμενοι πάντων διισχυρίζονται τοῦτο εἶναι μόνον ὃ παρέχει προσβολὴν καὶ ἐπαφήν τινα, ταὐτὸν σῶμα καὶ οὐσίαν ὁριζόμενοι, τῶν δὲ ἄλλων εἴ τίς ⟨τι⟩ φήσει μὴ σῶμα ἔχον εἶναι, καταφρονοῦντες τὸ παράπαν καὶ οὐδὲν ἐθέλοντες ἄλλο ἀκούειν.

Theaetetus, the interlocutor here, responds (246b4–5): "Terrible men you speak of; I've encountered many of them already" (ἦ δεινοὺς εἴρηκας ἄνδρας· ἤδη γὰρ καὶ ἐγὼ τούτων συχνοῖς προσέτυχον). Their opponents, the 'gods,' are the famous 'friends of the forms' (for the phrase, see 248a4).

The argument against the giants requires reforming a few of them to the point where they are at least willing to discuss things (246cd). They are made to admit that there is such a thing as a 'mortal animal' (θνητὸν ζῷον 246e5), that this is an ensouled body (σῶμα ἔμψυχον e7), that this involves positing a soul among the beings (τιθέντες τι τῶν ὄντων ψυχήν e9), and that one soul is just, another unjust, one intelligent and another unintelligent (247a2–4). We then read (247a5-c2):

> ES: But [do they] not [say] that it is by the possession and presence of justice that each [soul] comes-to-be such, and the contrary by the contraries?
>
> TH: Yes, they also agree to these things.
>
> ES: And yet that which is capable of becoming-present-to something and becoming-absent-from [it] they will say is altogether something.
>
> TH: So they say.
>
> b ES: So, whereas justice is, and intelligence and the rest of excellence and their contraries, and a soul in which these come-to-be as well, do they say any of them is visible and touchable, or all invisible?
>
> TH: Virtually none of them is visible.
>
> ES: And what of things like that [viz., invisible]? Do they say they have any body?
>
> TH: They no longer answer this entirely along the same lines, but [say] that while the soul itself seems to them to possess a body, as for intelligence and each of
> c the other things about which you asked, they are ashamed at daring either to agree that they are none of the things that are or to insist that they are all bodies.

> ΞΕ. Ἀλλ' οὐ δικαιοσύνης ἕξει καὶ παρουσίᾳ τοιαύτην αὐτῶν ἑκάστην γίγνεσθαι, καὶ τῶν ἐναντίων τὴν ἐναντίαν;

ΘΕΑΙ. Ναί, καὶ ταῦτα σύμφασιν.

ΞΕ. Ἀλλὰ μὴν τό γε δυνατόν τῳ παραγίγνεσθαι καὶ ἀπογίγνεσθαι πάντως εἶναί τι φήσουσιν.

ΘΕΑΙ. Φασὶ μὲν οὖν.

b ΞΕ. Οὔσης οὖν δικαιοσύνης καὶ φρονήσεως καὶ τῆς
ἄλλης ἀρετῆς καὶ τῶν ἐναντίων, καὶ δὴ καὶ ψυχῆς ἐν ᾗ
ταῦτα ἐγγίγνεται, πότερον ὁρατὸν καὶ ἁπτὸν εἶναί φασί τι
αὐτῶν ἢ πάντα ἀόρατα;

ΘΕΑΙ. Σχεδὸν οὐδὲν τούτων γε ὁρατόν.

ΞΕ. Τί δὲ τῶν τοιούτων; μῶν σῶμά τι λέγουσιν ἴσχειν;

ΘΕΑΙ. Τοῦτο οὐκέτι κατὰ ταὐτὰ ἀποκρίνονται πᾶν, ἀλλὰ
τὴν μὲν ψυχὴν αὐτὴν δοκεῖν σφίσι σῶμά τι κεκτῆσθαι,
φρόνησιν δὲ καὶ τῶν ἄλλων ἕκαστον ὧν ἠρώτηκας, αἰσχύ-
c νονται τὸ τολμᾶν ἢ μηδὲν τῶν ὄντων αὐτὰ ὁμολογεῖν ἢ
πάντ' εἶναι σώματα διισχυρίζεσθαι.

And so, as the Stranger points out, they have been considerably tamed (247c3–7), and in the process have conceded that something is, that there is something, that is incorporeal (c9–d1).

What is it that they have conceded is incorporeal but nonetheless exists? "Justice, intelligence, and the rest of excellence and their contraries" (247b1–2), by the *possession* (ἕξις 247a5) and *presence* (παρουσία a5) of which souls become just, and so on. They concede that what can *become-present-to or absent-from* something exists (a8–9), that justice and the others *are*, along with the soul *in* which they *come-to-be* (b2–3), and yet none of these is visible, and although the soul, they say, is corporeal, the others are not (bc).

These are surprising giants. Theaetetus seems to know a good deal about what they would say. They have an immanentist account of predication. They have quite sophisticated views about the soul, which they think is corporeal. It looks as if, had we asked them the same series of questions about whiteness and heat that are here asked about justice and intelligence, the refutation would not have been so successful. But then they would be accounting for something's being white or hot by saying it had whiteness or heat physically present in it. That is, they would have a Eudoxian view about those predications.

Curiously, for quite different reasons, Cherniss suggested that their opponents, the 'friends of the forms,' were opponents of Eudoxus.[202] I have little to say about that. But I see no reason against supposing that Eudoxus might have been one of the giants whom Plato here hoped to reform.

There used to be an industry that put out this sort of stuff,[203] so let me make it plain that I am not applying for a job in it. For example, A. E. Taylor once said about the *Sophist*: "The analysis of the actual argument of the dialogue presents few difficulties; our chief perplexities arise when we come to the problem of identifying the various groups of opponents who are mentioned as likely to dispute some of the positions laid down."[204] It is impossible for me to imagine the state of mind that led him to say that. The *Sophist* is a dialogue of incredible difficulty, and my suggestion about 246–247 and Eudoxus is not, to my mind, a major historical breakthrough that sheds light on any very important problem concerning its interpretation.

Rather, what I am suggesting is this. *Sophist* 246–247 contains an argument against certain materialists. It attacks them on a specific point. It is not just materialism in general that is under attack, for these materialists have something specific to say about the soul, and they accept a certain account of predication. The account of predication, at least verbally, is immanentist.

An objection is lodged against the materialists that turns on that account of predication. We have noticed from the beginning that Eudoxus' account of predication was open to this objection. It is generally accepted that Eudoxus was active before the time of writing of the *Sophist*. We cannot, or, at any rate, I do not, know whether this is so. But if it is so, I do not think Plato could have written the passage *without* thinking of Eudoxus' ideas about predication. I am inclined to suppose that the chronology is right, and that Plato is here attacking Eudoxus. We do not need to suppose this to understand the objection this passage raises against materialism. But it would explain why Plato felt it necessary to raise the issue at all. And it seems to me interesting.

Of course, the giants are described in somewhat scurrilous terms: they are 'terrible men,' whom Theaetetus has frequently encountered (246b);[205] it would be nice if we could improve them in fact, but if we cannot, we at least can pretend that they are amenable to discussion (246d), and so on. These are heavy things to say about someone who was, perhaps, the best mathematician of antiquity.

But perhaps the heaviness depends only on the way we read them. If we suppose that Eudoxus had a sense of humor, and that he was a party to the discussions in the Academy that led to the *Sophist*, the passage reads as comedy. (It is a particularly nice point that Theaetetus is then made to refer to his fellow mathematician Eudoxus as a 'terrible man,' especially given the ambiguity of δεινός among 'terrible,' 'marvelous,' and 'clever'). And I am perfectly prepared to suppose that Eudoxus, who thought pleasure was the good,[206] enjoyed laughing.

6. APPENDIX: ANAXAGORAS' SEEDS

Let us consider in more detail an issue broached earlier on p. 5: what, after all, did Anaxagoras call his 'elements,' 'principles,' or whatever? 'Seeds (σπέρματα)', I think, but this is a minority view.

It may be misleading to translate 'σπέρματα' as 'seeds': we tend to think of pellets.[207] But semen was also σπέρμα to a Greek, and even if

Clement's report (in DK 22B31) shows signs of Stoic mangling, there is nothing linguistically odd about supposing Heraclitus to have said that fire was transformed "into moisture, that [functions] as seed for the world-ordering" (εἰς ὑγρὸν τὸ ὡς σπέρμα τῆς διακοσμήσεως, DK i 158.9; see also 289.19 and .23 in connection with Empedocles).

Let us stick to the translation 'seeds' but bear in mind that seeds need not be pellets.

6.1. Anaxagoras Fr. 4

Then there are two occurrences of seeds in the text of Anaxagoras, both in fr. 4. This fragment comes from various citations in Simplicius; one of those citations (*in Physica* 156.2–9) represents Anaxagoras as saying:

> but since this is so, it is necessary to think that many, and of all sorts, are in among all [that are] mixed together, and seeds of all things[208] that also have all sorts of forms[209] and colors and tastes.[210] But before they were separated off, he says, when all were together, there was not even a color visible; for that was prevented by the mixture of all, of the moist and the dry and the hot and the cold and the bright and the dark and much earth that was in it and a plurality[211] of unlimited[ly many] seeds in no way resembling each other. For of the others none resembles any other either.

> τούτων δὲ οὕτως ἐχόντων, χρὴ δοκεῖν ἐνεῖναι πολλά τε καὶ παντοῖα ἐν πᾶσι τοῖς συγκρινομένοις καὶ σπέρματα πάντων χρημάτων καὶ ἰδέας παντοίας ἔχοντα καὶ χροιὰς καὶ ἡδονάς. πρὶν δὲ ἀποκριθῆναι, φησί, πάντων ὁμοῦ ἐόντων οὐδὲ χροιὴ ἔνδηλος ἦν οὐδεμία· ἀπεκώλυε γὰρ ἡ σύμμιξις πάντων χρημάτων τοῦ τε διεροῦ καὶ τοῦ ξηροῦ καὶ τοῦ θερμοῦ καὶ τοῦ ψυχροῦ καὶ τοῦ λαμπροῦ καὶ τοῦ ζοφεροῦ καὶ γῆς πολλῆς ἐνεούσης καὶ σπερμάτων ἀπείρων πλήθους οὐδὲν ἐοικότων ἀλλήλοις. οὐδὲ γὰρ τῶν ἄλλων οὐδὲν ἔοικε τὸ ἕτερον τῷ ἑτέρῳ.

On the face of it, this tells us that the Cosmic Soup contained an unlimited plurality of 'seeds,' and gives as examples of such seeds the moist, the dry, the hot, the cold, the bright, the dark, and earth; that none of these seeds resembles any other; and, in its last sentence,[212] that everywhere on the unending list of seeds the situation is the same as it is with the examples of seeds given: none resembles any other. It is possible to doubt that the last sentence in fact comes from Anaxagoras,[213] but that is not important, for the preceding one tells us that none of the seeds resembles any other. And that entails that there is no more than one seed for the moist, one for the dry, one for the hot, and so on. So there is no question of particles of the hot or of earth or of anything. The hot is one seed, and earth is another.

6.2. Aristotle

It is in this way that Aristotle understood Anaxagoras' seeds; he tells us (*De caelo* Γ 3. 302a28–b5):

> Anaxagoras speaks contrarily to Empedocles about the elements. For the one says fire and earth and things in that series are elements of the bodies, and all [bodies] are composed from them, but Anaxagoras says the contrary: that the
> 302b homoeomers are elements (I mean, e.g., flesh and bone and anything of that sort), and that air[214] and fire are mixtures[215] of these and all the other seeds; for each of these two is [composed] from all the invisible homoeomers collected.[216] This is why everything comes-to-be from these, for he uses 'fire' and 'ether' of the same thing.

> Ἀναξαγόρας δ' Ἐμπεδοκλεῖ ἐναντίως λέγει περὶ τῶν στοιχείων. ὁ μὲν γὰρ πῦρ καὶ γῆν καὶ τὰ σύστοιχα τούτοις στοιχεῖά φησιν εἶναι τῶν σωμάτων καὶ συγκεῖσθαι πάντ' ἐκ τούτων, Ἀναξαγόρας δὲ τοὐναντίον· τὰ γὰρ ὁμοιομερῆ στοιχεῖα (λέγω δ' οἷον σάρκα καὶ ὀστοῦν καὶ τῶν τοι-
> 302b ούτων ἕκαστον), ἀέρα δὲ καὶ πῦρ μίγματα τούτων καὶ τῶν ἄλλων σπερμάτων πάντων· εἶναι γὰρ ἑκάτερον αὐτῶν ἐξ ἀοράτων τῶν ὁμοιομερῶν πάντων ἠθροισμένων. διὸ καὶ γίγνεσθαι πάντ' ἐκ τούτων· τὸ γὰρ πῦρ καὶ τὸν αἰθέρα προσαγορεύει ταὐτό.

Let us set aside the special status accorded to fire (or ether) and air for a moment. In any case, Aristotle speaks of the homoeomers and *other* seeds, or, perhaps, of flesh, bone, and so on and the *other* seeds. If he means the former, the other seeds are presumably the opposites: the hot, the cold, and so on; in *Physics* A 4. 187a25–26 he contrasts Anaxagoras with Empedocles by saying:[217] "The one [makes] unlimited[ly many things]—the homoeomers and the contraries, the other only the so-called elements" (τὸν μὲν ἄπειρα, τά τε ὁμοιομερῆ καὶ τἀναντία, τὸν δὲ τὰ καλούμενα στοιχεῖα μόνον). Whichever he means, a homoeomer is a seed.

The special status allotted to air and fire/ether comes of Aristotle's understanding of texts such as fr. 1, part of which has this to say (Simplicius *in Physica* 155.28–30:[218]

> And when all were together, nothing was visible, by reason of smallness; for air and ether occupied[219] all, both being unlimited; for these are largest among them all together, both in plurality and in size.

> καὶ πάντων ὁμοῦ ἐόντων οὐδὲν ἔνδηλον ἦν ὑπὸ σμικρότητος· πάντα γὰρ ἀήρ τε καὶ αἰθὴρ κατεῖχεν ἀμφότερα ἄπειρα ἐόντα· ταῦτα γὰρ μέγιστα ἔνεστιν ἐν τοῖς σύμπασι καὶ πλήθει καὶ μεγέθει.

This is obscure enough, and I do not propose to unravel it here. But Aristotle is taking it to say that air and ether are not among the seeds (the homoeomers and the contraries), but, as we might say, are emergent. It is not clear that he is right about this. And further, he takes it that the same applies to the other two members of the Empedoclean triad; or, at least, he seems to suggest that here, and in *De generatione et corruptione* A 1. 314a28–29 he says so outright.[220]

It is even less clear that he is right about this. In fact, because earth is expressly given in fr. 4 as an example of a seed, he cannot be right about this.[221] But even if he is wrong on both scores, that does not affect his understanding of the seeds.

6.3. Simplicius

Simplicius shared that understanding. He says (*in De caelo* 603.17–19):

> Empedocles said the four were elements, and Anaxagoras called the homoeomers—e.g. flesh, bone, and such things—'seeds,' from which, he said, even the [things called] elements by Empedocles are mixed . . .
>
> Ἐμπεδοκλῆς τὰ τέσσαρα ἔλεγεν εἶναι στοιχεῖα, καὶ Ἀναξαγόρας τὰ ὁμοιομερῆ, οἷον σάρκα καὶ ὀστιοῦν καὶ τὰ τοιαῦτα, σπέρματα ἐκάλει, ἐξ ὧν καὶ τὰ ὑπὸ Ἐμπεδοκλέους στοιχεῖα μεμῖχθαι ἔλεγεν . . .

6.4. Conclusion

So it is not only natural to understand fr. 4 as identifying the seeds with what Aristotle called the homoeomers and the contraries, it is almost old hat. And furthermore, I cannot see anything wrong with it.[222] But it has received little more than passing mention for years.[223] A good example of the literature here is Guthrie's *History*: he mentions this interpretation in parentheses in an appendix concerned with the question whether Anaxagoras used the word *homoeomer*.[224] His own view is that a seed is "an imperceptibly small bit of any kind of substance."[225] At least he does not commit Anaxagoras to atomism, as he does Empedocles. But there is no reason even to go as far as 'imperceptibly small bits'; the seeds are just the homoeomers and the contraries.

STUDY • II

ANCIENT NON-BEINGS: SPEUSIPPUS AND OTHERS

1. Introduction

Speusippus, Plato's nephew and successor as head of the Academy, is sometimes thought to have held that the world of existent things depends upon a principle, the One, that is not itself an existent thing. This is a surprising view. My object here is to make it plausible that it was in fact his view, and to connect it with his attitude toward the Platonic theory of forms.

The first point to be made is that surprises are not necessarily absurdities. In 1904, Meinong said:[1] "Without doubt, metaphysics has to do with everything that exists. However, the totality of what exists, including what has existed and will exist, is infinitely small in comparison with the totality of Objects of knowledge." And a little later[2] he speaks of "Objects which do indeed subsist (*bestehen*), but which do not by any means exist (*existieren*), and consequently cannot in any sense be actual (*wirklich*)."

Meinong has recently been receiving favorable mention.[3] The authors who so mention him do not always intend to defend what was, historically speaking, Meinong's position, but they and he are united in their opposition to an orthodoxy. Meinong referred to the orthodoxy to which he was opposed as "the prejudice in favor of the actual."[4] This is a tendentious mouthful; I shall call it *Actualism*.[5] It tells us that only what exists or is actual can be talked about, or, more persuasively, that there is nothing that does not exist, that is not an existent.

We are not here concerned with the interpretation of Meinong, but I want to make use of his name. I shall refer to the denial of Actualism as *Meinongianism*.[6] The word is unpleasant, but so are alternatives such as the *theory of objects*[7] or *noneism*.[8] Meinongianism, then, is the view that there are things that don't exist,[9] or, more persuasively, that some of the things we can talk about are not existent things.

Meinongianism does not translate straightforwardly into the Greek of Speusippus' period, for that Greek did not possess separate verbs for *be* and *exist*, or a distinct word for *real*: all the work is done by the single verb *be* and its derivatives. I shall mostly be speaking a sublanguage of English, call it *Translator's English*, that mimics the Greek of that period as closely as possible: in particular, it does not contain the words *exist, real,* or their relatives. In Translator's English, the Meinongian idea that there are objects that do not exist might be stated as:

> (M) From 'x is something' it does not follow that x is (a being),

where the parentheses give us an alternative version of Meinongianism. Another alternative would be

> (Ma) From 'x is' it does not follow that x is a being.

Its denial, 'Actualism,' would read

> (A) From 'x is something' it follows that x is (a being)

or alternatively as

> (Aa) From 'x is' it follows that x is a being.

The rationale for these alternative formulations will emerge when we turn to some texts.

As now, so in antiquity, Actualism was the majority view. But the minority, even without Speusippus, is audible above the clamor. And the case of Speusippus, after all, is controversial. So let us listen to this audible minority before we turn to Speusippus.

To avoid arousing false hopes, or perhaps to dash such hopes early on if they are already formed, I should say that I shall not be pushing any further analogies between Meinong's views and those of ancient philosophers. Meinong's name gives us a useful label; how deep the resemblances go is not of present concern.

2. ANCIENT NON-ACADEMIC MEINONGIANISM

My primary aim here is to show that the rejection of Actualism was a live alternative in antiquity. Secondarily, I want to show that Aristotle, in particular, did not find that rejection absurd: this will be an important point when we turn to Speusippus.

2.1. Atomists

The arch-Actualist of all time was father Parmenides. He had this to say (DK 28B2):[10]

Come I shall tell you, and you carry off the story you've heard,[11]
[as to] which are the only ways of inquiry that can be thought:
the one, that [it] is and there is no way [for it] not to be,
is the road of conviction (for it follows truth[12]),
but the other, that [it] is not and there is necessity [for it] not to be,
I say to you this is an utterly inscrutable short cut,
for neither can you know what is not (that is not attainable)
nor can you say it.

εἰ δ' ἄγ' ἐγὼν ἐρέω, κόμισαι δὲ σὺ μῦθον ἀκούσας,
αἵπερ ὁδοὶ μοῦναι διζήσιός εἰσι νοῆσαι·
ἡ μὲν ὅπως ἔστιν τε καὶ ὡς οὐκ ἔστι μὴ εἶναι,
Πειθοῦς ἐστι κέλευθος (Ἀληθείηι γὰρ ὀπηδεῖ),
ἡ δ' ὡς οὐκ ἔστιν τε καὶ ὡς χρεών ἐστι μὴ εἶναι,
τὴν δή τοι φράζω παναπευθέα ἔμμεν ἀταρπόν·
οὔτε γὰρ ἂν γνοίης τό γε μὴ ἐὸν (οὐ γὰρ ἀνυστόν)
οὔτε φράσαις.

These verses are telling us that anything that can be thought about or spoken of must be; that is, in non-Translator's English, it must exist. So we have an instance of (A):

(A1) From 'x is thinkable' it follows that x is.

We actually have an instance of (Aa) as well. In line 7 'what is not' translates the participial phrase 'τὸ μὴ ἐόν', so that Parmenides' central claim comes through as 'you cannot think or speak of what is not.' We shall not be able to stick with this translation, as will become clear when we turn to Leucippus. An alternative translation, to accomodate Leucippus, would be 'you cannot think or speak of the not being'; that is, 'you cannot think or speak of any non-being.' This would give us

(Aa1) From 'x is thinkable' it follows that x is a being.

Even the most dedicated Actualist is likely to find this position unwelcome. Taken out of context, it makes anything you can dream up exist. Among the ancients, the favorite examples were such things as centaurs and the Chimaera, a fire-breathing, lion-headed, dragon-tailed goat.[13] In context, the story is somewhat different: Parmenides' own ultra-Actualism leads him to the astonishing view that fire-breathing, lion-headed, dragon-tailed goats are unthinkable. And so is just about everything else: coming-to-be and distinction, if there were such things, would involve that which is not, which is unthinkable, so they are likewise unthinkable, and so is fire-breathing, because it is a form of coming-to-be, and so is being dragon-tailed, because that is something that distinguishes the Chimaera from your pet cat.[14]

But neither acknowledging the existence of fire-breathing goats just because they are conceivable nor denying their conceivability and the conceivability of change and distinction along with it is going to be acceptable to the saner among the Actualists. Standardly, in the Actualist industry, (A1) is rejected. That means, if (A) is to be saved, that there have to be restrictions placed on the 'something' in (A). And a large part of the industry is devoted to manufacturing the appropriate restrictions.[15]

But sometimes, outside the industry, someone recommends just scrapping (A). It was so in antiquity. As often, to study this we are forced to read Aristotle. Here we must consider a report of his on atomism: *De generatione et corruptione* A 8. 324b35–325b5.[16]

From this point on, I shall translate the participle 'ὄν' as 'being.'

Aristotle mentions the atomism of Leucippus and Democritus in laudatory terms (324b35–325a2), and then gives an exposition of the view to which theirs was opposed (325a2–6):

> For to some of the ancients being seemed to be of necessity one and unchanging; for [it seemed to them that] the void [is] not a being, and that it is not possible [for anything] to change since there is no separated void,[17] nor again for there to be many [things] since there is not that which keeps them apart.

325a2 ἐνίοις γὰρ τῶν ἀρχαίων ἔδοξε τὸ ὂν ἐξ ἀνάγκης ἓν εἶναι καὶ ἀκίνητον· τὸ μὲν γὰρ κενὸν οὐκ ὄν, κινηθῆναι δ' οὐκ ἂν δύνασθαι μὴ ὄντος κενοῦ κεχωρισμένου, οὐδ' αὖ πολλὰ εἶναι μὴ ὄντος τοῦ διείργοντος.

This doctrine I shall call *Conventional Eleaticism*. Its progenitor is certainly Parmenides, who says (DK 28B8.22–25):

> Nor is it divisible, since it is all alike;[18]
> nor [is there] any more here [than there], that would keep it
> from holding together,
> nor any less, but all is full of being.
> So all is continuous, for being draws up to being.

> οὐδὲ διαιρετόν ἐστιν, ἐπεὶ πᾶν ἐστιν ὁμοῖον·
> οὐδέ τι τῇι μᾶλλον, τό κεν εἴργοι μιν συνέχεσθαι,
> οὐδέ τι χειρότερον, πᾶν δ' ἔμπλεόν ἐστιν ἐόντος.
> τῶι ξυνεχὲς πᾶν ἐστιν· ἐὸν γὰρ ἐόντι πελάζει.

This can be, and most often has been, understood as registering the denial of a void;[19] I happen to prefer other interpretations,[20] according to which Parmenides was not himself a Conventional Eleatic. Fortunately, this issue is of no importance here; we have, in any case, a text from one unambiguously Conventional Eleatic, namely Melissus, who argues (DK 30B7 sec. 7):[21]

> And nothing is void; for the void is nothing; nothing could not, in fact, be. And it does not change; for it cannot withdraw anywhere, but is full. For if there were

void, it would withdraw into the void; but since there is no void, it cannot withdraw anywhere.

(7) οὐδὲ κενεόν ἐστιν οὐδέν· τὸ γὰρ κενεὸν οὐδέν ἐστιν· οὐκ ἂν οὖν εἴη τό γε μηδέν. οὐδὲ κινεῖται· ὑποχωρῆσαι γὰρ οὐκ ἔχει οὐδαμῆι, ἀλλὰ πλέων ἐστιν. εἰ μὲν γὰρ κενεὸν ἦν, ὑπεχώρει ἂν εἰς τὸ κενόν· κενοῦ δὲ μὴ ἐόντος οὐκ ἔχει ὅκηι ὑποχωρήσει.

This[22] is what the atomists faced, and in *De generatione et corruptione* A 8 Aristotle tells us in particular about Leucippus (325a23–32):

> But Leucippus thought he had arguments which, stating [things] in agreement with perception, do not destroy coming-to-be or passing-away or motion and the plurality of things that are. Having agreed in these [matters] with appearances,[23] [he agrees] with those who establish the one that there could not be motion without a void and that the void [is a] non-being, and says that nothing of being is a non-being.[24] For being, taken strictly, is fully a being; but there is not [just] one [thing] like that, [he says,] but [many,] unlimited in plurality, and invisible through the smallness of their masses. And these move in the void (for a void is), and when they are put together they make coming-to-be, and when they are separated, passing-away.

325a23 Λεύκιππος δ' ἔχειν ᾠήθη λόγους οἵ τινες πρὸς τὴν αἴσθησιν ὁμολογούμενα λέγοντες οὐκ ἀναιρήσουσιν οὔτε γένεσιν οὔτε φθορὰν οὔτε κίνησιν καὶ τὸ πλῆθος τῶν ὄντων. ὁμολογήσας δὲ ταῦτα μὲν τοῖς φαινομένοις, τοῖς δὲ τὸ ἓν κατασκευάζουσιν ὡς οὔτε ἂν κίνησιν οὖσαν ἄνευ κενοῦ τό τε κενὸν μὴ ὄν, καὶ τοῦ ὄντος οὐθὲν μὴ ὄν φησιν εἶναι· τὸ γὰρ κυρίως ὂν παμπληρὲς ὄν· ἀλλ' εἶναι τὸ τοιοῦτον οὐχ ἕν, ἀλλ' ἄπειρα τὸ πλῆθος καὶ ἀόρατα διὰ σμικρότητα τῶν ὄγκων. ταῦτα δ' ἐν τῷ κενῷ φέρεσθαι (κενὸν γὰρ εἶναι), καὶ συνιστάμενα μὲν γένεσιν ποιεῖν, διαλυόμενα δὲ φθοράν.

Leucippus wants to save motion. He concedes to the Conventional Eleatics that (a27)

(1) There is no motion without void.

But he also concedes that (a27–28)

(2) The void is a non-being.

Then how can he find room for motion? Has he not conceded everything Melissus could ask?

On the face of it, the rest of the passage does not clarify matters but only makes the difficulty more explicit. Leucippus apparently[25] adds (a28)

(3) Nothing of being is not a being[26]

and (a28–29)

(4) Being, taken strictly, is being throughout.

The latter provides a reason for (3); this is easier to see if we rewrite (3) to read "No [part] of [a] being is [a] non-being." Then (3), so understood, seems to be intended to explain the sense or the truth of (2): the void is not a being, for it has parts that are non-beings, but, according to (4), any being must be a being through and through. As an argument for the claim that the void is not a being, this looks circular. At least it is tolerably clear. But, in any case, it does nothing to show us how Leucippus can stay out of Melissus' clutches.

Finally (325a29–32), we are told that the difference between the Eleatics and Leucippus is that Leucippus thinks there is not just one such being; rather there are lots of them, moving in a void, "for a void is" (325a31: κενὸν γὰρ εἶναι). There are in fact three things unacceptable to Conventional Eleaticism here: first, the plurality of the beings; second, their motion; and third, what allows for that plurality and motion; the void. So we must add to Leucippus' position, as the crucial point of disagreement:

(5) The void is.

This is deliberately translated starkly, to bring out the apparent contradiction between (5) and (2)-(4). I hope it is clear now why we must translate the participle 'ὄν' as 'being' rather than as (say) 'a thing that is': if we had followed the latter translation, (2) would read 'The void is something that is not,' and the contradiction would be direct.

It is bad enough as it is. There is a temptation to squirm out of it by translating one of the occurrences of 'is' by 'exists': we might then hope to make out a distinction between (say) the atoms, which really exist, and the void, which merely is.[27] But nothing in our passage suggests that Leucippus was drawing such a distinction. There is another temptation to manufacture different senses of 'to be'; this is to be resisted for the same reason.[28]

Indeed, nothing in our passage suggests anything about how Leucippus might have motivated his distinction. But it is clear what the distinction must be, however unmotivated. And it is clear that it entails what I have been calling *Meinongianism*. The apparent contradiction is between (2) and (5). If it is not a real contradiction, it must be that

(Ma1) From 'a void is' it does not follow that a void is a being.

And that is an instance of one our formulations of Meinongianism.

Aristotle mentions atomistic Meinongianism frequently. In *Metaphysics* A 4. 985b4–9, he says:[29]

> Leucippus and his companion Democritus say that the elements are the full and the void, calling the one being and the other non-being, and of these the full and solid is being and the void and rare is non-being (which is why they also say that being no more is than non-being, because body [is no more] than the void[30]).

> **985**b4 Λεύκιππος δὲ καὶ ὁ ἑταῖρος αὐτοῦ Δημόκριτος στοιχεῖα μὲν τὸ πλῆρες καὶ τὸ κενὸν εἶναί φασι, λέγοντες τὸ μὲν ὂν τὸ δὲ μὴ ὄν, τούτων δὲ τὸ μὲν πλῆρες καὶ στερεὸν τὸ ὄν, τὸ δὲ κενόν γε καὶ μανὸν τὸ μὴ ὄν (διὸ καὶ οὐθὲν μᾶλλον τὸ ὂν τοῦ μὴ ὄντος εἶναί φασιν, ὅτι οὐδὲ τοῦ κενοῦ τὸ σῶμα).

Aristotle may here be referring to a text preserved by Plutarch (*Adversus Colotem* 1109a):[31] "Hing no more is than nothing" (μὴ μᾶλλον τὸ δὲν ἢ τὸ μηδὲν εἶναι) (where the first word is derived from 'nothing' by dropping 'not').[32] Aristotle (assuming that the reconstruction of 985b9 is correct: see note 30) represents this as the conclusion of an argument:

(1) Body is no more than void.
(2) Body = being.
(3) Void = non-being.
∴ (4) Being no more is than non-being.

We can extend this argument; presumably it is tautologous that

(5) Being is,

so we can conclude

∴ (6) Non-being is.

That is precisely the way the position is phrased in *Physics* A 3. 187a2:[33] "non-being is" (ἔστι τὸ μὴ ὄν). A page later (A 5. 188a22–23), Aristotle speaks of Democritus' "solid and void, of which he says the one is as [a] being and the other as not [a] being" (τὸ στερεὸν καὶ κενόν, ὧν τὸ μὲν ὡς ὂν τὸ δ' ὡς οὐκ ὂν εἶναί φησιν).[34]

Again, according to Aristotle (*apud* Simplicius *in De caelo*, Heiberg [1893] 294.33 ff.),[35] Democritus used the term *nothing* of his void.

The first thing to notice is that in none of the many passages in which Aristotle cites this view does he pronounce it an absurdity. He has arguments against atomism, but this is not one of them. Indeed, he thinks the atomists provided the most systematic theory of corporeal structure and one that has a principle or starting point that accords with nature, and he says so in the same breath in which he introduces Leucippus' claim that the void is, but is not a being (*De generatione et corruptione* A 8. 324b35–325a2).

The second thing to be clear about is the exact formulation of Aristotle's atomists' Meinongianism: they want to drive a wedge between finite and participial occurrences of 'to be.' The wedge is given formulation in (Ma1): there are some things that are not beings.

2.2. *Hellenistic Meinongians*

Well, one might think, that is the Presocratics for you: you never know what they will say next. But this is a formulation that survived into Hellenistic philosophy; and the form in which it survived shows Platonic influence.

The rest of this section is, at most, dimly relevant to Speusippus. But it is of interest in its own right, and turns on a passage in the *Sophist* we have already considered in connection with the views of Eudoxus.

2.2.1. Being as the Power of Acting in the *Sophist*. The *Sophist*'s lead character, the "Eleatic Stranger"—who, if he does not directly represent Plato, at least is on the side of the angels—is, in the middle of the dialogue, concerned precisely with the question what it is for something to *be*. He falls to arguing with some people whom we may call 'materialists'; they

> drag all things to earth out of the heavens and the invisible, crudely grasping stone and oak[36] in their hands. For seizing on all such things they insist that that only is which offers some contact and touch, delimiting body and being as the same, and if any of the others should say that anything that does not have body is, they hold him in complete disdain and will hear nothing else (246a7-b3).

246a7 εἰς γῆν ἐξ οὐρανοῦ καὶ τοῦ ἀοράτου πάντα
ἕλκουσι, ταῖς χερσὶν ἀτεχνῶς πέτρας καὶ δρῦς περιλαμ-
βάνοντες. Τῶν γὰρ τοιούτων ἐφαπτόμενοι πάντων διισχυρί-
ζονται τοῦτο εἶναι μόνον ὃ παρέχει προσβολὴν καὶ ἐπαφήν
b τινα, ταὐτὸν σῶμα καὶ οὐσίαν ὁριζόμενοι, τῶν δὲ ἄλλων εἴ
τίς [τι] φήσει μὴ σῶμα ἔχον εἶναι, καταφρονοῦντες τὸ
παράπαν καὶ οὐδὲν ἐθέλοντες ἄλλο ἀκούειν.

These rowdy types undergo reformation at the Stranger's hands; they end up conceding that justice, intelligence, and other virtues and vices are (οὔσης, 247b1), along with the soul in which these come-to-be (247b1–3); and, although they think of the soul itself as possessing body, when it comes to intelligence and the rest, "they are too embarrassed either to refuse to admit them as beings or to maintain that they are all bodies" (247b9–c2) (αἰσχύνονται τὸ τολμᾶν ἢ μηδὲν τῶν ὄντων αὐτὰ ὁμολογεῖν ἢ πάντ' εἶναι σώματα διισχυρίζεσθαι). They will, then, concede that there is at least some small portion of the beings that is bodiless (τι καὶ σμικρὸν ἐθέλουσι τῶν ὄντων συγχωρεῖν ἀσώματον, 247c9–d1), and the Stranger returns to his main task by asking (247d2–4) what is common to the bodiless things and to the ones with body "looking at which they say that both *are*" (εἰς ὃ βλέποντες ἀμφότερα εἶναι λέγουσι). He answers for them (247d8–e4):

> I say that that which has any power whatever, either that which is of a nature to act on another in any way or that [which is of a nature] to undergo even in the smallest way by the meanest thing, even if only for once, all this really *is*; for I'm positing as a delimiter to delimit the things that are that [they] are not anything but power.[37]

247d8 Λέγω δὴ τὸ καὶ ὁποιανοῦν τινα κεκτημένον δύναμιν
e εἴτ' εἰς τὸ ποιεῖν ἕτερον ὁτιοῦν πεφυκὸς εἴτ' εἰς τὸ παθεῖν
καὶ σμικρότατον ὑπὸ τοῦ φαυλοτάτου, κἂν εἰ μόνον εἰς ἅπαξ,
πᾶν τοῦτο ὄντως εἶναι· τίθεμαι γὰρ ὅρον ὁρίζειν τὰ ὄντα
ὡς ἔστιν οὐκ ἄλλο τι πλὴν δύναμις.

We must first notice that in this passage there is no tendency on Plato's part to allow the verb 'to be' to behave in one way while the participle 'being' goes another. We shall return to this point later.

The definition[38] we are given for 'to be' or 'being' is not something the Stranger offers as his own; a fortiori, Plato does not offer it as his own. Nor is it a definition he formulates as materialistic, for it is constructed explicitly to include the counterexamples of 246e–247c: by the wording of 247d2–4, it covers what is common to things that have body and things that are bodiless. Yet it had influence on post-Platonic materialism: on Epicureanism, and, more important, on Stoicism.

2.2.2. Epicurus. Epicurus followed Leucippus[39] in working with atoms and the void. He first argues that there are bodies (σώματα μὲν . . . ὡς ἔστιν, DL x 39);[40] perception tells us this. He will subsequently explain that these bodies are composed of indivisible parts, atoms (ἄτομα, DL x 41);[41] this is not our present concern. After trying to show that bodies are, he argues that the void must be on the Leucippean ground[42] that, if there were no void (εἰ δὲ μὴ ἦν ὃ κενὸν καὶ χώραν καὶ ἀναφῆ φύσιν ὀνομάζομεν: "if there were not what we call void, space, and untouchable nature" DL x 40),[43] there would be no room for bodies to be or to move.[44] Leucippus would have added: but the void is not a being. Epicurus does not deny this outright, but neither does he say it; what he does say is that he conceives bodies and the void, and nothing else "as natures in their entireties" (καθ' ὅλας φύσεις, DL x 40).[45]

Later he says (DL x 67):[46]

> But we must furthermore note this, that we use the term 'bodiless' in accordance with the widest usage for whatever is conceived in its own right; but it is not possible to conceive the bodiless in its own right except for the void. But the void can neither act nor undergo, but only provides for motion through itself for bodies. So that those who say the soul is bodiless speak in vain. For it could neither act nor undergo if it were such; but as things are, both of these attributes are distinguished for the soul.

Ἀλλὰ μὴν καὶ τόδε γε δεῖ προσκατανοεῖν, ὅτι τὸ ἀσώματον
526 λέγομεν κατὰ τὴν πλείστην ὁμιλίαν τοῦ ὀνόματος ἐπὶ τοῦ καθ' ἑαυτὸ νοηθέντος ἄν· καθ' ἑαυτὸ δὲ οὐκ ἔστι νοῆσαι τὸ ἀσώματον πλὴν τοῦ κενοῦ. τὸ δὲ κενὸν οὔτε ποιῆσαι οὔτε παθεῖν δύναται, ἀλλὰ κίνησιν μόνον δι' ἑαυτοῦ τοῖς σώμασι παρέχεται. ὥστε οἱ λέγοντες ἀσώματον εἶναι τὴν ψυχὴν ματαιίζουσιν. οὐθὲν γὰρ ἂν ἐδύνατο ποιεῖν οὔτε πάσχειν, εἰ ἦν τοιαύτη· νῦν δ' ἐναργῶς ἀμφότερα ταῦτα διαλαμβάνεται περὶ τὴν ψυχὴν τὰ συμπτώματα.

So Epicurus, at any rate, refuses to accept the Eleatic Stranger's proffered definition of being: he instead uses it as a definition for 'body,' but allows that there is at least one stand-alone thing that is not a body: the void. Perhaps, if he had had to explain to the Eleatic Stranger what it is that he sees in common between bodies and the void that leads him to say they both *are*, he would have said: they are extended in space.[47]

Compare Lucretius on the same point (i 440–442):[48] "Further whatever is to be in its own right either will act on something or will itself have to undergo[49] when other things act on it, or will be such that things can be and carry on in it" (*praeterea per se quodcumque erit, aut faciet quid aut aliis fungi debebit agentibus ipsum aut erit ut possint in eo res esse gerique*). Here the Eleatic Stranger's definition has been expanded by a clause to accommodate the void among the beings.[50]

Here, then, is one important difference between the Epicureans and the earlier atomists: the Epicureans remain Actualist where Leucippus and Democritus had gone Meinongian, and in doing that they accept the Eleatic Stranger's offering but put it to a use he had not intended: they use it to define a subclass of beings, the bodies. And then they are led to count all sorts of things as bodies that the Stranger employed as counterexamples to crude materialism; especially, as we have seen, souls.

2.2.3. Stoics. Not so the Stoics: they accept the Stranger's offering and use it as directed, and end up going Meinongian.[51]

As with Leucippus and Democritus, we must fall back on hearsay. Plutarch, in his polemic against the Epicurean Colotes, speaks of 'more recent' philosophers who (*Adversus Colotem* 1116bc)[52]

> deprive many quite important objects of the appellation 'being': void, time, place, in a word, the class of sayables, in which are all the [things] that are true. For they say these are not beings, but are somethings, and they continue to use them in life and in philosophizing as subsisting and obtaining.

> πολλὰ γὰρ καὶ μεγάλα πράγματα τῆς τοῦ ὄντος ἀποστεροῦσι προσηγορίας, τὸ κενόν, τὸν χρόνον, τὸν τόπον, ἁπλῶς τὸ τῶν λεκτῶν γένος, ἐν ᾧ καὶ τἀληθῆ πάντα ἔνεστι. ταῦτα γὰρ ὄντα μὲν μὴ εἶναι, τινὰ δὲ εἶναι λέγουσι, χρώμενοι δὲ αὐτοῖς ὡς ὑφεστῶσι καὶ ὑπάρχουσιν ἐν τῷ βίῳ καὶ τῷ φιλοσοφεῖν διατελοῦσιν.

It is Stoics to whom Plutarch here refers,[53] as is clear from other passages (some will be quoted later).

Plutarch talks of 'subsisting' (ὑφεστάναι, ὑφεστηκέναι) and 'obtaining' (ὑπάρχειν); here we encounter a larger ontological vocabulary than was employed by Plato and Aristotle, at least in any official capacity.[54] 'Obtain,' ὑπάρχειν, occurs in both Plato and Aristotle in contexts in which the correct translation is plainly 'be': sometimes existential (e.g., *Republic* i 347a4, *Cratylus* 434a7–b1, *De generatione animalium* Γ 10. 760b17, 762a2) and sometimes predicative (e.g., *Republic* iii 412c12, *Meteorology* B 8. 365b24).[55] But neither of them makes use of the term in discussions of ontological questions (*Phaedo* 76e1 is close). The other verb, ὑφίστασθαι, is not used in a relevant sense by Plato[56] or, I think,[57] by Aristotle: there is an occurrence of the word in this sense that might be Aristotelian in Alexander, quoting from or paraphrasing the lost *On Ideas*.[58] But that occurrence could be due to Alexander, who uses the word frequently.[59]

Ὑφεστηκέναι meaning 'to subsist' can be found in Epicurus (341–271),[60] which takes it back close to the time of Plato and Aristotle, and the occurrences just quoted from Plutarch go back to the early Stoa. Chrysippus even drew a distinction between 'obtaining' (ὑπάρχειν) and 'subsisting' (ὑφεστηκέναι):[61] the present, he said, obtained but the past and the future merely subsisted: this makes it sound as if some non-beings are farther away from being than others. But it is dangerous to lean too hard on matters of vocabulary such as this.

What we have, in any case, is a distinction between 'obtaining' or 'subsisting,' on the one hand, and 'being,' on the other, that overlays the older, simpler division between 'to be' and 'to be a being':[62] things that are but are not beings are in the newer terminology said to subsist.

Sextus Empiricus, after discussing a view according to which time is a body, says (*Adversus mathematicos* x 218):[63]

> but the philosophers from the Stoa think it obtains as bodiless; for they say that of the somethings some are bodies and others bodiless, and of the bodiless [ones] they count four forms: sayable, void, place, and time.
>
> οἱ δὲ ἀπὸ τῆς Στοᾶς φιλόσοφοι ἀσώματον αὐτὸν ᾠήθησαν ὑπάρχειν· τῶν γὰρ τινῶν φασι τὰ μὲν εἶναι σώματα τὰ δὲ ἀσώματα, τῶν δὲ ἀσωμάτων τέσσαρα εἴδη καταριθμοῦνται ὡς λεκτὸν καὶ κενὸν καὶ τόπον καὶ χρόνον.

This passage classes the same four things that Plutarch said were not beings as not bodies. It does not contain the claim that they are not beings,[64] but pretty clearly the Stoics both denied that they were bodies and denied that they were beings; indeed, the latter was a conclusion from the former. Proclus (*in Timaeum* 271d)[65] tells us that the philosophers from the Stoa had a view of time vastly inferior to Plato's,

> exhibiting it as [a] bare conception, feeble and right next to non-being; for time was one of their bodiless [things], which were despised by them as inactive, not beings, and subsisting in bare conceptions.
>
> κατ' ἐπίνοιαν ψιλὴν αὐτὸν συνιστάντες ἀμενηνὸν καὶ ἔγγιστα τοῦ μὴ ὄντος· ἓν γὰρ ἦν τῶν παρ' αὐτοῖς ἀσωμάτων ὁ χρόνος, ἃ δὴ καταπεφρόνηται παρ' αὐτοῖς ὡς ἀδρανῆ καὶ οὐκ ὄντα καὶ ἐν ἐπινοίαις ὑφιστάμενα ψιλαῖς.

The Stoics were, notoriously, materialists: Plotinus, for example, refers to them as "those who posited that only bodies are the beings" (οἱ . . . σώματα μόνον τὰ ὄντα εἶναι θέμενοι, *Enneads* ii 4, 1.7).[66] But they recognized a broader genus than that of beings: 'something' was the name of this genus. Alexander tells us (*in Topica*, Wallies [1891] 301.20–21, 22–23):[67] "those from the Stoa posit 'something' as a genus of being; . . . they legislated for themselves that being is said of bodies alone" (τὸ τὶ οἱ ἀπὸ τῆς Στοᾶς γένος τοῦ ὄντος τίθενται· . . . ἐκεῖνοι νομοθετήσαντες αὑτοῖς τὸ ὂν κατὰ σωμάτων μόνων λέγεσθαι).

And their materialism involved accepting the Eleatic Stranger's gift.[68] Proclus echoed this when we quoted him as saying that time was inactive, but we have no need to rely on echoes: many sources are explicit about this.

One of the best is Plutarch's dialogue *On Common Concepts, against the Stoics* (*De Communibus Notitiis adversus Stoicos*). The Stoics had charged that the skeptical Academy "philosophize against the common concepts" (παρὰ τὰς κοινὰς φιλοσοφεῖν ἐννοίας, 1058ef); that is, very roughly,[69] that their skepticism flies in the face of common sense. Plutarch's character Diadumenus tries to rebut this charge by showing that the Stoics are even worse off on this score; at one point he lights on their views about being (1073de):[70]

> In general it is absurd and against the [common] concept for something to be but not be a being, and, while [they] say [that many things are somethings][71] but are not beings, what they say about the all is most absurd. For, having put an unlimited void outside around the cosmos, they say the all is neither a body nor bodiless. It follows from this that the all is the non-being; for they call bodies alone beings, since it [is a mark] of a being to act or to undergo something.
>
> καθόλου μὲν ἄτοπον καὶ παρὰ τὴν ἔννοιάν ἐστιν εἶναι μέν τι, μὴ ὂν δ' εἶναι, ⟨τούτων δὲ πολλά τιν' εἶναι⟩ μὲν οὐκ ὄντα δ' εἶναι λεγόντων ἀτοπώτατόν ἐστι τὸ ἐπὶ τοῦ παντὸς λεγόμενον. κενὸν γὰρ ἄπειρον ἔξωθεν τῷ κόσμῳ περιθέντες οὔτε σῶμα τὸ πᾶν οὔτ' ἀσώματον εἶναι λέγουσιν. ἕπεται δὲ τούτῳ τὸ μὴ ὂν εἶναι τὸ πᾶν· ὄντα γὰρ μόνα τὰ σώματα καλοῦσιν, ἐπειδὴ ὄντος τὸ ποιεῖν τι καὶ πάσχειν.

That is, they accepted the definition of being as what can act or undergo from the Eleatic Stranger, agreed with the Epicureans that the void, anyway, did neither, and concluded that it was not a being.

It looks as if it was Zeno himself who accepted the gift. Cicero (*Academica* i 39) has Varro say:[72]

> [Zeno] differed from those [*viz.* his predecessors] in that he thought it in no way possible for anything to be acted on by that which has no share in body, in which genus Xenocrates and already previous [philosophers] had said the soul was [placed], and, in fact, not possible for what acts on anything or what is acted on[73] not to be [a] body.
>
> *Discrepabat etiam ab iisdem quod nullo modo arbitrabatur quidquam effici posse ab ea quae expers esset corporis, cuius generis Xenocrates et superiores etiam animum esse dixerant, nec vero aut quod efficeret aliquid aut quod efficeretur posse esse non corpus.*

This suggests that the Stranger's gift was employed by Zeno, as it was by Epicurus, in an argument for the corporeality of the soul. Tertullian ascribes just such an argument to Zeno (*De anima* 5):[74]

> Zeno, in fact, defining soul as entwined spirit, teaches as follows: that by which, when it departs, the living thing dies, is a body; but it is by the entwined spirit departing that the living thing dies; but the entwined spirit is the soul; therefore the soul is a body.
>
> *denique Zeno consitum spiritum definiens animam hoc modo instruit, quo, inquit, digresso animal emoritur, corpus est: consito autem spiritu digresso animal emoritur: ergo consitus spiritus corpus est: consitus autem spiritus anima est: ergo corpus est anima.*

Similar arguments employing the Stranger's gift are ascribed by Tertullian and Nemesius to Cleanthes and Chrysippus.[75]

So the Stoics take the same line as Epicurus in the face of the first of the Stranger's counterexamples to crude materialism: the soul, they all say, is a body. They go further: they also say that the rest of the Stranger's purported counterexamples, the virtues and vices, are bodies.[76] Alexander of Aphrodisias, in the course of polemic against this view, expresses it as follows (*De anima libri mantissa*, Bruns [1887] 115.36–38, 116.13–14):[77] "the qualities of the soul are bodies, according to them, as well as those of the body . . . (αἱ τῆς ψυχῆς ποιότητες σώματα κατ' αὐτοὺς καὶ αἱ τοῦ σώματος . . .). . . .even the virtues and the arts [are] bodies . . . (. . . καὶ αἱ ἀρεταὶ σώματα καὶ αἱ τέχναι . . .)." The argument for this view, as it appears in Seneca, is only what we would expect:

> The good acts; for it benefits; what acts is a body. (*Epistulae morales* 106.4:[78] *Bonum facit; prodest enim; quod facit corpus est.*)
>
> Doesn't fear hold back? Doesn't audacity impel forward? Doesn't courage incite and give impulse? Doesn't moderation restrain and keep back? Doesn't joy raise up? Doesn't sadness lead down?[79] In fact, however we act, we behave under

> the command of either vice or virtue; what commands a body is a body, what brings force to a body [is] a body. (106.9:[80] *non timor retinet? non audacia inpellit? non fortitudo inmittit et impetum dat? non moderatio refrenat ac revocat? non gaudium extollit? non tristitia deducit? Denique quidquid facimus aut malitiae aut virtutis gerimus imperio: quod imperat corpori corpus est, quod vim corpori adfert, corpus.*)
>
> It is our [*sc.* the Stoics'] view that what is good is a body, because what is good acts; whatever acts is good. What is good benefits; but something must act in order to benefit; if it acts, it is a body. (117.2:[81] *Placet nostris quod bonum est corpus esse, quia quod bonum est facit, quidquid facit corpus est. Quod bonum est prodest; faciat autem aliquid oportet ut prosit; si facit, corpus est.*)

It sometimes sounds as if the Stoics wanted to say that the virtue of justice (say) was a body because justice is the soul in a certain condition, and the soul is a body. The train of thought can be found in Seneca; he is arguing for the closely related claim that the virtues are not only bodies but living things (*animalia*); he says:

> The soul is evidently a living thing, since it itself brings it about that we are living things, [and] since from that living things have acquired this name. But virtue is nothing other than a soul in a certain condition; therefore it is a living thing. (*Epistulae morales* 113.2:[82] *Animum constat animal esse, cum ipse efficiat ut simus animalia, cum ab illo animalia nomen hoc traxerint; virtus autem nihil aliud est quam animus quodam modo se habens; ergo animal est.*)

Either they are confused, or our sources, most of whom[83] are unsympathetic, are confused. We need not try to straighten things out now; what is of present interest is the Stoics' Meinongianism.

We may note two points before turning to Speusippus.

First, the formulation of the Stoics' Meinongianism, however it may be decked out with modern terminology like 'subsist' and 'obtain,' is at bottom that of the ancient Atomists: certain things are, or are something, but are not beings.[84]

Second, when Plutarch notes that the Stoics make use of their non-beings in living and in philosophizing, he probably means to point to an absurdity: that the Stoics make heavy use of things they do not even count as beings. He may even be pointing to a rather neat ad hominem argument: the Stoics, who adopt as their mark of a being that it can act or undergo, make use of the void, time, and so forth, and so those things do some undergoing.[85] But if this is his point, he does not hammer it home. In any case, he points to something of relevance to our concerns. The things that the Stoics and the Atomists describe as non-beings are not trivial, or even out-of-the-way: for the atomists, the void, and for the Stoics, the void and sayables, were central to their theories. Calling something a non-being is not necessarily dismissing it.

3. SPEUSIPPUS

Reconstructing the thought of Speusippus is a painful business. Aristotle frequently mentions his colleagues from the Academy, but he rarely names them. So figuring out what they said is a matter of nailing down what explicit references there are and triangulating. Some of what follows is standard stuff in that regard: it is, perhaps, only a little more explicit than usual. This crossing the t's and dotting the i's is humbling; the whole enterprise is very tenuous, and I find it astonishing to encounter the word *certainty* in various scholarly accounts of it.[86] The following, then, is conjecture; if we are fortunate, it may all be plausible conjecture; if we are very fortunate, it may also be interesting conjecture. But we cannot hope for much more.

Not all of it is standard stuff. I intend to provide Speusippus with arguments for his Meinongian attitude toward the One that connect that attitude to discussions current in the Academy at the time.

When it comes to Speusippus' metaphysics, we have two[87] explicit references in Aristotle to work with: one at *Metaphysics* Z 2. 1028b21, and the other at Λ 7. 1072b31. I shall take these up in the next two subsections, and expand from there.

3.1. The Levels of Speusippus' Universe

In *Metaphysics* Z 2,[88] Aristotle lists various candidates for the title *substance* or *reality* (οὐσία). This word is another word for *a being*, cognate with the verb *to be*. It would have been best to translate it in a way that made that clear, but there are not enough 'being' words in English to go around.

Aristotle nominates his own favorite 'substances': perceptible bodies, such as 'animals, plants, their parts' and so on (1028b8–13). He signals his intention to consider whether these in fact are substances (b13–15) and refers to alternatives (b15–24). He first says (b15–18):

> The limits of a body, e.g., surface, line, point, and unit, are thought by some to be substances, and more so than the body and the solid.

> δοκεῖ δέ τισι τὰ τοῦ σώματος πέρατα, οἷον ἐπιφάνεια καὶ γραμμὴ καὶ στιγμὴ καὶ μονάς, εἶναι οὐσίαι, καὶ μᾶλλον ἢ τὸ σῶμα καὶ τὸ στερεόν.

The people who think this way are standardly classed as *Pythagoreans*, where that is meant to contrast them with Academics.[89] I think they are in fact Academics,[90] and that Speusippus would at least have been sympathetic to them.[91] But here we can leave them on the shelf.

Aristotle next mentions unidentified people[92] who think that there are no substances apart from the perceptible ones (1028b18–19)[93] and then turns to views that are unmistakably Academic (b19–24):

> but others think there are many [of them][94] and more so [substances],[95] as they are eternal:[96] so Plato, [who thinks that] the forms and the mathematicals [are] two substances, and that the substance of the perceptible bodies is a third.
>
> b21 and Speusippus, who, starting from the one,[97] [thinks there are] even more substances and principles for each substance, one for numbers, another for magnitudes, then for soul; and in this way he extends the substances.

> **1028**b19 οἱ δὲ πλείω καὶ μᾶλλον ὄντα ἀίδια, ὥσπερ Πλάτων τά τε εἴδη καὶ τὰ μαθηματικὰ δύο οὐσίας, τρίτην δὲ τὴν τῶν αἰσθητῶν σωμάτων οὐσίαν, Σπεύσιππος δὲ καὶ πλείους οὐσίας ἀπὸ τοῦ ἑνὸς ἀρξάμενος, καὶ ἀρχὰς ἑκάστης οὐσίας ἄλλην μὲν ἀριθμῶν, ἄλλην δὲ μεγεθῶν, ἔπειτα ψυχῆς· καὶ τοῦτον δὴ τὸν τρόπον ἐπεκτείνει τὰς οὐσίας.

The view ascribed to Plato is that there are three substances, that is, three sorts of substance:[98] forms, perceptibles, and mathematical objects (elsewhere called *intermediates*[99]). We are not here concerned with this view, but it will help us see what is being ascribed to Speusippus.

Speusippus thinks there are "even more substances." This is no more a counting of heads than it was in the case of Plato: Speusippus thinks there are many types of substances.

He starts these types of substance from the One, or perhaps derives (some of) them from the one as principle.[100] Nothing is said about the character of the One; in particular, nothing is said that implies that the One is itself to be counted as one of the substances;[101] it is simply characterized as where Speusippus takes off from. The substances expressly so characterized are numbers, magnitudes, and soul. We may add perceptible things as a fourth level of substances, because Speusippus is here being listed along with Plato as one of those who thought that there were eternal substances apart from the perceptible ones, and that should mean that there are eternal substances in addition to, not to the exclusion of, sensible ones. Anyway, elsewhere (*Metaphysics* Λ 1. 1069a30ff.), in commenting on the available options, one of which is Speusippus' (1069a36), Aristotle remarks that everyone agrees on there being perceptible substances (1069a31).

The levels of substances Aristotle mentions have, he says, different principles: one for numbers, another for magnitudes, another for soul. If we add perceptible things, presumably we must add a new principle or principles for them.

There is not a lot here, in particular not much that helps characterize the top-drawer principle, the One. We learn a little more about it in the other of our two explicit references to Speusippus.

3.2. *The One Not Good or Beautiful*

In *Metaphysics* Λ 7. 1072b30–1073a3, we read:[102]

> Those who suppose, as do the Pythagoreans and Speusippus, that the most beautiful and best is not in [the] principle, because of the fact that whereas the principles for both plants and animals are causes, the beautiful and the good are in the [things] from these, do not think rightly. For the seed is from other prior complete [things], and the first is not a seed, but the complete [thing]; e.g. one may say that a man is prior to the seed, not that which has come-to-be from this, but another from which the seed [has come-to-be].

1072b

ὅσοι δὲ
ὑπολαμβάνουσιν, ὥσπερ οἱ Πυθαγόρειοι καὶ Σπεύσιππος,
τὸ κάλλιστον καὶ ἄριστον μὴ ἐν ἀρχῇ εἶναι, διὰ τὸ καὶ
τῶν φυτῶν καὶ τῶν ζῴων τὰς ἀρχὰς αἴτια μὲν εἶναι, τὸ
δὲ καλὸν καὶ τέλειον ἐν τοῖς ἐκ τούτων, οὐκ ὀρθῶς οἴονται.
τὸ γὰρ σπέρμα ἐξ ἑτέρων ἐστὶ προτέρων τελείων, καὶ τὸ
1073 πρῶτον οὐ σπέρμα ἐστίν, ἀλλὰ τὸ τέλειον· οἷον πρότερον
ἄνθρωπον ἂν φαίη τις εἶναι τοῦ σπέρματος, οὐ τὸν ἐκ τούτου
γενόμενον, ἀλλ' ἕτερον ἐξ οὗ τὸ σπέρμα.

Principle (ἀρχή) is a term with temporal connotations; 'beginning' is the more common rendering in this passage. We shall consider the issue this raises and then turn to the analogy between principles and seeds.

It is important to be clear from the outset that Aristotle is ascribing to Speusippus the claim that, just as with plants and animals there is no beauty or goodness in their principles or beginnings, but only in the fully developed organisms, so in the universe at large we encounter things that are beautiful and good only farther down the road, not at the level of first principles.[103] In particular, Aristotle is not merely ascribing to Speusippus the view that the One is not *the* Good.

3.2.1. The Language of Generation. The Pythagoreans and Speusippus think that "the most beautiful and best is not in the principle" (1072b32). This peculiar phrasing is only slightly normalized by the more standard rendering, "in the beginning," and in that rendering the continuity with Z 2 is lost. Aristotle has here been discussing his own first principle, the unmoved mover (or one of the unmoved movers) and that is not a 'beginning' in any temporal sense. He is saying that Speusippus is wrong in believing that the first principle of everything is not beautiful and good, and that should not be taken to import a temporal beginning into Speusippus' universe. Anyway, Speusippus is talking about the derivation of *numbers*, in the first instance, and he could not have supposed this was a temporal process, if we put any stock in Z 2: there Speusippus' numbers were classed, along with Plato's forms, as eternal substances.

We are in what follows going to encounter talk of beginnings, generation, things coming first, so-and-so not appearing until such-and-such has happened, and so on: the description of Speusippus' universe is shot through with temporal metaphors. We had better try to get straight on how the language of generation is to be understood.

It is sometimes written off as a mere device to ease communication.[104] This has a foothold, or, anyway, a toehold, in the ancient tradition.

Plato's *Timaeus* presents a creation story. There is a dispute over whether this should be taken literally. Fortunately we need not enter into that arena.[105] But, from the grandstand, we can see the dispute is an ancient one: it goes back to the Early Academy itself. In *De caelo* A 10 Aristotle mentions a tactic employed by "some" (τινές, 279b32) who speak of the universe as coming-to-be but who want that discounted (279b33–280a2):[106]

> for they say that they have spoken of coming-to-be in the way that [mathematicians] draw diagrams, not as if it ever did come-to-be, but for the sake of teaching, so that they will more easily gain knowledge, just as those who behold the diagram coming-to-be
>
> ὁμοίως γάρ φασι τοῖς τὰ διαγράμματα γράφουσι καὶ σφᾶς εἰρηκέναι περὶ τῆς γενέσεως, οὐχ ὡς γενομένου ποτέ, ἀλλὰ διδασκαλίας χάριν ὡς μᾶλλον γνωριζόντων, ὥσπερ τὸ διάγραμμα γιγνόμενον θεασαμένους.

Aristotle goes on to argue against the idea that creation stories can be treated like mathematical constructions, and Simplicius' commentary ad loc. (*in De Caelo*, Heiberg [1893], p. 303.33–34[107]) says "The argument is thought to be directed against Xenocrates and the Platonists" (δοκεῖ μὲν Ξενοκράτην μάλιστα καὶ τοὺς Πλατωνικοὺς ὁ λόγος τείνειν). This is confirmed by Plutarch in *De animae procreatione in Timaeo* 3. 1013a, where the tactic Aristotle mentions is treated as a device applied by Xenocrates and Crantor to the interpretation of the *Timaeus*. Xenocrates' name also comes up most often in the scholia as a source for this idea,[108] but Speusippus is mentioned in one of them.[109] It looks as if at least Xenocrates, and perhaps Speusippus,[110] said of the creation story in the *Timaeus* that it was told in the language of generation only for pedagogical purposes (διδασκαλίας χάριν *De caelo* A 10. 280a16; θεωρίας ἕνεκα Plutarch, *De animae procreatione in Timaeo* 1013a[111]), even as a geometrical construction should not be taken as a description of a process in time.

But Aristotle's argument against this in *De caelo* A 10. 280a2–10[112] is that, whereas in a typical creation story, you start with disorder and end with order, in a geometrical construction the initial stages are preserved in the result: you start, say, with a line and end up with an equilateral triangle on that line; in the creation story, because the antecedent state of affairs conflicts with the later one, there *must* be a temporal process; not so in the case of the geometrical construction. This is not an argument against anybody's interpretation of the *Timaeus*; it is an argument against the viability of putting out creation stories and then saying you only meant them for pedagogical purposes.[113] So somebody was doing more than just interpreting the *Timaeus*: somebody was talking in the language of generation and claiming that it was legitimate to treat that language this way.

Might Speusippus have been doing this?

We happen to have a little information about Speusippus' attitude toward geometrical constructions. Proclus, commenting on Euclid, says (Friedlein [1873] p. 77.7–12, 15–78.6)[114]

> Again, the [things that follow] from the principles are divided into problems and theorems, the former including the comings-to-be of figures, their sectionings, subtractions, additions, and in general the undergoings that come-to-be concerning them, the latter showing the attributes that belong to them by virtue of themselves. . . .
>
> 15 But already among the ancients, some demanded we call all [of the things that follow from the principles] theorems, as [did] Speusippus, Amphinomus, and those around them, thinking that for the theoretical branches of knowledge the appellation 'theorems' was more appropriate than 'problems,' especially in that they make their accounts about eternal [things].
>
> 20/21 For there is no coming-to-be among the eternal [things], so that the problem could have no place with them, it requiring [the] coming-to-be and making of that which was not before, e.g. constructing an equilateral triangle or describing a square when a line is given, or placing a line at a given point.
>
> **78**.3/4 So they say it is better to say that all these [things][115] are, but that we look at their comings-to-be not by way of producing [them] but by way of knowing [them], treating the things that always are as if they were coming-to-be.

> Πάλιν δ' αὖ τὰ ἀπὸ τῶν ἀρχῶν εἰς προβλήματα διαρεῖται καὶ θεωρήματα, τὰ μὲν τὰς γενέσεις περιέχοντα τῶν σχημάτων καὶ τὰς τομὰς καὶ τὰς ἀφαιρέσεις ἢ προσθέσεις καὶ ὅλως τὰ παθήματα τὰ γιγνόμενα περὶ αὐτά, τὰ δὲ καθ' αὑτὰ συμβεβηκότα ἑκάστοις δεικνύοντα. . . .
>
> ἤδη δὲ τῶν παλαιῶν οἱ μὲν πάντα θεωρήματα καλεῖν ἠξίωσαν, ὡς οἱ περὶ Σπεύσιππον καὶ Ἀμφίνομον, ἡγούμενοι ταῖς θεωρητικαῖς ἐπιστήμαις οἰκειοτέραν εἶναι τὴν τῶν θεωρημάτων προσηγορίαν ἢ τὴν τῶν προβλημάτων, ἄλλως τε καὶ περὶ ἀϊδίων ποιουμέναις τοὺς λόγους. οὐ γάρ ἐστι γένεσις ἐν τοῖς ἀϊδίοις, ὥστε οὐδὲ τὸ πρόβλημα χώραν ἐπὶ τούτων ἂν ἔχοι, γένεσιν ἐπαγγελλόμενον καὶ ποίησιν
> **78** τοῦ μήπω πρότερον ὄντος, οἷον ἰσοπλεύρου τριγώνου σύστασιν, ἢ τετραγώνου δοθείσης εὐθείας ἀναγραφήν,

> ἢ θέσιν εὐθείας πρὸς τῷ δοθέντι σημείῳ. ἄμεινον οὖν φασι λέγειν, ὅτι πάντα ταῦτα ἐστι, τὰς δὲ γενέσεις αὐτῶν οὐ ποιητικῶς ἀλλὰ γνωστικῶς ὁρῶμεν ὡσανεὶ γιγνόμενα λαμβάνοντες τὰ ἀεὶ ὄντα . . . .

Speusippus is not, according to this, excluding the language of generation from mathematics altogether, because he (and Amphinomus,[116] and whoever else[117] is in this camp) are telling us at the end of the passage that it is all right to 'treat the things that are as if they were coming-to-be,' as long as we realize what we are talking about.[118] Where the mathematician presents us with a construction, such as that of an equilateral triangle (cf. Euclid i 1), what we are actually getting is a proof that there is in the realm of eternal mathematical objects an equilateral triangle, or perhaps that an equilateral triangle depends for its existence on the existence of certain types of lines. Speusippus and Amphinomus[119] construe constructions as proofs of the existence of the entities constructed, or proofs that the eternal objects of mathematics have certain properties.

Speusippus is so far presumably following Plato's lead:[120] in *Republic* vii 527ab Socrates seems to say that the mathematician's talk of squaring, adding, etc. is ridiculous (γελοίως 527a6)—it makes it sound as if what was going on was for the sake of action (πράξεως ἕνεκα a7), whereas in fact it is for the sake of knowing (γνώσεως ἕνεκα b1), which is of what always is (τοῦ ἀεὶ ὄντος b5)—but unavoidable (ἀναγκαίως a6).[121]

So there is some reason to think Speusippus would have found the demythologizing of the language of generation acceptable.[122] But what is left after this demythologization? If we stick with phrases like "for pedagogical purposes," it may seem that there is nothing left. But this is not so.

A larger look at some of the options will clarify matters. First consider the alternative to the Speusippus-Amphinomus position as it is described by Proclus (78.8–9): "Others, contrariwise, held it right to say that all [of the things that follow from the principles] are problems, as did Menaechmus and the mathematicians around him" (οἱ δὲ ἀνάπαλιν πάντα προβλήματα λέγειν ἐδικαίουν ὡς οἱ περὶ Μέναιχμον μαθηματικοί), but they distinguished among types of problem (78.10–13).

Both parties are right, Proclus thinks (78.13ff.); what he says about Speusippus, Amphimomus, and the rest adds nothing, but he does say something that may carry a little new information about Menaechmus and his camp (78.17–79.2):

> And Menaechmus and those around him [speak rightly]—for not without proceeding forth into matter as well are there the discoveries of the theorems. But I am speaking of matter that is intelligible. So our concepts (λόγοι)[123] going forth into this and shaping it are plausibly said to be like comings-to-be.

For we say that the motion of our thought and the projection of the concepts (λόγοι) in it are a coming-to-be of the figures and the features of them. For there [*sc*. in the imagination] there are the constructions, the sections, the placings, the juxtapositions, the additions, and the subtractions, but all the things in thought are at rest, without coming-to-be or any change.

καὶ οἱ περὶ τὸν Μέναιχμον —οὐ γὰρ ἄνευ τῆς εἰς ὕλην προόδου καὶ αἱ τῶν θεωρημάτων εἰσὶν εὑρέσεις. λέγω δὲ ὕλην τὴν νοητήν. εἰς ἐκείνην οὖν οἱ λόγοι προϊόντες καὶ μορφοῦντες αὐτὴν εἰκότως δήπου ταῖς γενέσεσιν ἐοικέναι λέγονται. τὴν γὰρ τῆς διανοίας ἡμῶν κίνησιν καὶ τὴν προβολὴν τῶν ἐν αὐτῇ λόγων γένεσιν τῶν ἐν φαντασίᾳ σχημάτων εἶναί φαμεν καὶ τῶν περὶ αὐτὰ παθημάτων. ἐκεῖ γὰρ αἱ συστάσεις καὶ αἱ τομαὶ καὶ αἱ θέσεις καὶ αἱ παραβολαὶ καὶ αἱ προσθέσεις καὶ αἱ
79 ἀφαιρέσεις, τὰ δὲ ἐν τῇ διανοίᾳ πάντα ἕστηκεν ἄνευ γενέσεως καὶ πάσης μεταβολῆς.

There are, in the abstract, many positions that can be taken about the objects of mathematics. Here two are in question.

Some think mathematics describes an antecedent reality that is eternal and unchanging. That is certainly the position here being ascribed to Speusippus and Amphinomus. As a consequence, they think the propositions[124] of mathematics should be referred to as *theorems*: 'objects of contemplation' (θεωρήματα, from θεωρεῖν, 'to contemplate'). Let us call this position *realism*.

Menaechmus disagrees with them about what to call the propositions of mathematics: he thinks they should be called *problems*: 'objects thrown forward' or perhaps 'produced' (προβλήματα, from προβάλλω). That, with some of Proclus' comments in the sequel, seems to imply that the objects of mathematics are products of the mathematicians' minds:[125] Proclus' comments about matter, intelligible matter, our λόγοι and their 'going forth', and so on, are in Proclus' vocabulary and not Menaechmus',[126] but it sounds as if Proclus, in trying to say what is true about Menaechmus' view, is attempting to accommodate a view according to which, when the mathematician describes a construction in temporal terms, he is to be taken seriously: when he says he is constructing an equilateral triangle, that is (unless he is lying, hallucinating, or whatever) exactly what he is doing.

Let us call this position *constructivism*.

Both the labels *realism* and *constructivism* are easily misused. The present labeling is merely a temporary expedient.[127]

In the abstract, many positions can be taken about the constructions of mathematics. Here are two.

One might suppose that constructions are merely pedagogic devices. The order in which they are presented is arbitrary, in the sense that anything goes if it will help get the point across. Let us call this *pragmatism*.

One might, on the other hand, suppose that some constructions have to precede others. You cannot construct an equiangular triangle without first constructing circles and lines. Call this *determinism*.

These labels are even more obviously temporary expedients than the others.

One might suppose that determinism is tied to realism and pragmatism to constructivism. This is false. You could be a deterministic constructivist: the objects of mathematics are constructs of the mathematician's mind, but constraints are set on the constructs by the very structure of the mind doing the constructing. Brouwer was plainly such a constructivist. On the other hand, you could be a pragmatistic realist: the independent reality mathematics describes is all there at once, in a block, and any way into it is as good as any other provided it gets you there. Amphinomus may have been a pragmatistic realist. Proclus tells us (Friedlein [1873] 202.9–12): "Geometry seemed to many not to contemplate the cause, the 'why'—Amphinomus is of this belief, although Aristotle started it off" (τήν γε μὴν αἰτίαν καὶ τὸ διὰ τί πολλοῖς μὲν ἔδοξεν ἡ γεωμετρία μὴ θεωρεῖν—ταύτης γάρ ἐστι καὶ ὁ 'Αμφίνομος τῆς δόξης 'Αριστοτέλους κατάρξαντος). There is something fishy here: it sounds very odd to suppose that Aristotle was the progenitor of this view.[128] Short of tampering with the text, or supposing that Proclus is referring to something of Aristotle's that we do not possess,[129] we might suppose that Aristotle started the view off in the sense that he brought it up, perhaps only to argue against it.[130] But let us suppose it is correctly ascribed to Amphinomus. Then his realism does not prevent him from supposing that mathematics does not really explain *why* certain things are so. It might proceed, for all that it matters, entirely in terms of reductiones ad absurdum, very few of which look genuinely explanatory (especially to a constructivist). (The use of reductio arguments is mentioned by Proclus in connection with this position in 202.19–21).

But plainly Amphinomus' position is not the only possible one here. One might believe that mathematical arguments are explanations in that their premises reflect truths somehow more fundamental than their conclusions, and the entities dealt with in their premises are more fundamental than the ones that appear in subsequent constructions, and so on: points, one might think, are more fundamental than lines, and lines than triangles, and so on.

Then we must ask, Was Speusippus allied with Amphinomus on this score as well as on the score of realism? Or was he, to change labels for greater clarity, not just a realist but an explanatory realist, thinking that the demonstrations of mathematics reflected something inherent in the structure of the mathematical world, the entities dealt with in earlier demonstrations explaining why subsequent entities are as they are?[131]

It is important to remind oneself that causality, in the broad sense required here, in which a cause is simply what you invoke whenever you try to explain *why* something is so, does not require temporal succession. The eternal dependence of Aristotle's eternal universe on its eternal unmoved mover(s) is enough to show that. So it would have been perfectly consistent for Speusippus to think that the numbers were causally or ontologically dependent on the One and Plurality, and even to describe their derivation as if it were a temporal process, without supposing that there is in fact any temporal process involved.

Then the answer to our question is plain. Everything we hear about Speusippus indicates that he was talking about causes. In *Metaphysics* Λ 7 we found Aristotle crediting Speusippus (and the Pythagoreans) with an analogy between the principles of things that are and seeds; that analogy is plainly intended to shed light on what is responsible for the existence of what. Speusippus is an explanatory realist.

Then the language of generation may be amenable to demythologization, but there will remain an obvious sense in which the way things are ordered in the generation story reflects the way things are ordered in reality. The earlier entities in the generation story are prior to the later ones in that they are causes for them; the latter depend for their existence on the former.[132]

This will require a qualification, as we shall see: Speusippus' universe does not show as much causal connectedness as some (in particular, Aristotle) thought it should. But plainly the things that are 'generated' from certain principles are causally dependent on those principles.

3.2.2. Seeds and Principles. Speusippus or the Pythagoreans or both are credited in the passage from Λ 7 with an analogy: the causes of animals and plants, 'seeds,' are not good or beautiful, but the animals and plants that come from them are. The biological terms in which this analogy is cast are ones Aristotle would have liked himself. But so would any member of the Academy, whose interest in biological classifications was well enough known to be the subject of comic parody. There is a famous fragment of Epicrates[133] that portrays Plato, Speusippus, and others laboring to classify a pumpkin.[134] This is no less absurd, if it is absurd at all, than the twenty-odd fragments[135] preserved from Speusippus' book *Likes* (Ὅμοια), in which he took up the radish and the turnip[136] along with male and female tunny-fish.[137] There is no reason against supposing that he subscribed to the analogy Aristotle gives.

Aristotle confronts that analogy with a favorite view of his own: the 'seeds' had to come from fully formed turnips and tunny-fish; so the turnips and the tunny-fish are prior, and if the beautiful and the good are in them, they are in the principles. At this point, the issue between him and Speusippus sounds like a chicken-and-egg question, with Speusippus opting for the priority of the egg and Aristotle for that of the chicken. And it certainly is Aristotle's view that the 'seed' is only a go-between: the real cause of any given chicken is a chicken.[138] This has been aptly called[139] a *Transmission Theory* of causality: the cause of things that are F is itself F, and transmits being F to them. We might speak of a 'transmitting cause' as a cause that satisfies the following schema:

(T) c causes x to be F inasmuch as c is itself F.

A Transmission Theory then says: all causes, or perhaps all causes of a certain important type, are transmitting causes.

Our passage might be seen as offering a counterexample to that view: seeds are responsible for beautiful plants and animals, but are not themselves beautiful. It can hardly be said that the passage *requires* this interpretation or constitutes crushing evidence that Speusippus had considered a Transmission Theory and rejected it, but it is clear that he could not have accepted it as an account of the causal activity of his first principle. That principle, the One, causes things to be good and beautiful, but it is not itself good and beautiful. Its effects are complete or perfect in some way in which it is not itself complete or perfect. So it is not a transmitting cause of their goodness, beauty, or perfection.

3.3. The One Not a Being

In *Metaphysics* N 4–5, Aristotle castigates various unnamed Academics for their views on principles. Prominent among these views is the Speusippean one that the good and the beautiful are not to be ascribed to the principle or principles but to their products[140] (see, e.g., 4. 1091a34–b3, b32–35, 5. 1092a9).[141]

An abbreviated account of Speusippus' view, without the name *Speusippus* attached, appears in *Metaphysics* N 4. 1091a29–36:[142]

> There is a puzzle, and a reproach for one who is unpuzzled, as to how the elements and the principles are related to the good and the beautiful; this is [the] puzzle: whether any of those [elements] is such as we want to call the good itself and the best, or not, but rather [these] are later in origin.
>
> a33/34 For from the theologians there seems to be agreement with some of those now, who say [the good is] not [among the principles], but that when the nature of the beings has come forward the good and the beautiful show up.

> ἔχει δ' ἀπορίαν καὶ εὐπορήσαντι ἐπιτίμησιν πῶς ἔχει πρὸς τὸ ἀγαθὸν καὶ τὸ καλὸν τὰ στοιχεῖα καὶ αἱ ἀρχαί· ἀπορίαν μὲν ταύτην, πότερόν ἐστί τι ἐκείνων οἷον βουλόμεθα λέγειν αὐτὸ τὸ

ἀγαθὸν καὶ τὸ ἄριστον, ἢ οὔ, ἀλλ' ὑστερογενῆ. παρὰ μὲν γὰρ τῶν θεολόγων ἔοικεν ὁμολογεῖσθαι τῶν νῦν τισίν, ὅι οὔ φασιν, ἀλλὰ προελθούσης τῆς τῶν ὄντων φύσεως καὶ τὸ ἀγαθὸν καὶ τὸ καλὸν ἐμφαίνεσθαι.

As the position is stated here, the good and the beautiful enter 'later'; specifically, "when the nature of the beings has come forward." When is that? It could be really quite unspecific: 'once the nature of the beings has got on a little further.' But it could easily be read as: 'once the nature of *beings* has entered the picture.'[143] That would mean that the beautiful and the good do not enter until we have some beings, and it would follow that there are no beings to begin with.

The sequel is certainly compatible with this reading; it may even support it. Aristotle says, in N 5. 1092a11–17:[144]

> And one does not rightly understand either if one compares the principles of the whole to that of animals and plants, on the ground that from indefinite, incomplete things the more complete always [arise], which is why he says it holds thus for the first [things], so that the one itself is not even a being. For even here the principles from which these [arise] are complete: for a man begets a man, and it is not that the seed is first.

> **1092**a11 οὐκ ὀρθῶς δ' ὑπολαμβάνει οὐδ' εἴ τις παρεικάζει τὰς τοῦ ὅλου ἀρχὰς τῇ τῶν ζῴων καὶ φυτῶν, ὅτι ἐξ ἀορίστων ἀτελῶν δὲ ἀεὶ τὰ τελειότερα, διὸ καὶ ἐπὶ τῶν πρώτων οὕτως ἔχειν φησίν, ὥστε μηδὲ ὄν τι εἶναι τὸ ἓν αὐτό. εἰσὶ γὰρ καὶ ἐνταῦθα τέλειαι αἱ ἀρχαὶ ἐξ ὧν ταῦτα· ἄνθρωπος γὰρ ἄνθρωπον γεννᾷ, καὶ οὐκ ἔστι τὸ σπέρμα πρῶτον.

This certainly sounds like Speusippus. Aristotle portrays him as applying his analogy to the first principles and again as, at least implicitly, denying the Transmission Theory. And the clause "so that the one itself is not even a being" seems to be telling us that Speusippus is a Meinongian: he thought the one was not a being.

But this has been denied.[145] The clause "so that the one itself is not even a being" is not necessarily governed by the verb phrase *he says*;[146] it could be that it is Aristotle who is drawing this conclusion, and Speusippus might have found it unwelcome.

Tarán insists that this is so:[147] that Aristotle is in this passage extracting the conclusion that the One is not a being from Speusippean premises to show, by the absurdity of that conclusion, the absurdity of the premises.

This interpretation labors under two quite severe difficulties: first, the passage supplies no argument that Aristotle would himself accept for the extraction of the allegedly absurd conclusion; and, second, Aristotle does not allege that the conclusion is absurd.

On the first point, the only Speusippean premises Aristotle supplies are those involved in the familiar analogy about animals, plants, and seeds. Suppose Aristotle were trying to reduce these premises to absurdity by deriving from them the conclusion that the One is not a being. He would have to be saying that Speusippus thinks that seeds are not turnips but are the principles of turnips, and that, in general, the principles of things that are F are not themselves F, so he is *forced* to the conclusion that the One, his principle of beings, is not a being. This argument would have to be Aristotle's rather than one supplied by Speusippus. But Aristotle's considered position is that 'being' and 'turnip' are different sorts of terms in that 'being' does not, while 'turnip' does, mark out a *kind* of things.[148] The generalization that the principles of things that are F are not themselves F would not have as an instance the claim that the principles of things that are beings are not themselves beings. By Aristotle's lights,[149] then, the argument would fail.

On the other hand, suppose Speusippus did not subscribe to the Aristotelian claim that 'being' is not a kind-term. Then the generalization would be instantiable with 'being' replacing 'F.' But then Speusippus' own principles *do* commit him to the claim that the One is not a being. But then he can hardly have missed the point: it would be a part of his position.

And then there is the second point. This actually affects more than just Tarán's peculiar interpretation of the text. For it is agreed by parties on both sides of this dispute that Aristotle, when he says that Speusippus' one is not even a being, intends to be pointing to an absurdity: the only difference is that those who think the conclusion Aristotle's see him as attempting a *reductio ad absurdum* and those who think it Speusippus' see Aristotle as brandishing it by way of ridicule.[150]

And yet there is not the slightest suggestion in the passage that the conclusion is absurd. The argument Aristotle actually gives against Speusippus here is the same as the one we found in Λ, based on the Transmission Theory, and has nothing to do with the ontological status, or rather nonstatus, of the One. And we must remember that Aristotle is not in a very good position for making trouble over the point that the one is 'not even a being.' Recall his treatment of Leucippus and Democritus: theirs was a theory to be reckoned with despite its Meinongianism, and Aristotle did not profess to find anything absurd in it because of that Meinongianism.[151] Aristotle is, no doubt, an Actualist at heart, but his Actualism is not so well-entrenched that he can see in Meinongian consequences an obvious refutation of their antecedents.[152]

But, of course, if Aristotle is not drawing the conclusion from Speusippus' position by way of showing the absurdity of that position, there is not the slightest reason for him to be drawing it at all, unless it was in fact a part of Speusippus' position. He can hardly be helping Speusippus out by furnishing a theorem Speusippus neglected to prove. So I shall suppose it was Speusippus' own conclusion: the One is not a being.

The form of Meinongianism here is the participial one we were led to expect from our examination of the atomists.

There is another text to be considered in this connection.[153] About 600 years after Aristotle, Iamblichus compiled a book *On Universal Mathematical Science*.[154] *Compiled* is the right word here: Iamblichus notoriously excerpted from other authors without attribution.[155] About 1600 years after Iamblichus, Philip Merlan read the fourth chapter of *Universal Math* (as I shall refer to it) and noticed striking similarities between it and what little we have about Speusippus and striking dissimilarities between it and what we know about Iamblichus.[156] (The text of the chapter and a translation of it form the Appendix to this study.) Merlan concluded that that chapter may have been bodily lifted from Speusippus.[157] Perhaps that is too strong; but we are at least entitled to try out the hypothesis that Iamblichus was relying heavily on Speusippean material.

We must once more confront the doctrines of Tarán: he has, he thinks, 'conclusively proved' that Speusippus is not the source for *Universal Math* iv.[158] Fortunately, his 'conclusive proofs' have been rebutted in the literature,[159] and I shall not take up space in the text of this study with most of them.[160] But one of them is directly on our topic. It runs as follows. When Aristotle says of Speusippus that "he says" the principle that the more complete comes from the less complete holds for the first principles as well, "so that the one is not even a being," the "so that" clause is not governed by the verb phrase *he says*, as we saw; according to Tarán, it is an inference of Aristotle's that the one is not a being; it conclusively follows, Tarán thinks, that Speusippus did not make that inference. But in *Universal Math* iv the one is explicitly said not to be a being. Therefore, *Universal Math* iv cannot go back to Speusippus.

But, of course, it does not follow from Aristotle's text that Speusippus did not himself infer that the one is not a being. The presumption, as we have seen, is exactly the opposite.

So let us look at some passages from *Universal Math* iv.

The first comes from the middle of the chapter (16.10–14); it puts us on familiar ground:

> But it is fit to call the one neither beautiful nor good, because of the fact that it is above the beautiful and the good;
> 12 for it was when nature proceeds farther away from the things in the principle[161] that, first, the beautiful appeared, and, second, when the elements had an even longer distance, the good.

(For the text, see the Appendix to this study.)

This certainly has a Speusippean ring. The phrasing in 16.12–13 is particularly reminiscent of Aristotle's in *Metaphysics* N 4. 1091a33–36 (see p. 86).[162] It adds a detail that we cannot get from Aristotle: that the beautiful and the good are not only late to arrive, they do not arrive together; the beautiful comes first.[163]

A passage later in the chapter may allow us to be more specific about this (18.1–12):

> **18.**1/2 But the elements out of which the numbers [are produced] do not yet obtain there as either beautiful or good;[164]
>
> 3 but out of the combination of the one and the matter that is [the] cause of plurality number subsists, and first in these being and beauty appear,
>
> 6 while next out of the elements of lines geometrical substance appears, in which in the same way there is being and the beautiful, but in which there is nothing either ugly or bad;
>
> 9 but at the extreme, among the fourths and fifths, which are combined from the last elements, [it is possible] for badness to come-to-be, not directly,[165] but from something's falling away from and failing to retain possession of that which accords with nature.

Putting this together with 16.12–14, it appears that beauty and being both come in at the level of number and goodness comes in later. The passage does not say outright where goodness turns up, but it ought to be there by 'the fourths and fifths,' as there badness, its contrary, is to be found. (Badness, according to the author of this scheme, does not come about there 'directly', i.e., as a result of the interaction that produces everything else at these levels: whatever causes are responsible for the existence of everything else here is not responsible for bad stuff.)

If this passage is giving us Speusippus by and large, the fourth level ought to be that of soul and the fifth that of body.

Aristotle tells us *in propria persona*, and without reference to Speusippus, that there is no goodness among mathematical objects, because the good always requires action, whereas mathematical objects are unchanging (*Metaphysics* M 3. 1078a31–b2; see also B 2. 996a22–b1).[166] In the scheme we are looking at, there is no room for action until we get to soul and body. So it might have been precisely on this basis that Speusippus had beauty coming at the level of mathematical objects and goodness only on some lower level.

Let us consider one more passage, from earlier in the chapter (15.6–12):

> **15.6** For the mathematical numbers one must posit two [things], the first and highest principles,
>
> 7/8 the one (which indeed one ought not yet even call a being,
>
> 8 because of the fact that it is simple

8/9 and because of the fact that it is a principle for the things that are, while the principle is not yet such as are the things of which it is a principle),

10/11 and again another principle, that of plurality, which can by virtue of itself provide division as well,[167]

The terminology of this passage is Speusippean enough: as we shall see later, he was devoted to "the mathematical numbers" and employed a principle he apparently referred to as *plurality* (rather than the *indefinite dyad*) in generating them.

And here, at last, we have something that looks like an *argument* for the conclusion that the one is not a being. In fact, we have two arguments for that conclusion, one from simplicity:

(1a) The one is simple.
∴ (2a) The one is not a being.

And one from the explicit rejection of the Transmission Theory:

(1b) The one is a principle of beings.
(2b) A principle of Fs is not yet F.
∴ (3b) The one is not a being.

I shall from here on refer to (2b) as the *Principle of Alien Causality*. It is quite vague; clarification will come later.

I want to suppose that these two arguments, the Argument from Simplicity and the Argument from the Principle of Alien Causality, are Speusippus' and see what happens.

But, before we get to that, there is a question connected with Speusippus' One that we must deal with.

3.3.1. Ranking the One and Being. Should the One be thought of as *above* being or just outside the scope of the term *being*?[168] At first sight, here there is conflicting evidence.

(1) What we already have from Aristotle makes it sound as if the One is somehow incomplete: somehow inferior to being.

(2) In *Universal Math* iv, the One is referred to as one of the two first and highest principles (δύο τὰς πρώτιστας καὶ ἀνωτάτω . . . ἀρχάς, 15.6–7) and as up above both the beautiful and the good (καὶ τοῦ καλοῦ καὶ τοῦ ἀγαθοῦ ὑπεράνω εἶναι, 16.11).

(3) In a section of Proclus' commentary on the *Parmenides* preserved only in a Latin translation, Proclus tells us that Speusippus said, "as if reporting the sentiments of the ancients" (*narrans tamquam placentia antiquis*, Klibansky and Labowsky [1953] 38.33), the following (Klibansky and Labowsky [1953] 40.1–5):[169]

> For thinking the one better than being and that from which the being [derives], they even deliver it from the status that accords with a principle. But, judging that if one posits the one itself conceived as separate and alone, without [the?] others, in its own right, adding no other element to it, nothing of the others would be made, they introduced the indefinite duality as principle of the beings.

> *Le unum enim melius ente putantes et a quo le ens, et ab ea que secundum principium habitudine ipsum liberaverunt. Existimantes autem quod, si quis le unum ipsum seorsum et solum meditatum, sine aliis, secundum se ipsum ponat, nullum alterum elementum ipsi apponens, nichil utique fiet aliorum, interminabilem dualitatem entium principium induxerunt.*

Let us begin with the last text. If we could suppose that Speusippus was endorsing the 'sentiments of the ancients,' our question would be answered. But we cannot suppose that: those sentiments make the One *better* than being and deny that it can be thought of as a principle; both of these ideas fly in the face of what we already have from Aristotle.

But it is conceivable that what Proclus quotes from Speusippus was anticipating an argument in Speusippus *against* those very sentiments. The argument would have been a reductio ad absurdum; it might have looked something like this. Suppose the principle of beings were better than being. Then (see later on this inference) we should in the end have to deny it the status of a principle. This is represented in the preceding text by the clause translated "they even deliver it from the status that accords with a principle"; they do this, Speusippus would be saying, without intending to. The result is an absurdity: a principle that is not a principle. So we must say it is *not* better than being; but we can hardly say it is worse; so we should deny that it falls within the scope of the predicate *good*.

This, then, would give an argument for the position Aristotle tells us Speusippus took. But, of course, a major piece is missing: how do we get from the claim that the principle of beings, the One, is better than being to the claim that it cannot after all be a principle?

For this the argument might have been one that Aristotle echoes in *Metaphysics* N 4. Aristotle is arguing against the view that the One is a principle (ἀρχή); in 1091b30–35[170] he says:

> Then these absurdities follow, and that the contrary element, whether it is plurality or the unequal and great and small, is the evil itself (for which reason one [thinker] avoided attaching the good to the one, inasmuch as it is necessary, since coming-to-be is from contraries, that the nature of plurality would be the evil . . .).

1091b

ταῦτά τε δὴ συμβαίνει ἄτοπα, καὶ τὸ ἐναντίον στοιχεῖον, εἴτε πλῆθος ὂν εἴτε τὸ ἄνισον καὶ μέγα καὶ μικρόν, τὸ κακὸν αὐτό (διόπερ ὁ μὲν ἔφευγε τὸ ἀγαθὸν προσάπτειν τῷ ἑνὶ ὡς ἀναγκαῖον ὄν, ἐπειδὴ ἐξ ἐναντίων ἡ γένεσις, τὸ κακὸν τὴν τοῦ πλήθους φύσιν εἶναι . . .).

Aristotle does not say what the thinker in question, who certainly sounds like Speusippus again, thought was absurd about making Plurality evil. But *Universal Math* iv 15.23–16.9 argues, albeit somewhat foggily, that it is absurd. In the fog, at least this much is discernible: if we make Plurality evil or ugly but take it to be responsible for numbers, various qualities of soul such as magnanimity, and so on, then, because Plurality is the cause of many things that are good or beautiful, it is not in every way blameworthy; but the bad and the evil must be in every way blameworthy.

This might be put together into the following argument. Suppose

(1) The One is better than being.

But we also want to have

(2) The One is the first principle.

If (1) is true, then the One is the best there is; if (2) is true, it is responsible for other things being as they are. (1) and (2) amount, in Platonist language, to

(3) The One is the good itself.

But

(4) Plurality is the principle contrary to the One,

so

∴ (5) Plurality is the evil itself.

But

(6) Plurality is responsible for many good things,

and

(7) What is responsible for good things cannot be all bad.
∴ (8) Plurality cannot be all bad.

But (8) contradicts (5).

This is speculative, perhaps even wildly speculative. But it is worth noting that the premise labeled (7) is not actually in conflict with the Principle of Alien Causality, although it is close to being in conflict with it. In the first place, it does not depend on the generalization that what causes things to be F must itself be F. It is rather the special case: what causes things to be good is, on that ground, praiseworthy, and so cannot be the evil itself or the worst thing there is. And, in the second place, we have left the phrasing of the Principle of

Alien Causality very loose: it is not simply the claim that whatever causes anything to be F must itself not be F. We shall get back to this later.

In any case, I do not put much stock in the preceding reconstruction. But, however speculative it is, it has one advantage that any viable reconstruction must have: it does not make Speusippus adopt the 'sentiments of the ancients' wholesale. He cannot do that. The sentiments of the ancients make the One better than being, and Speusippus' One is not better than being.

Then what of *Universal Math* iv's claims that the One is a 'highest' principle that is 'up above'[171] the beautiful, the good, and, presumably, being? Does this in fact conflict with what Aristotle has to say about Speusippus? It does not. Even in Aristotle's version of Speusippus, the One was in an obvious sense 'first,' and so 'before' being: it is somehow responsible for everything else's being.

In fact, the question we have posed is close to meaningless. If saying that the One is 'above' being means anything more than that it is outside the scope of the predicate 'being', all it can mean is what Aristotle gives us: the One is Speusippus' first principle, the cause of beings. It *cannot* mean that the One is *better* than being, given what we have from Aristotle, so if that is what is meant by calling it *above* being, it is not above being.

Much of the vigor in the discussion of this question is due to a supposed connection between Speusippus' views and a famous passage in Plato's *Republic*, *viz.* vi 509b2–10:

> You will say, I think, that the sun not only provides to the visibles their power of being seen, but also their coming-to-be, growth, and nurture, not itself being coming-to-be.
>
> How could it be?
>
> And then say to the knowables not only is their being known present by the agency of the good, but also their being and substance is present to them by the agency of that, while the good is not substance, but goes over yet beyond substance in dignity and power.

509b2 Τὸν ἥλιον τοῖς ὁρωμένοις οὐ μόνον οἶμαι τὴν τοῦ ὁρᾶσθαι δύναμιν παρέχειν φήσεις, ἀλλὰ καὶ τὴν γένεσιν καὶ αὔξην καὶ τροφήν, οὐ γένεσιν αὐτὸν ὄντα.

Πῶς γάρ;

Καὶ τοῖς γιγνωσκομένοις τοίνυν μὴ μόνον τὸ γιγνώσκεσθαι φάναι ὑπὸ τοῦ ἀγαθοῦ παρεῖναι, ἀλλὰ καὶ τὸ εἶναί τε καὶ τὴν οὐσίαν ὑπ' ἐκείνου αὐτοῖς προσεῖναι, οὐκ οὐσίας ὄντος τοῦ ἀγαθοῦ, ἀλλ' ἔτι ἐπέκεινα τῆς οὐσίας πρεσβείᾳ καὶ δυνάμει ὑπερέχοντος.

I have here translated οὐσία as 'substance'; this is the translation it usually receives in Aristotle; in Plato it is more often rendered 'being.' But here again we come up against the shortage of 'being' words in English, and I am trying to keep 'being' for parts of the Greek verb εἶναι. Still, when Socrates here is made to say that the good is 'beyond substance,' what he means is that it is beyond being.

This is a text that I do not think is relevant in understanding Speusippus, although others[172] think it is. The central question for us is this: does Socrates mean that the good is not a being? Is he a Meinongian about the good?

So later Pythagoreans and Platonists thought; this passage was a favorite among them.[173] The Pythagorean Moderatus of Gades (first century A.D.) "shows that the first one is above being and all substance" (Simplicius *in Physica* 230.36–37:[174] τὸ μὲν πρῶτον ἓν ὑπὲρ τὸ εἶναι καὶ πᾶσαν οὐσίαν ἀποφαίνεται). The Middle Platonists who taught Justin Martyr in the second century A.D. apparently made much of 509b.[175] Of all the passages Plotinus quotes from Plato, this is the one he quotes more than any other,[176] and he is certainly Meinongian about his One (*Enneads* vi 9.3.36–38):[177] "And it [*sc.* the one] is not mind, but before mind; for mind is something among beings, but that is not something, but before each [thing], and not [a] being" (οὐδὲ νοῦς τοίνυν, ἀλλὰ πρὸ νοῦ· τὶ γὰρ τῶν ὄντων ἐστὶν ὁ νοῦς· ἐκεῖνο δὲ οὔ τι, ἀλλὰ πρὸ ἑκάστου, οὐδὲ ὄν).

But, I think, the Neoplatonists are wrong; even, perhaps, plainly wrong.

Much of what Socrates has to say about the good he does not say outright, but suggests by the analogy with the sun. Here he says something outright about the good—that, although it makes it possible for things that are knowable to be known and to be in the first place, it is not itself being but is beyond being. This last is obscure. So let us look at the analogous claim about the sun.

The analogous claim about the sun is that it is the cause of visible things' coming-to-be, and of their being seen; but it is not itself coming-to-be. (It is, of course, itself something that is seen.)

Socrates does *not* say that the sun does not come-to-be. If Plato had meant this, he would have had to be saying either (1) that the sun has never come into existence, but has always existed, or (2) that it is not subject to the conditions of coming-to-be: it does not change, shows no relativity, and so forth. Of these, Plato would have thought (2) obviously false, and probably would have rejected (1) as well; in any case, Socrates could hardly presuppose Glaucon's agreement with (1).

I conclude that Plato did not intend this. He certainly did not intend to be applying the Principle of Alien Causality, because he allows the sun to be the cause of visible things' being seen while it itself is a visible object.

But then the parallel point for the Good is this: it is the cause of knowable things' being, and of their being known: this corresponds to the sun's not itself being coming-to-be, so it must mean at least that the Good is not itself being, but, as the cause of everything else's being, has a privileged status.[178] And, just as prima facie the sun remains something that comes-to-be, the Good remains something that is.

But Plato says it is 'beyond being' (ἐπέκεινα τῆς οὐσίας), and this is what makes things so exciting. Does this mean any more than that the Good is not Being but is the cause of everything else's being and so transcends them in power and dignity? It is not, presumably, 'beyond knowledge' in the sense that it cannot be known: it is itself known, if the sun is itself seen.[179] So is it 'beyond being' in the sense that it does not exist?

The first thing to notice is that the translation 'beyond' is not to be relied on: the word ἐπέκεινα (= ἐπ' ἐκεῖνα) can mean 'on the far side of.' So in *Phaedo* 112b5 εἰς τὸ ἐπ' ἐκεῖνα τῆς γῆς, 'in the direction of the further side of the earth' (Burnet [1911], 136), does not imply '*beyond* the earth'.[180] So 509b9 does not have to be read as saying that the good is *beyond* being: it is only, perhaps, on or at the far side of it. And then the second thing to notice is that the good is repeatedly listed as one form among others: in v 476a4, a passage in which the realm of forms is described as the realm of *being*,[181] in vi 484d2, which with c6 implies that there is a *being* corresponding to good things, in 507b5, where it gets the mark 'ὃ ἔστιν' in b7 (see also vii 531c6–7, 538e1). At vii 518cd Socrates speaks of turning the soul around "until it is able to hold up looking at that which is, indeed, the brightest [part] of being; and this we say to be the good" (c9–d1) (ἕως ἂν εἰς τὸ ὂν καὶ τοῦ ὄντος τὸ φανότατον δυνατὴ γένηται ἀνασχέσθαι θεωνένη· τοῦτο δ' εἶναί φαμεν τἀγαθόν). This is echoed in 526e, which refers, clearly to the Good, as 'the happiest [part] of that which is' (τὸ εὐδαιμονέστατον τοῦ ὄντος, e3–4). There is no room in the *Republic* for Meinongianism about the Good.

But then we must allow that the Good is something that is, just as the sun had to be something that comes-to-be. In 509b Socrates says the Good provides being to the realm of forms, itself being 'beyond' substance. If he means that the Good is not a being, he is contradicting himself. It seems to me fortunate that this is not what he says. The Good provides being to all the forms—presumably, except itself. The Good is 'beyond' substance, 'beyond' being, but beyond need only mean 'on the far side of.' This is plainly not a natural way of reading the text. But the natural reading of this unnatural text gives an outright contradiction, and it stands in splendid isolation on this score. I suspect Plato came to wish he had not written it.

Read so as to erase the contradiction, there remains on this point no direct connection with Speusippus' view.

Nor is there any connection on another quite important score: the cause of beings is here said to be the Good, and Speusippus could not have tolerated that.[182]

We may now turn to the first of our two arguments for the claim that the One is not a being.

3.3.2. The Argument from Simplicity. This is the less interesting of the two, and I shall spend proportionally less time on it. We made it read:

(1a) The one is simple.
∴ (2a) The one is not a being.

One curious feature of this argument is plain on the surface: it goes from a predication of the form 'the One is F' to a conclusion of the form 'the One is not': its author would reject the Aristotelian or Platonic inference to the contrary (see also note 164).

It is less interesting than the other argument in that we hardly needed *Universal Math* to get it: it was frequently used by Neoplatonists, who derived it from Plato's *Parmenides* (thereby supporting their view of *Republic* 509b).

The first 'antinomy' of Plato's *Parmenides* part ii (137c–155e) comes in (roughly)[183] two parts.

In the first, Parmenides argues that "if [the] one is" (εἰ ἕν ἐστιν, 137c4) all sorts of negative results follow, including ultimately that "the one in no way is" (οὐδαμῶς ἄρα ἔστι τὸ ἕν, 141e9–10). The first step in this derivation is the denial of parts to the one on the ground that if it had parts it would no longer be one (137cd); from there on, its lack of plurality is used to rule out all predications of it, including finally the predication of 'is' itself (and even 'one').

Parmenides and his interlocutor treat this as an impossible result (142a), and start over again from the same hypothesis (142b1–2): "if [the] one is" (ἓν εἰ ἔστιν, 142b3). But whereas, in the preceding derivation, Parmenides was leaning on the characterization of the one as *one*, this time the emphasis goes on its *being* (142bc); it is referred to occasionally as "the one being" (τὸ ὂν ἕν, e.g. 144e5). And so it turns out to be many (143a6–7): it has parts, since it both *is* and *is one*, where *being* and *being one* are not the same (142d).

These are two sides of the same coin. Something's being both F and G where F $\neq$ G makes it more than one thing, pluralizes it. In the first derivation, Parmenides is employing that point in a proof that the One cannot have a plurality of predicates. That would make it no longer be *one*, but that rules out its existing at all. (This is not precisely how Parmenides performs his derivation, but is pretty close to the surface.) In the second, he employs the same point to conclude that if the one exists, it must be many.

There is an echo of this in *Sophist* 244b–245e: the Eleatic Stranger argues, against the monists, that if 'one,' 'being,' and 'whole' mean different things, they must be wrong in supposing that there is only one thing; his central premise seems to be (245a8–9): "Surely one must say according to the correct account that that which is truly one is entirely partless" (ἀμερὲς δήπου δεῖ παντελῶς τό γε ἀληθῶς ἓν κατὰ τὸ ὀρθὸν λόγον εἰρῆσθαι).

And the Argument from Simplicity is another echo: the One, to be so characterized, cannot be more than one thing: since to be is not the same as to be one, it cannot be.

The characterization of Speusippus' position we have been getting from Aristotle so far leads toward this argument: complexity, in the universe, comes in later. Existence involves complexity. If we start with the One, we must be starting with something that does not exist.

The interesting argument is the other one, however, and the entire remainder of this study is devoted to it.

3.3.3. The Argument from the Principle of Alien Causality. This read:

(1b) The one is a principle of beings.
(2b) A principle of Fs is not yet F.
∴ (3b) The one is not a being.

The argument makes explicit, in (2b), Speusippus' rejection of a Transmission Theory. But, as here formulated, the rejection of the Transmission Theory is generalized: it is not just that something can cause Fs without itself being an F, but rather that in all or at least in the most important cases the cause of Fs is not itself F. This is the foggy claim I call the *Principle of Alien Causality*.

Why might Speusippus have accepted it? One hopes he would have been able to do more than recite the analogies about turnips, tunny-fish, and their seeds.

Consider the background of the Transmission Theory: it is not just Aristotle's. It is, in fact, Plato's: the theory of forms is a Transmission Theory. It tells us that the cause of things being beautiful is the form, the beautiful: things get to be beautiful by coming to be like that supremely beautiful thing. The form is, then, a transmitting cause: the beautiful causes other things to be beautiful inasmuch as it is itself beautiful.

That the theory of forms is a Transmission Theory becomes important when we remind ourselves of one other thing we may know about Speusippus: he rejected the theory of forms.

For this we need to do some more triangulating.

3.4. Speusippus' Rejection of the Theory of Forms

Aristotle, we saw (in Z 2. 1028b18–21, p. 78 earlier), attributed to Plato the view that there were three sorts of substances: the forms, the mathematicals, and the perceptibles. It becomes clear from other passages that the theory he is here ascribing to Plato involves not just the two levels of forms and mathematicals, but, more particularly, two levels of *numbers*: some of them occur at the level of forms, Aristotle calls them *formal numbers* (in *Metaphysics* M 9. 1086a4–5, N 2. 1088b34, and cf. 3. 1090b35); the others are 'mathematical' numbers.[184] The mathematical ones are different from the formal ones in that there are many instances for the same number (*Metaphysics* A 6. 987b14–18, 9. 991a4 = M 4. 1079a35);[185] each formal number is unique, and the units of which one of them, say five, conceived as a pentad of units, is composed are not combinable with the units of any other, such as three, conceived as a triad of units. If you could put, say, three of the units from the five together with two of the units from the three, you would have another way of getting a five at the level of the forms, and that is what is ruled out. But, after all, we do add and subtract in just this sort of way: we can add three dollars from your wallet together with two from mine to get five, even though you had five already. And we can add three and five to get eight even if we are penniless. Apparently the mathematical numbers are what we are operating on or with when we do this.

At any rate, this is the way Aristotle portrays at least one stage in the development of Plato's views. Reigning dogma has it that Aristotle's portrait is based on confusion, outright lying, or both. Here we must let sleeping dogmas lie, for our target is not Plato but Speusippus. When it comes to Speusippus, we have almost nothing by way of independent check on Aristotle, so the only effect of the dogma is a presumption that, when Aristotle says something about a Platonist, he is wrong. I do not subscribe to the dogma, so I am free of the presumption. Those who do subscribe can regard this as an exercise in constructing straw men for Aristotle to refute.

In the same passage in which Aristotle ascribes a three-tier universe to Plato, as we saw (*Metaphysics* Z 2. 1028b21–24, p. 78 earlier), he says that Speusippus thought there were even more sorts of substance. He listed three: numbers, magnitudes, and souls; we added perceptible objects. There was no mention of forms, and we have encountered none since.

Aristotle often[186] mentions a view to the effect that there were no forms, only numbers—mathematical, not formal, numbers. For example, in *Metaphysics* M 9 he discusses conflicting theories about number (1085b36–1086a2); the following outlines one of them (1086a2–5):[187]

> For those who make only the mathematicals apart from the perceptibles, seeing the difficulty and fabrication about the forms, gave up formal number and made [only] mathematical number, . . .

> **1086a2** οἱ μὲν γὰρ τὰ μαθηματικὰ μόνον ποιοῦντες παρὰ τὰ αἰσθητά, ὁρῶντες τὴν περὶ τὰ εἴδη δυσχέρειαν καὶ πλάσιν, ἀπέστησαν ἀπὸ τοῦ εἰδητικοῦ ἀριθμοῦ καὶ τὸν μαθηματικὸν ἐποίησαν, . . .

And in M 8. 1083a20–24[188] he says

> But yet the way that some others speak about numbers is not a good one either. These are those who think there are not ideas, either simply or as being certain

numbers, but that there are mathematicals and that the numbers are first among the beings, and their principle is the one itself.

1083a

20 ἀλλὰ μὴν ουδ' ὡς ἕτεροί τινες λέγουσι περὶ τῶν ἀριθμῶν λέγεται καλῶς. εἰσὶ δ' οὗτοι ὅσοι ἰδέας μὲν οὐκ οἴονται εἶναι οὔθ' ἁπλῶς οὔτε ὡς ἀριθμούς τινας οὔσας, τὰ δὲ μαθηματικὰ εἶναι καὶ τοὺς ἀριθμοὺς πρώτους τῶν ὄντων, καὶ ἀρχὴν αὐτῶν εἶναι αὐτὸ τὸ ἕν.

Two texts, one from *Metaphysics* Λ 10 and one from N 3, connect this with Speusippus.

First, Λ 10. 1075b37–1076a3[189] (broken up for ease of reference):

1075

b37/38 And those who say that first[190] is the number that is mathematical
b38 and thus that there is always another, next, substance,
1076a1 and different principles for each,
a1 make the substance of the all episodic
a2 (for one substance contributes nothing to another by being or not being)
a3 and many principles . . .

1075b37 οἱ δὲ λέγοντες τὸν ἀριθμὸν πρῶτον τὸν μαθηματικὸν καὶ οὕτως ἀεὶ ἄλλην ἐχομένην οὐσίαν καὶ ἀρχὰς
1076 ἑκάστης ἄλλας, ἐπεισοδιώδη τὴν τοῦ παντὸς οὐσίαν ποιοῦσιν (οὐθὲν γὰρ ἡ ἑτέρα τῇ ἑτέρᾳ συμβάλλεται οὖσα ἢ μὴ οὖσα) καὶ ἀρχὰς πολλάς· . . .

At Z 2. 1028b21–23, we found (see p. 78) Aristotle saying that Speusippus thinks there is a plurality of substances "starting from the one, and principles for each substance, one for numbers, another for magnitudes, then for soul; and in this way he extends the substances." The echoes of Z 2 in Λ 10 are distinct.

The passage at Λ 10 speaks of "those who say that first is the number that is mathematical" (b37–38): Z 2 does not outright say that mathematical number is 'first,' but the first group of substances mentioned is that of numbers.

The position described in Λ 10 has it that "there is always another, next, substance, and different principles for each" (b38–1076a1); Z 2 speaks of a sequence of groups of substance with principles for each.

So it is generally supposed that Λ 10 is speaking of Speusippus.[191] Let us suppose that. Then Λ 10 makes it sound as if Speusippus is the one who made mathematical number first and denied the existence of ideas. And this receives some confirmation from our second text.

The passage at Λ 10 accuses the position it describes of making everything 'episodic.'[192] In N 3, we first read this (1090b5–7):[193]

> There are some who, from the fact that the limits and extremes are: of a line the point, of a plane the line, and of a solid the plane, think it a necessity that there be such natures.

1090b

> εἰσὶ δέ τινες οἳ ἐκ τοῦ πέρατα εἶναι καὶ ἔσχατα τὴν στιγμὴν μὲν γραμμῆς, ταύτην δ' ἐπιπέδου, τοῦτο δὲ τοῦ στερεοῦ, οἴονται εἶναι ἀνάγκην τοιαύτας φύσεις εἶναι.

There follows criticism of this view: these are limits, not substances, Aristotle says (b8–9); various absurdities would follow if they were substances (b10–11); and no reason has been given for separating them (b11–13). Aristotle goes on (b13–20):[194]

> b13 Again, someone who was not easily satisfied might look into the fact that, where all of number and the mathematicals are concerned,
>
> b15 they contribute nothing to each other, the prior to the posterior; for where number is not, the magnitudes will no less be,
>
> b17 for those who say that the mathematicals alone are, and where these are not, the soul and the perceptible bodies [will no less be]. But nature does not, from the appearances, come out as being episodic, like a bad tragedy.

1090b13

> ἔτι δὲ ἐπιζητήσειεν ἄν τις μὴ λίαν εὐχερὴς ὢν περὶ μὲν τοῦ ἀριθμοῦ παντὸς καὶ τῶν μαθηματικῶν τὸ μηθὲν συμβάλλεσθαι ἀλλήλοις τὰ πρότερα τοῖς ὕστερον· μὴ ὄντος γὰρ τοῦ ἀριθμοῦ οὐθὲν ἧττον τὰ μεγέθη ἔσται τοῖς τὰ μαθηματικὰ μόνον εἶναι φαμένοις, καὶ τούτων μὴ ὄντων ἡ ψυχὴ καὶ τὰ σώματα τὰ αἰσθητά. οὐκ ἔοικε δ' ἡ φύσις ἐπεισοδιώδης οὖσα ἐκ τῶν φαινομένων, ὥσπερ μοχθηρὰ τραγῳδία.

And he goes on to observe that these problems do not beset those who posit ideas (b20–24).

Speusippus, then, rejects Plato's theory of ideas, and ends up with an episodic universe whose first principle is not a being.

On the first score, of course, Aristotle was sympathetic. Earlier we heard him saying that the Academic whom we are taking to be Speusippus arrived at his position "seeing the difficulty and fabrication about the forms" (M 9. 1086a3–4; see p. 99). That Speusippus' first principle is not a being is something about which Aristotle expresses neither sympathy nor antipathy. But the claim that Speusippus' universe was 'episodic' is a criticism, and one to which Aristotle adverts more than once. *Metaphysics* N 2. 1090a7–15 (cited later, pp. 108–109), for example, is another passage in which we can see the same mixture of agreement and complaint: Speusippus was right about the difficulties that face the theory of ideas, but his views on causality are all wet.

We can bring this picture into better focus.

3.5. The Transmission Theory and Self-Predication: Aristotle

We have noticed that a large part of Aristotle's disagreement with Speusippus about causality centers on Aristotle's accepting and Speusippus' rejecting a Transmission Theory. We have noticed that the Platonic theory of forms, which both reject, is a Transmission Theory: the form named 'the F' is also F, and participation in it, which makes a thing here below F, is a matter of likeness to it. Aristotle sees himself and Speusippus as agreeing in spotting a difficulty in this theory. So we need to ask, Which of the many difficulties Aristotle sees in the theory of ideas is relevant here?

A family of arguments in Aristotle suggest themselves; the most prominent member of that family[195] is the argument known as the 'third man.'[196] We can find this argument stated at length, not in the standard corpus of Aristotle, but in what are probably very nearly Aristotle's words, in Alexander's commentary on the *Metaphysics*, at a point in the *Metaphysics* (A 9. 990b17) where Aristotle mentions the argument without explaining it. There Alexander either has in his hand or has recently read Aristotle's lost book *On Ideas*, and he is either quoting from that book or paraphrasing it. He gives more than one version of the argument; the following is the one he says (Hayduck [1891] 85.11) Aristotle "himself used in the fourth book of *On Ideas*" (84.21–85.3):

21/22 [197]The third man is also shown as follows.

22/23 If what is truly predicated of some many [things][198] is also something else apart from the [things] of which it is predicated, separated from them (for this is what those who posit the ideas think they show; for there is according to them some man-itself because of this, that man is truly predicated of the many particulars[199] that are men and is different from the particular men)—but if this is so, there will be some third man. For if what is predicated is different from the [things] of which it is predicated, subsisting on its own,[200] and man is predicated both of the particulars and of the idea, there will be some third man apart from the particular [men][201] and the idea. But so also a fourth which is predicated of this and of the idea and of the particulars, and in a like way also a fifth, and so on to infinity.

84.21 δείκνυται καὶ οὕτως ὁ τρίτος ἄνθρωπος. εἰ τὸ κατηγορούμενόν τινων πλειόνων ἀληθῶς καὶ ἔστιν ἄλλο παρὰ τὰ ὧν κατηγορεῖται, κεχωρισμένον αὐτῶν (τοῦτο γὰρ ἡγοῦνται δεικνύναι οἱ τὰς ἰδέας τιθέμενοι· διὰ τοῦτο γάρ ἐστί τι αὐτοάνθρωπος κατ' αὐτούς, ὅτι ὁ ἄνθρωπος κατὰ τῶν καθ' ἕκαστα ἀνθρώπων πλειόνων ὄντων ἀληθῶς κατηγορεῖται καὶ ἄλλος τῶν καθ' ἕκαστα ἀνθρώπων ἐστίν)—ἀλλ' εἰ τοῦτο, ἔσται τις τρίτος ἄνθρωπος. εἰ γὰρ ἄλλος ὁ κατηγορούμενος ὧν κατηγορεῖται, καὶ κατ' ἰδίαν ὑφεστώς, κατηγορεῖται δὲ κατά τε τῶν καθ' ἕκαστα καὶ κατὰ τῆς ἰδέας ὁ ἄνθρω-

85 πος, ἔσται τρίτος τις ἄνθρωπος παρά τε τοὺς καθ' ἕκαστα καὶ τὴν ἰδέαν. οὕτως δὲ καὶ τέταρτος ὁ κατά τε τούτου καὶ τῆς ἰδέας καὶ τῶν καθ' ἕκαστα κατηγορούμενος, ὁμοίως δὲ καὶ πέμπτος, καὶ τοῦτο ἐπ' ἄπειρον.

The crucial assumption that this argument attributes to the theory of forms is that where something is predicated of many things, it is different from them *and* predicated of itself as well. We may put this a little more formally as a 'One over Many' assumption incorporating two subclauses, 'Non-Identity' and 'Self-Predication':[202]

(OM) If some things x, y, z are F, there is one form, the F, by virtue of which they are all F,
(NI) distinct from them,
(SP) and itself F.

Suppose now

(P_0) a, b, and c are all F.

Then, by (OM),

(1) There is something, the F_1, by virtue of which a, b, and c are all F, and
(1a) the $F_1 \neq$ a, b, or c, and
(1b) the F_1 is F.

So

(P_1) a, b, c, and the F_1 are all F, and by (OM)
(2) There is something, the F_2, by virtue of which a, b, c, and the F_1 are all F; and
(2a) the $F_2 \neq$ a, b, c, or the F_1, and
(2b) the F_2 is F.

And so on.

At each stage, (OM) supplies us with a new F, and so a new group of F's; the form for each group is unique to that group, so that although (e.g.) a, b, and c turn out at stage (2) to be F because of the F_2, there is no conflict with the results at stage (1): it is not just a, b, and c that are all F because of F_2, but a, b, c, and the F_1.

This argument first appeared in "print" in Plato's own dialogue, the *Parmenides* (132a1–b2, 132c12–133a7).[203] The preceding analysis was rediscovered by Gregory Vlastos in 1954,[204] but it first appeared twenty-three centuries earlier in Aristotle's lost work *On Ideas*. We can assume that Aristotle's analysis emerged from Academic discussions: Plato and Aristotle can hardly have been the only ones who took the Third Man seriously.

One wants to ask: is the Third Man a good argument against the Theory of Forms?[205] But this is not the right question to ask; it makes it sound as if there was a single well-defined theory, *The* Theory of Forms,[206] against which the Third Man either is or is not a knock-down argument. There is certainly material in Plato's dialogues that can be read as supplying the assumption (OM) with its two subclauses. That assumption leads to a plurality, in fact, an unending plurality, of forms where there should be only one.[207] If someone, in the name of a Theory of Forms, wants to defend the spirit of (OM) but avoid pluralizing the forms, the next move is his: he must say how he wants to restrict (OM), and what motivates his restrictions.

He need not respond in any simple way: he need not say either that (NI) is no good or that (SP) is no good. He is perfectly free to accept (NI) for some predicates, (SP) for others, and reject the applicablity of (OM) in general for yet others. All he has to do is explain why he makes whatever choices he does.

On one reading,[208] Aristotle, at one stage, accepted (SP) and rejected (NI) for some cases (the essential predications) and went the opposite way for others (the accidental ones); on this reading, what explains the truth of

(1) Socrates is a man

is just Socrates, the man—there is nothing other than that man to be the bearer of the predicate *man*, by contrast with

(2) Socrates is [a] white [thing]

where there is something other than that white thing that is the bearer of the predicate *white*; namely, Socrates, the man. Put another way, (2) leaves room for the question, What is that white thing? in a way that (1) does not leave room for What is that man? On this reading, what is required to explain the truth of (2) is two non-identical things: the man Socrates and the color white, and the color white is not itself predicatively white, whereas what is needed to explain the truth of (1) is just the one thing, Socrates, who is predicatively a man.[209] It is worth recalling that, in Aristotle's jargon, this makes reference to Socrates' *form*: Aristotle himself has a theory of forms, however different it may be from Plato's.

There is another way in which (SP) survives, or anyway has a descendent, in Aristotle, as we have already seen: he accepts a Transmission Theory of efficient causality. Here what explains the fact that we have Socrates, a man, is something distinct from Socrates, namely, Sophroniscus, his father, and this something else is, predicatively, a man. So what explains the presence of a man must itself be a man, but another one. And this leads us on to a regress, but, one that Aristotle seems to think is harmless: because there always were (and always will be), in his view, men, there is no harm in having to trace one's ancestry back to infinity.[210]

Both these curious trains of thought require further examination. Here our concern is not with Aristotle but with Speusippus. What we see in Aristotle is a Theory of Forms: not the one he ascribes to Plato, but one that bears some resemblances to that theory and that must have resulted from his pondering over the difficulties raised in the Academy and the ways of avoiding such difficulties. We might expect something parallel in the case of Speusippus.

3.6. *The Construction of Speusippus' Universe*

It looks as if Speusippus simply rejected (SP), and replaced it with the Principle of Alien Causality (for which see p. 91 and p. 98 earlier, and the next section). He apparently retains, as does Aristotle, a use for the notion of a form: in [Iamblichus'] comments preceding his quotation from Speusippus' book *On Pythagorean Numbers*, after describing the first half of the book, he says (De Falco [1975] pp. 82.20–83.5):[211]

> straightaway [Speusippus] makes the other remaining half of the book about the decad, showing that it is the most natural and most mystically completing[212] of the beings, a sort of artistic form for the cosmic accomplishments, obtaining in its own right and not because we use it or suppose that it happens [to be so], and lying before the god that is maker of the all as an all-complete[213] paradigm.

> μετὰ ταῦτα λοιπὸν θάτερον τὸ τοῦ βιβλίου
> **83** ἥμισυ περὶ δεκάδος ἄντικρυς ποιεῖται φυσικωτάτην αὐτὴν ἀποφαίνων καὶ τελεστικωτάτην τῶν ὄντων, οἷον εἶδός τι τοῖς κοσμικοῖς ἀποτελέσμασι τεχνικὸν ἀφ' ἑαυτῆς ἀλλ' οὐχ ἡμῶν νομισάντων ἢ ὡς ἔτυχε θεμένων ὑπάρχουσαν καὶ παράδειγμα παντελέστατον τῷ τοῦ παντὸς ποιητῇ θεῷ προεκκειμένην.

Here the number ten is called a *form* (εἶδος) and a *paradigm* (παράδειγμα).

One difficulty with this text must be borne in mind: according to [Iamblichus], Speusippus composed his book in the following way (De Falco [1975] p. 82.12–15):

> from the Pythagorean lectures, which had always been particularly interesting [to him], especially the writings of Philolaus,[214] he compiled a neat booklet and entitled it *On Pythagorean Numbers*.

> ἐκ τῶν ἐξαιρέτως σπουδασθεισῶν ἀεὶ Πυθαγορικῶν ἀκροάσεων, μάλιστα δὲ τῶν Φιλολάου συγγραμάτων, βιβλίδιόν τι συντάξας γλαφυρὸν ἐπέγραψε μὲν αὐτὸ Περὶ Πυθαγορικῶν ἀριθμῶν.

So it is possible he did not endorse every detail. And the word *form*, εἶδος, appears in the fragments of Philolaus (DK 44B5, i 408.8)[215] and Archytas (DK 47B1, i 432.9;[216] 47B4, i 438.10, 11[217]). *Paradigm*, παράδειγμα, does not occur in any Pythagorean material that has a chance of being genuine.[218] But conceivably Speusippus is seeing the same resemblance between Philolaus' views and Plato's that Aristotle emphasizes in *Metaphysics* A 6. 987b10–13: what Plato called *participation*; the Pythagoreans called *imitation*. If this is right, the use of the term *paradigm* would be natural, whether it derives from Philolaus (or some other Pythagorean) or only from Speusippus.

In any case, there is no incompatibility between Speusippus' rejection of a Theory of Forms he took to be Plato's and his accepting another; the case of Aristotle shows that much.

But if he is adopting any of these views as his own, he must be thinking of the number 10 as very different in its ultimate functioning from a Platonic form: perhaps the difference is that the god here mentioned, in fashioning whatever he does with this as paradigm, is not making an *instance* of the number 10; that is, supposing that he fashions the universe with his eye on the number 10 as paradigm, he does not make, in the universe, an example of a decad.

In his universe, the beings have for their principle the One, but the One is therefore not itself a being. The first beings are numbers; the One, not itself a number, in some ill-defined way gets together with another principle, plurality, and generates, nontemporally, the numbers. "In some ill-defined way" is certainly unsatisfying, but it may be the best that can be done: Aristotle says (*Metaphysics* M 9. 1085b4–6): "Again, as to how it is possible for number to be from the one and plurality, no attempt is made" (ἔτι πῶς μὲν ἐνδέχεται εἶναι ἐκ τοῦ ἑνὸς καὶ πλήθους τὸν ἀριθμὸν οὐθὲν ἐπιχειρεῖται). If this is to be taken at face value,[219] Speusippus himself was not helpful here.

One feature of the fragment from *On Pythagorean Numbers* tells us something about the relationship between the One and the numbers. At first, we might expect that the One is the first term of the number-sequence; when it emerges that the One is not a being, but the numbers are, this expectation is overthrown. We might then reflect that Aristotle explicitly says that 1 is *not* a number, but the measure of number (*Metaphysics* N 1. 1088a6–8; cf. I 1. 1052b20–24, 1053a24–30, 2. 1054a6–7, 6. 1057a2–7), that there are passages in Plato in which 1 is apparently not thought of as a term in the number sequence (*Republic* vii 524d7, *Phaedo* 104a7–b4),[220] and that even in Euclid *number* is so defined as to exclude 1 (vii defs. 1–2).[221] This would have the number sequence starting with 2. But *On Pythagorean Numbers*, if it is presenting views that Speusippus himself espoused, shows that this is not right either.[222]

According to *On Pythagorean Numbers*, the number 10 is 'complete' or 'perfect' for the following three reasons among others:

(1) it has in it as many odds as evens (De Falco [1975], p. 83.11–14).[223]

(2) it has in it as many primes and incomposites as secondaries and composites (De Falco [1975] pp. 83.14–84.1);[224] and

(3) it has in it as many multiples as submultiples (De Falco [1975] p. 84.1–7).[225]

It is a mathematically relatively uninteresting[226] notion of 'completion' or 'perfection' that operates here;[227] what is historically interesting is this.

Speusippus explicitly includes 10 as one of the numbers in 10 in discussing property (3) (De Falco [1975] p. 84.4–5). So to verify property (1), we must either count both 1 and 2 as, respectively, odd and even, or leave both out as not terms of the number sequence.[228] But to verify property (2), we must count as primes both 2 and 1.[229] Similarly, for property (3), the multiples turn out to be 6, 8, 9, and 10, the submultiples 1, 2, 3, and 5.[230]

The upshot is that 1 counts as a number. So it cannot be this that is referred to as 'the One,' if any of the preceding is right.

But 1, the number, could not have been the One anyway. Aristotle tells us that Speusippus rejected the formal numbers and retained only the mathematical numbers. The difference between the formal numbers and the mathematical numbers is just that there are many instances of each mathematical number, but only one for each formal number. So when Speusippus counts 1 as a number, he is not speaking of the unique (but nonexistent) One, but of a plurality. 'The' number 1 is not unique; in adding 1 + 1 to get 2, two ones are required. There are, in fact, unlimitedly many of them, and, when grouped together in various ways, they constitute the rest of the numbers, which are collections of these ones or units.

The nontemporal generation of the numbers, then, requires the interaction of the One with the principle to which Speusippus opposes the One; namely, Plurality. This interaction is required even to generate 'the' number 1, the units from which other numbers are constructed.[231] This renders apposite Aristotle's complaints in *Metaphysics* M 9. 1085b12–17:

> One could additionally ask, especially, if each unit [is] one, from what it is [derived]; for each [unit] is not the one *itself*. Necessarily it is [derived] from the one itself and plurality or [a] part of plurality. Now to say that the unit is a particular plurality [is] impossible, as it is indivisible; while [saying] that [it derives] from [a] part of plurality has many difficulties . . .

1085b μάλιστα δ' ἄν τις ἐπιζητήσειεν, εἰ μία ἑκάστη μονάς, ἐκ τίνος ἐστίν· οὐ γὰρ δὴ αὐτό γε τὸ ἓν ἑκάστη. ἀνάγκη δὴ ἐκ τοῦ ἑνὸς αὐτοῦ εἶναι καὶ πλήθους ἢ μορίου τοῦ πλήθους. τὸ μὲν οὖν πλῆθός τι εἶναι φάναι τὴν μονάδα ἀδύνατον, ἀδιαίρετόν γ' οὖσαν· τὸ δ' ἐκ μορίου ἄλλας ἔχει πολλὰς δυσχερείας· . . .

It does not render those complaints altogether intelligible, but at least their target is the claim that the units that compose numbers derive from the one and plurality.[232]

When we turn to the geometrical magnitudes, we have a new departure. Aristotle had told us (*Metaphysics* Z 2. 1028b22–23) that Speusippus had "principles for each" of his types of substance, "one for numbers, another for magnitudes."

Universal Math iv 15.6–7, 10–12 starts out with two principles, the One and the principle of plurality: let us just refer to the latter as *Plurality*. These are the principles for "the mathematical numbers" (15.6), and they are generated once Plurality "has taken from the part of the One" (16.18; cf. 15.17–18), once Plurality has become a 'receptacle' for the One (16.15). But, according to our author, if there were only "one unlimited matter and receptacle for all [things]" (16.18–20), there would be no way to generate the rest of the universe; the One, acting on this single principle, would never get us anything but numbers (16.20–17.1). And he rejects the idea that the principle of plurality might be somehow internally differentiated (17.1–13).

He is then led to the conclusion that Plurality and the cause of geometrical magnitudes are different (17.13–14). He does not clearly say what he wants to call this new principle, but it may be that he is referring to it under the labels *position* (θέσις) and *interval of places* (διάστασις τόπων) in 17.16. Let us call it *Extension*.

The result of the interaction of Plurality and the One was, he says, "*unit*, corresponding to the One" (μονάδα κατὰ τὸ ἕν, 17.14–15); in the same way, the result of the interaction of the One with Extension is *point* (17.15–16).

This does not, as far as I can see, conflict in the slightest with Aristotle's comment in Z 2. That chapter is sometimes read as saying that there is a different 'formal principle' for each layer of Speusippus' universe: the One for numbers, the point for geometrical magnitudes, and so on.[233] But it does not say that. It says that Speusippus starts from the one, and has different principles for his different types of substance. That is what the author of *Universal Math* iv has: he starts from the One, which then realizes itself in different ways depending on the corresponding 'material principle,' so that its representative or embodiment at each level is also different.

Aristotle complains, as we saw (*Metaphysics* Λ 10. 1076a1–2, N 3. 1090b19–20: earlier, pp. 100–101), that Speusippus' universe is 'episodic,' 'like a bad tragedy.' Perhaps the justice of his complaint can be seen here: there is no causal relation between the level of numbers and that of geometrical magnitudes; the process of generation is merely repeated at each level. Aristotle says (*Metaphysics* N 2. 1090a2–15):[234]

> One might also attend to the question about numbers why one might hold the belief that they are.
>
> a4 For the one who posits ideas, they provide a certain cause for the beings, since each of the numbers is a certain idea while the idea is for the other [things] a cause of their being in whatever way (for let this assumption be [granted] to them);
>
> a7 but for the one who does not think in this way, due to his seeing the inherent difficulties about the ideas, so that he does not make numbers for these reasons, and makes number mathematical, why should one believe that there is such number,
>
> a11 and what use [is it] for the other [things]? For neither does he who says that there is say that it is [a cause] of anything[235], but he speaks of it as being a

certain nature by virtue of itself, nor is it plain that it is [a] cause; for the theorems of the arithmeticians all will hold for the perceptibles, as has been said.

1090a2 ἐπιστήσειε δ' ἄν τις τὴν σκέψιν καὶ περὶ τῶν ἀριθμῶν πόθεν δεῖ λαβεῖν τὴν πίστιν ὡς εἰσίν. τῷ μὲν γὰρ ἰδέας τιθεμένῳ παρέχονταί τιν' αἰτίαν τοῖς οὖσιν, εἴπερ ἕκαστος τῶν ἀριθμῶν ἰδέα τις, ἡ δ' ἰδέα τοῖς ἄλλοις αἰτία τοῦ εἶναι ὃν δή ποτε τρόπον (ἔστω γὰρ ὑποκείμενον αὐτοῖς τοῦτο)· τῷ δὲ τοῦτον μὲν τὸν τρόπον οὐκ οἰομένῳ διὰ τὸ τὰς ἐνούσας δυσχερείας ὁρᾶν περὶ τὰς ἰδέας ὥστε διά γε ταῦτα μὴ ποιεῖν ἀριθμούς, ποιοῦντι δὲ ἀριθμὸν τὸν μαθηματικόν, πόθεν τε χρὴ πιστεῦσαι ὡς ἔστι τοιοῦτος ἀριθμός, καὶ τί τοῖς ἄλλοις χρήσιμος; οὐθενὸς γὰρ οὔτε φησὶν ὁ λέγων αὐτὸν εἶναι, ἀλλ' ὡς αὐτήν τινα λέγει καθ' αὐτὴν φύσιν οὖσαν, οὔτε φαίνεται ὢν αἴτιος· τὰ γὰρ θεωρήματα τῶν ἀριθμητικῶν πάντα καὶ κατὰ τῶν αἰσθητῶν ὑπάρξει, καθάπερ ἐλέχθη.

The one who posits Ideas is presumably Plato; he has a reason for supposing numbers to exist, for he identifies each number with an Idea and makes each Idea a cause. Despite Aristotle's rejection of this last claim elsewhere (*Metaphysics* A 9. 991a8ff. = M 5. 1079b12ff., etc.), he is here prepared to allow it for purposes of argument (a6–7): Plato at least has some ostensible reason for supposing numbers exist. But for the one who sees 'the inherent difficulties about the Ideas' (a8) and confines the numbers to the mathematical ones (a9–10)—if this is not Speusippus, we may as well turn in our texts and take up something more profitable—there is not even that much, for he does not say that numbers are a cause of anything further (a11–12), and it is not plain independently that numbers are causes either (a13–15).

Geometrical objects, in *Universal Math* iv, take their start from the One and a new material principle; they do not depend on the numbers for their existence. "Where number is not, the magnitudes will no less be" is the way Aristotle put it (N 3. 1090b16–17; earlier p. 101).

From here on in Speusippus' universe, things are even more mysterious: we hear nothing about the construction of the levels of soul and perceptible body.[236]

Fortunately, I have not promised any demystification about soul and body.

3.7. The Principle of Alien Causality

Let us ask once more, Why might Speusippus have accepted the Principle of Alien Causality? It is, on the face of it, a poor principle: are there not piles of cases in which one F is the cause of other things' being F? And in addition it looks vastly undermotivated by the difficulties the theory of forms got itself into.

But perhaps things are not quite so bad. Look again at the 'third man' argument. The theory of forms attempts to explain why things are F, and introduces a new thing that is F to do it. The third man develops this into a regress. It is really quite natural to take this situation as pointing in the direction of saying, whatever you introduce to explain why things are F, it had better not itself be F.

And if we stop to think of the *context* in which Speusippus is applying his principle, it is independently plausible. Certainly, we can think of cases in which one thing that is F causes something else to be F. But then we are not trying to construct the entire universe. If we want to explain the entire universe, our question becomes, Why are there F's *at all*? And then it is only too obvious that we cannot introduce something that is F as the answer to this question. Speusippus is generating numbers, geometrical magnitudes, souls, and bodies, in that order. The One and its mysterious counterpart, Plurality, are supposed to explain how it is that there are numbers. So the One cannot very well be a number, nor, for that matter, can Plurality be a number.

The oddity is that Speusippus thinks the first *beings* in his universe are the numbers. We can make a sort of genealogical sense of this if we recall that in the High Platonic Theory of Forms, the Forms were the first, and, really, the only beings: the rest were things-that-come-to-be. But then (it is not clear when) the mathematical objects enter the picture, and these do not come-to-be. So there are now at least two levels of beings. Speusippus revises this picture by dropping the Forms and is left with the mathematical objects as the first beings.

This kind of explanation is intrinsically incapable of putting us actually into the picture: it gives us only in the most indirect way the reasons Speusippus might have had for adopting it. Some of them can be filled in by tracing our way through the motivations for the High Theory of Forms in the first place, the reasons for modifying the picture, and so on. But that is a long story. Perhaps the genealogical explanation, without quite putting us into the picture, enables us to get a slightly better view of it.

Speusippus' One is supposed to explain not only how it is that there are numbers, but how it is that there are geometrical magnitudes, and so on: it is to explain how it is that there are any beings at all. And so the same point that holds of it in connection with the numbers must now be generalized to cover all the beings. As what accounts for the numbers, it could not be a number; as what accounts for the beings, it cannot be a being. This suggests a formulation of the Principle of Alien Causality:

(PAC) x causes whatever is F to be F $\rightarrow \neg$Fx.

This is not implausible at all.[237] Indeed, if we reject the possibility that anything can cause itself to be F, it is true.[238] Of course, we may wonder, at least for certain cases of F, whether there is anything that causes whatever is F to be F. And if we replace *F* by *a being*, we get a case that really causes puzzlement, for that is precisely what leads to Speusippus' conclusion.

Where are we? It remains fashionable to assign grades: some think Speusippus was a towering intellect; some think the loss of his writings is not greatly to be regretted. This is a pointless exercise: it is like trying to gauge Milo's wrestling style on the basis of Aristotle's comments[239] on his diet. But we can say a little.

A willingness to go against the swim, although not in itself either praiseworthy or blameworthy, in a philosopher is hardly out of place. If what I have said is right, Speusippus possessed this quasi-virtue. His Meinongianism may illustrate the questionability of the quasi-virtue: many would suppose it takes not courage but madness to make the foundation of reality something that does not exist. But, first, Speusippus is at least reacting to difficulties: he is not as complacent a Platonist as are most twentieth-century defenders of 'The Unity of Plato's Thought.' And, second, even if the Principle of Alien Causality goes too far, it starts off in the right direction. For the Transmission model, so dear to the heart of Aristotle and many others in the history of philosophy, is a thoroughly awful picture of causality. Speusippus rejected it. We are in no position to wish that there had been more Speusippeans in the history of philosophy. But that history would at least have been different, and might even have contained fewer mistakes, if more philosophers had followed him in the rejection of that model.

And last, even if we are not prepared to follow Speusippus all the way, we can follow him in drawing an intermediate conclusion. It may be profound, or may be a triviality, or may be both, but the Heideggerian-sounding insight is at any rate true[240]—that if there is an answer to the question "why are there any beings at all?", the answer cannot involve another being.

4. APPENDIX: IAMBLICHUS, *UNIVERSAL MATH* IV

De communi mathematica scientia iv 15.6–18.12 has been claimed[241] for Speusippus. This much of the chapter appears in Tarán (1981), pages 90–92, but not as a fragment, because Tarán rules it out (see earlier). It also appears in Isnardi Parente (1980), but split up: 15.6–16.14 and 18.1–12 constitute 72IP, and 16.15–17.29 is 88IP. She thinks the chapter is a Neopythagorean reworking of Aristotle's testimony about Speusippus (see Isnardi Parente [1975], Isnardi Parente [1980] pp. 305–306). I stand somewhere in between: it seems to me likely that this material descends from Speusippus, but it may have suffered damage in the descent. I have included the whole thing here, as I refer to it several times, and it is something of a rarity; it seems to me the reader should have the opportunity to form his or her own opinion.

The notes I have provided do not purport to be a complete commentary. The text and lineation are as in Festa (1975);[242] the translation is my own.[243]

14.18 Εἰ δὲ δεῖ καὶ τὰς ἰδίας ἀρχὰς καθ' ἕκαστον τῶν μαθημάτων ἀφορίσασθαι, τίνες τέ εἰσι καὶ ὁποῖαι καὶ τίνα ἔχουσαι τὴν καθ' αὑτὰς ἰδιότητα καὶ τὴν πρὸς ἀλλήλας διαφορὰν καὶ τὴν πρὸς ἁπάσας τὰς ἄλλας ἀρχὰς πάντων τῶν ὄντων, καιρός ἐστιν ἤδη καὶ περὶ τούτων διελθεῖν. πάντων δὲ ἄριστον, ἐπεὶ τάξις τίς ἐστιν ἐν αὐτοῖς, καὶ τὰ μὲν ὡς πρότερα προηγεῖται οὐ τῇ τάξει μόνον ἀλλὰ καὶ τῇ φύσει (συναναιρεῖ μὲν γὰρ οὐ συναναιρεῖται δέ, καὶ συνεπιφέρει μὲν οὐ συνεπιφέρεται δέ),
15.1 τὰ δὲ ἐν ἀμφοτέροις τούτοις ἀπολείπεται πρεσβείᾳ καὶ ἁπλότητι, τούτων δὴ ἕνεκα καὶ ἡμῖν προσήκει τῇ κατὰ φύσιν αὐτῶν τάξει συνακολουθῆσαι, καὶ πρῶτον μὲν εἰπεῖν περὶ τῶν πρώτων, ἔπειθ' οὕτω περὶ τῶν ἄλλων.

Τῶν δὴ ἀριθμῶν τῶν μαθηματικῶν δύο τὰς πρωτίστας καὶ ἀνωτάτω ὑποθετέον ἀρχάς, τὸ ἓν (ὅπερ δὴ οὐδὲ ὄν πω δεῖ καλεῖν, διὰ τὸ ἁπλοῦν εἶναι καὶ διὰ τὸ ἀρχὴν μὲν ὑπάρχειν τῶν ὄντων, τὴν δὲ ἀρχὴν μηδέπω εἶναι τοιαύτην οἷα ἐκεῖνα ὧν ἐστιν ἀρχή), καὶ ἄλλην πάλιν ἀρχὴν τὴν τοῦ πλήθους, ἣν καὶ διαίρεσιν οἷόν τ' εἶναι καθ' αὑτὸ παρέχεσθαι, καὶ διὰ τοῦτο ὑγρᾷ τινι παντάπασι καὶ εὐπλαδεῖ ὕλῃ, προσηκόντως εἰς δύναμιν παραδεικνύντες, ἀποφαίνοιμεν ἂν ὁμοίαν εἶναι· ἐξ ὧν ἀποτελεῖσθαι, τοῦ τε ἑνὸς καὶ τῆς τοῦ πλήθους ἀρχῆς, τὸ πρῶτον γένος, ἀριθμῶν ἐξ ἀμφοτέρων τούτων μετά τινος πιθανῆς ἀνάγκης συντιθεμένων. καὶ χρὴ καθ' ἕκαστον ἐπεξιόντα τῶν ἀριθμῶν διαίρεσιν μὲν ἅπασαν λέγειν ἅπαντι ἀριθμῷ καὶ μέγεθος ὡς καθόλου εἰρῆσθαι ταύτην τὴν φύσιν παρέχεσθαι, τὸ δὲ ποιὸν εἶναι ἕκαστον αὐτῶν, ἔτι δὲ ὡρισμένον καὶ ἕν, τὴν ἀδιάφορον καὶ ἄτμητον ἀρχὴν ἐπισφραγιζομένην ἀποτυποῦν. κακὸν δὲ ἢ αἰσχρὸν τὸ τοιοῦτον οὐ προσῆκον ἴσως ἐστὶ τιθέναι, ᾧ συμβαίνει μεγέθους τε καὶ διαιρέσεως, ἔτι δὲ αὔξης, καθ' ἑαυτὸ αἰτίῳ εἶναι· οὔτε γὰρ ἐν τοῖς ἄλλοις τὸ τοιοῦτο γένος εἰς κακὴν μοῖραν εἰώθαμεν τιθέναι, ἔστιν ὅτε δὲ τοῦ μεγαλοπρεποῦς καὶ ἐλευθερίου μετὰ ποιότητος συμπλεκόμενόν τινος τὸ μέγα αἴτιον λέγοιμεν ἂν ἴσως ἀληθεύοντες·
16.1 ὥστε πολλοῦ δέον ἂν εἴη κακὸν προσαγορεύεσθαι αὐτό. εἰ γὰρ δὴ καὶ τὴν τοῦ ἑνός τις φύσιν ἐπαινῶν τυγχάνοι δι' αὐτάρκειάν τε καὶ τὸ καλῶν τινων ἐν τοῖς ἀριθμοῖς αἴτιον εἶναι, πῶς οὐκ ἄλογον ἂν εἴη λέγειν τὸ κακὸν ἢ τὸ αἰσχρὸν δεκτικὸν κατὰ φύσιν τοῦ τοιούτου πράγματος εἶναι; οὐ γὰρ ἂν ἔτι πάντῃ συμβαίνοι ψεκτὸν εἶναι τὸ κακὸν καὶ τὸ αἰσχρόν, εἴπερ τὸ δεκτικόν τινος ἐπαινετοῦ καὶ αὐτὸ δεῖ ἐπαινετὸν προσαγορεύειν. αὕτη μὲν οὖν οὕτως ἡμῖν νοείσθω

14.18 But if one has also[244] to demarcate the unique principles for each of the mathematical sciences, both what and what sort they are and what uniqueness they have by virtue of themselves and [what] difference relative to each other as well as that [difference] relative to all the other principles of all the beings, it is opportune to cover these matters at this point. And it is best of all, since there is a certain order in them, and some lead off as prior not only in order but also in nature (for they coabolish but are not coabolished,[245] and they coimport but are not coimported[246]), while others are left behind in both these respects, in rank and in simplicity,[247] so for these reasons it is appropriate for us also to follow their natural order, and first to speak about the first [ones], and so on about the rest.[248]

15.6 For the mathematical numbers one must posit two [things] as the first and highest principles, the One (which indeed one ought not yet even call a being, because of the fact that it is simple and because of the fact that it is a principle for the things that are, while the principle is not yet such as are the things of which it is a principle),[249] and again another principle, that of plurality,[250] which can by virtue of itself provide division as well,[251] and for this reason we may, by way of making a comparison appropriate to its capacity,[252] assert it to be like some moist and easily molded matter; from which, the one and the principle of plurality, there is produced the first kind, [that] of numbers, from both of these when combined in accordance with some persuadable necessity.[253] And one must say that, for each of the numbers as it goes forth, this nature[254] provides every division for every number and, to speak universally, magnitude,[255] while the undifferentiated and indivisible principle by impressing itself stamps out each of them so as to be of the sort [it is], and again determinate and one.

15.23 It is perhaps inappropriate to posit as bad or ugly such a thing, to which it belongs to be by virtue of itself responsible for magnitude as well as division, and again for increase;[256] for neither in the other [cases] are we accustomed to place such a kind in the bad part, and sometimes we might perhaps be right in saying that the large is a cause of [someone's being] magnificent[257] or liberal when interwoven with some quality;[258] so that it would miss a lot to say that it is bad. For if indeed one may even in fact praise the nature of the One because of its self-sufficiency and its being [the] cause of certain beautiful [things] among the numbers,[259] how could it fail to be irrational to say that the bad or the ugly is naturally receptive of such a thing?[260] For the bad and the ugly would no longer turn out to be in every way blamable,[261] if what is receptive of something praiseworthy must also itself be called praiseworthy.[262]

16.9 So let this be thought of as a principle for us in that way.

ἀρχή. τὸ δὲ ἓν οὔτε καλὸν οὔτε ἀγαθὸν ἄξιον καλεῖν, διὰ τὸ καὶ τοῦ καλοῦ καὶ τοῦ ἀγαθοῦ ὑπεράνω εἶναι· προϊούσης γὰρ πορρωτέρω ἀπὸ τῶν ἐν ἀρχῇ τῆς φύσεως πρῶτον μὲν τὸ καλὸν ἐφάνη, δεύτερον δὲ καὶ μακροτέραν ἀπόστασιν ἐχόντων τῶν στοιχείων τἀγαθόν. ἡ τοίνυν πρώτη ὑποδοχή τε καὶ μέγεθος, ἢ ὅ τι δήποτε δεῖ προσαγορεύειν αὐτήν, τὸ τῶν ἀριθμῶν εἶδος ἀπετύπωσε πλήθει μὲν ἀόριστον εἰκότως εἴδει δὲ πως ὡρισμένον ἐκ τῆς τοῦ ἑνὸς παραλαβοῦσα μοίρας. εἰ μὲν οὖν μίαν ἄπειρον ἅπασιν ὑποθήσει τις ὕλην τε καὶ ὑποδοχήν, ἄλογον ὡς τὸ εἰκὸς συμβήσεται τό, τῆς ἕνος ἰδέας ἐγγιγνομένης ἐν αὐτῇ, εἴπερ ὁμοία διὰ παντός, μὴ οὐ τὰ αὐτὰ καὶ γένη πάλιν ἀποτελεῖσθαι. ὥστε πάντα ἀριθμοὺς τὰ γένη παντελῶς συμβήσεται εἶναι· διαφορὰν γὰρ οὐχ ἕξομεν ἁρμόττουσαν προσάψαι, διὰ τί δήποτε ἐνθάδε μὲν ἀριθμῶν ἐγεννήθη φύσις, μετὰ δὲ τοῦτο γραμμῶν καὶ ἐπιπέδων καὶ σχημάτων, καὶ οὐκ ἀεὶ τὸ αὐτὸ γένος, ἀπό γε τῶν ὁμοίων καὶ κατὰ τὸν αὐτὸν τρόπον ἀλλήλοις συμπλεκομένων
17.1 στοιχείων. εἰ δέ τις μίαν μὲν ὑποθήσεται τὴν ἅπαντος πλήθους τε καὶ μεγέθους αἰτίαν πρώτην, διαφορὰς δὲ πολλὰς ἐν αὐτῇ παρεχομένην, δι' ὅπερ ἄλλα καὶ ἄλλα γένη κατὰ πᾶσαν τὴν φύσιν ἀποτίκτειν πεφυκέναι, καίπερ τοῦ ἑνὸς ὁμοίου ἐγγιγνομένου διὰ παντός, οὐδὲ μὴν οὐδὲ τούτου διὰ τὴν παχύτητα τῆς ὕλης ἀκριβῆ τὴν ἑαυτοῦ φύσιν ἐμφαίνοντος ἀεί, καθάπερ ἔν τισιν εἰκαίοις ξύλοις σχῆμα, ταῦτα μὲν οὖν οὐκ ἀλόγως ἂν ἴσως συμβαίνοι αὐτῷ, τὸ δὲ πρῶτον στοιχεῖον εἰς τοσαύτας διαφορὰς διαιρέσεις ἔχειν δυσχεραίνοι ἄν τις προσηκόντως ἴσως, ἄλλως τε καὶ εἰ παντάπασιν εἴη διήκων κατὰ ταῦτα τὰ παραδείγματα· τὸ γὰρ ἁπλούστατον πανταχοῦ στοιχεῖον εἶναι. λοιπὸν οὖν τινα ἑτέραν μεγέθους αἰτίαν ὑποθεμένους, ὡς ἐν ἀριθμοῖς μονάδα κατὰ τὸ ἕν, οὕτως στιγμὴν ἐν γραμμαῖς τιθέναι, θέσιν δὲ καὶ διάστασιν τόπων περί τε γραμμὰς καὶ χωρία καὶ στερεὰ πρῶτον, κατὰ τὰ αὐτὰ δὲ καὶ τόπον ἐνταῦθα φανῆναι παρὰ τὸ τὴν τῆς ὑποδοχῆς διαφορὰν ἴδιόν τι παραδιδόναι τῷ ἀπ' αὐτῆς γένει. ἔτι δὲ καὶ τὸ συνεχὲς καὶ τὸ συμμεμολυσμένον μᾶλλον τῶν ἀριθμῶν καὶ παχύτερον ἐκ ταύτης ἄν τις αἰτιώμενος καὶ λέγων, ἴσως οὐ διαμαρτάνοι. καὶ μέχρι μὲν δὴ τούτων γένος ἂν εἴη ἀποτετελεσμένον δεύτερον· εἰς ταὐτὸ γὰρ τίθημι γραμμάς τε καὶ στερεὰ καὶ πλάτη χωρίων. πρώτη μὲν οὖν ἡ τῶν ἀριθμῶν ἐστιν ὕλη, δευτέρα δὲ ἡ τῶν γραμμῶν τε καὶ τῶν ἐπιπέδων καὶ

10 But it is fit to call the one neither beautiful nor good, because of the fact that it is above the beautiful and the good; for it was when nature proceeds farther away from the things in [the] principle[263] that, first, the beautiful appeared, and, second, when the elements had an even longer distance, the good.

15 So then the first receptacle, that is magnitude, or whatever indeed one ought to call it, stamped out the form of the numbers, which is, as you might expect,[264] indefinite in plurality, but in a way definite in form,[265] since it took[266] from the part of the One.[267]

18 So if one is to posit one unlimited matter and receptacle for all [things], then, as one might expect,[268] it will turn out inexplicable that, when the idea of One comes-to-be in it, if it is alike throughout all,[269] the same kinds are not also produced again.[270] So that all the kinds will turn out to be numbers, from first to last; for we shall not be able to fasten on to an appropriate difference because of which here, indeed, the nature of numbers was generated, but after this [the nature] of lines, planes, and shapes, and not always the same kind, from like elements woven together with each other in the same way.

17.1 But if one is to posit the first cause of all plurality and magnitude as one but provided with many differences in itself, for just which reason it is of a nature to procreate ever different kinds throughout all nature, even though the One comes-to-be-present alike through all, and yet does not always show its own exact nature because of the denseness of the matter, just as a shape in some random sticks, then while these things might not turn out irrationally for it [i.e., the One], one might perhaps appropriately feel qualms that the first element has divisions into so many differences, both in general and especially going through these examples; for an element is everywhere the simplest [thing].

13 So it remains having posited a different cause for magnitude,[271] to posit, as in numbers, unit, conforming with the One, so point in lines, but position and interval of places[272] pertaining to lines and areas and solids first [appear here],[273] and, conforming with them,[274] place appears here as well, because of the differentiation of the receptacle transmitting[275] something unique to the kind [derived] from it.[276]

20 And again one who, giving causes, says that [*sc*. the geometricals'] being continuous and tougher[277] than numbers and denser is based on this [receptacle][278] would perhaps not be in error.[279]

22 And the second kind would have been produced as far as [to include] these [things]; for I place in the same [kind] lines and solids and flat areas.[280]

25 So first is the matter of the numbers, and second that of the lines, planes, and solid figures. And also for the other mathemati-

στερεῶν σχημάτων. καὶ τῶν ἄλλων δὲ ὡσαύτως μαθημάτων, ὅσα ἂν καὶ ὁποῖα ἂν εὕρῃ ὁ λόγος, τὰς οἰκείας ὑποδοχὰς προϋποθετέον.

18.1 Καὶ τοῦτο μὲν οὖν οὕτως ἡμῖν ἐχέτω. τὰ δὲ στοιχεῖα ἐξ ὧν οἱ ἀριθμοί, οὐδέπω ὑπάρχει οὔτε καλὰ οὔτε ἀγαθά· ἐκ δὲ τῆς συνθέσεως τοῦ ἑνὸς καὶ τῆς τοῦ πλήθους αἰτίας ὕλης ὑφίσταται μὲν ὁ ἀριθμός, πρώτοις δὲ ἐν τούτοις τὸ ὂν φαίνεται καὶ κάλλος, ἐφεξῆς ἐκ τῶν στοιχείων τῶν γραμμῶν τῆς γεωμετρικῆς οὐσίας φανείσης, ἐν ᾗ ὡσαύτως τὸ ὂν καὶ τὸ καλόν, ἐν οἷς [οὔτε] οὐδὲν οὔτε αἰσχρόν ἐστιν οὔτε κακόν· ἐπ' ἐσχάτῳ δὲ ἐν τοῖς τετάρτοις καὶ πέμπτοις τοῖς συντιθεμένοις ἀπὸ τῶν στοιχείων τῶν τελευταίων κακίαν γενέσθαι οὐ προηγουμένως, ἐκ δὲ τοῦ ἐκπίπτειν καὶ μὴ κατακρατεῖν τινα τοῦ κατὰ φύσιν.

Ἐκ δὴ τούτων φανερόν ἐστι καὶ τίνα ἔχουσι τὴν διαφορὰν αἱ μαθηματικαὶ ἀρχαὶ πρὸς τὰς ἄλλας· τῶν μὲν γὰρ τελευταίων προέχουσι, διότι σωματικῶν πως ἐκείνων οὐσῶν αὗταί εἰσιν ἀσώματοι, τῶν δὲ κατὰ τὴν ζωὴν θεωρουμένων, διότι κατὰ κίνησιν ἐκείνων χαρακτηριζομένων αὗταί εἰσιν ἀκίνητοι, τῶν δὲ νοητῶν, διότι ἀμερίστων ἐκείνων προϋπαρχουσῶν αὗται συνθέσεως καὶ διαιρέσεως ἀρχὴν παρέχονται. οὕτως ἡμῖν ὁ κοινὸς λόγος περὶ τῶν μαθηματικῶν ἀρχῶν καὶ ὁ ἴδιος περὶ ἑκάστων ἐχέτω διορισμόν· πῇ τε διαφέρει τῶν ἄλλων ἀρχῶν, οὑτωσὶ διακεκρίσθω.

cal studies, for as many as the account[281] finds and of whatever sort, in the same way one must posit their own receptacles beforehand.

18.1 Let this then be how this stands for us.

1 But the elements out of which the numbers [are produced][282] do not yet obtain there as either beautiful or good; but out of the combination of the One and the matter that is [the] cause of plurality number subsists,[283] and first in these being and beauty appear, while next out of the elements of lines geometrical substance[284] appears, in which in the same way there is being and the beautiful, but in which there is nothing either ugly or bad; but at the extreme, among the fourths and fifths, which are combined from the last elements, [it is possible] for badness to come-to-be, not directly, but from something's falling away from and failing to retain possession of that which accords with nature.

13 From these things it is plain what difference the mathematical principles have relative to each other; for they precede the last [things], because they are bodiless [principles] of those [things], which are bodily, and the things contemplated with regard to life, because they are motionless [principles] of those [things], which are characterized by motion, and the intelligibles, because they provide a principle of combining and division for those partless preexisting [things]. Let that be our general account concerning the mathematical principles and the specific determination for each severally; and how they differ from the other principles, let be distinguished in this way.[285]

Notes

Introduction

1. These are conventional dates, gathered from sources such as Hammond and Scullard (1970) and Guthrie (1978). Detailed discussion is unnecessary for present purposes.

2. According to some, before the death of Plato.

3. This is discussed in a little more detail in the introduction to the first study.

I. Predication and Immanence

1. See Dancy (1978).

2. Particularly over the question whether the entities that are 'in' things but 'said of' nothing are (what are sometimes called) 'abstract particulars,' each logically (or metaphysically or somehow or other) tied to the individual in which it is to be found: see Ackrill (1963), pp. 74–75, Owen (1965a), Matthews and Cohen (1967–68), Allen (1969, 1973), Jones (1972), Annas (1974), M. Frede (1978), Heinaman (1981). I remain, as in Dancy (1975b), p. 345, inclined to Owen's view that they are not, but are shared or at least shareable; see Furth (1988) pp. 16, 41–47.

The most controversial claim in Dancy (1975b) was (pp. 349–351 et passim) that, in Aristotle's terminology in the *Categories*, stating that that stick is white is saying *white* of that stick, and the white(ness) that is in the stick if the statement is true is simply the whiteness that corresponds to the predicate-term *white* in the statement. At least, judging by the negative response to that claim, it was the most controversial one: see e.g. Wedin (1980), and, more recently, Cresswell (1987), p. 141, n. 10, Furth (1988), pp. 10–11 w. n. 4, Irwin (1988), p. 505, n. 29. As far as I know, only Brakas (1988), p. 84 (see all of pp. 77–85) accepts this claim. I am unmoved, but that is not an issue here. This claim has a tangential bearing on the question of abstract particulars: it makes the idea that the stick has a whiteness peculiar to it less plausible.

3. Dancy (1975b), pp. 346–347 gives more detail here.

4. The text of Minio-Paluello (1956), but not quoting his 6b–c. The textual difficulties are not here relevant.

5. Although the Stoics apparently did say something like this: virtue, anyway, is a 'part' of the upright man (Sextus Empiricus, *AM* xi 24 = SVF iii 75, p. 18.37–38, Long & Sedley (1987), Vol. 1, p. 371 t60G(4), Vol. 2, p. 368 t60G.12–13), knowledge and truth are said to be body (Sextus, *HP* ii 81 = Long & Sedley (1987), Vol. 1, p. 198 t33P(2), Vol. 2, p. 203 t33P.3–5), and so on.

6. Started, it seems, by Jacoby (1902), p. 324 n. 18; and taken up by Sachs (1914), pp. 17–18, n.2; Jaeger (1948), pp. 16–17, n. 2; Düring (1957), pp. 159–160 and (1966), p. 1; Merlan (1960b), p. 99, n. 14. For dissent, see Friedländer (1958), p. 353, n. 15, Gigon (1958), p. 159, n. 22 and (1962), p. 49; Leszl (1975), p. 339. Huxley (1963), pp. 84–85, expresses qualified assent, but the story is absent from Huxley (1970). See also Lasserre (1966), p. 138 (it is incompatible with Lasserre's favored birthdate for Eudoxus, 391/390 [pp. 138–139], as Leszl [1975], p. 339 points out); Isnardi Parente (1979), pp. 132–133, n. 186 (the article was first published in 1977); Guthrie (1978), pp. 447–448, n. 1 p. 448.

7. The *Vita Marciana* has (Rose [1886] 428.18–429.1 = Düring [1957], p. 99 §(11) = Gigon [1987] 29b14–16), after restoration based on the *Vita Latina* (R 444.8 = D 152 § (11) = G 32a28): οὐκ ἄρα οὖν, ὡς αὐτοὶ συκοφαντοῦντές φασιν, ⟨τεσσαρ⟩α⟨κο⟩ντούτης 'Αριστοτέλης φ⟨οιτᾷ Πλάτωνι ἐπὶ Εὐδ⟩όξου ("So, then, Aristotle did not, at the age of forty, as some falsely allege, go to Plato in the time of Eudoxus"). The phrase ⟨ἐπὶ Εὐδ⟩όξου, "in the time of Eudoxus," is odd. The *VM* elsewhere uses ἐπὶ + genitive to date an event by the name of the archon of Athens for the year of the event (ἐπὶ Διοτίμου ἄρχοντος R 428.12 = D 98 § (10) = G 29b7, ἐπὶ Διοτρέγους R 428.14 = D 98 § (10) = G 29b9–10, ἐπὶ Φιλοκλέους R 428.14 = D 98 § (10) = G 29b10–11, ἐπὶ Ναυσιγένους R 428.15 = D 98 § (10) = G 29b11–12, Θεοφίλου ἐφ' οὗ R 428.16 = D 98 § (10) = G29b12: most of these are the result of restoration based on *VL*); the *VL* translates most of these with *sub* + ablative. But here it has *tempore Eudoxi*. The support for the phrase ἐπὶ Εὐδόξου is correspondingly shaky, and, anyway, in this

context would sound very like 'when Eudoxus was archon', which is impossible, because there was no archon by that name.

Merlan (1960b), p. 90, n. 14, accepting the text and the conjecture based on it, says, of Friedländer and Gigon, who do not, "Unfortunately, no reasons for their dissent are given nor is an alternative explanation offered." Given the nature of the evidence, I cannot see that any reason need be given for refusing to follow along, with or without an alternative explanation.

8. E. Frank (1955), pp. 145–150, makes much of this.

9. Leszl (1975), pp. 335–340, would deny this: he thinks that a theory of forms is incompatible with Eudoxus' known hedonism and that the dating is against it (see above, n. 6). See below, pp. 26–27.

10. Guthrie (1965), pp. 282–283 (adopting an idea from Peck [1931], pp. 28–29) says: "there is no reason to think that Aristotle intends in these passages to saddle him (*sc.*, Anaxagoras) with any doctrine that however far one divides any of his elements the parts will be like the whole." This quite fails to do justice to 314a20, which Guthrie cites (p. 283) for its definition of *homoeomer*, but without mentioning that the passage is concerned directly with Anaxagoras.

The question is not, of course, whether Anaxagoras used the term ὁμοιομερής: I suppose he did not (see references in next note).

11. Bailey (1928), pp. 551–556, thought it did, but see Mathewson (1958), pp. 77–81, Guthrie (1965), pp. 325–326.

12. The question is dealt with more fully in an appendix to this study, where the passages from *De caelo*, Simplicius' commentary, Anaxagoras fr. 4, etc. are quoted.

13. As was emphasized long ago by Becker (1936), pp. 395 ff. It has recently been reemphasized by Brentlinger (1972), pp. 63–69; see also Furley (1976), pp. 80–83 = Anton and Preus (1983), pp. 83–86.

14. The analogies prompted Furley (1976), p. 82 = Anton and Preus (1983), p. 84, to speak of Anaxagoras' ingredients as 'forms'; for his purposes it does no harm. But it might here, so I shall not follow him.

Becker (1936), p. 395, n. 15, drew attention to the phrase σπέρματα πάντων χρημάτων καὶ ἰδέας παντοίας ἔχοντα καὶ χροιὰς καὶ ἡδονάς in 59B4 at DK ii 34.7–8.

15. *Pace*, e.g., Cherniss (1935), p. xi: "We know that certain concepts and theories were introduced by Aristotle and others by Plato. If a Presocratic theory is presented in a way which involves such a notion, there is clearly something wrong with the statement." Suppose someone says "what things are depends on what is in them," and someone else describes this as a (partial)

immanentist theory of predication. There need be nothing wrong with this, even if the terms *immanent* and *predication* were not available to the first speaker. This is what we have here; see Aristotle, *Physics* A 4. 187b2–7 and Anaxagoras fr. 12 (quoted on pages 8–9).

16. With εἴη ἐν, ἔνεστι, etc. in these places cf. *Categories* 2. 1a20–21, etc.

17. With χωρίς, χωρισθῆναι, etc. in these places cf. χωρίς in *Categories* 2. 1a25.

18. In these places the words are ἀποκρίνεσθαι and its cognates: often translated using the English *separate* (e.g., Kirk and Raven (1957), impressions of 1957 through 1963, p. 376; Kirk, Raven, and Schofield (1983), p. 366). Elegance has been sacrificed in favor of uniformity in translating words for separation.

19. διακρίνεσθαι and cognates: see nn. 17 and 18.

20. The phrase, which seems peculiarly apt for Anaxagoras, in fact comes from Weinberg (1977), p. 6. But Weinberg's recipe for Cosmic Soup calls for particles; Anaxagoras' does not (see the appendix on seeds).

21. There are many other passages in which Aristotle says this: see Bonitz (1870), 49a58–61. But Schofield is reluctant to accept it as an interpretation of fr. 1: see Schofield (1980a), p. 77, w. n. 12 p. 156 and pp. 78–79. If the identification mentioned in n. 12 above were accepted, this would follow from 59B4 at 35.1–2, where Anaxagoras speaks of "seeds unlimited in plurality in no way resembling each other" (σπερμάτων ἀπείρων πλῆθος οὐδὲν ἐοικότων ἀλλήλοις) as being present in the Cosmic Soup.

22. See Furley (1976), pp. 64–66 = Anton and Preus (1983), pp. 73–74 et passim. I am not entirely clear what Furley's solution to the problem is.

23. So also, I take it, Schofield (1980a), pp. 89–94.

24. Kerferd (1969), in Mourelatos (1974), p. 491.

25. Again, I think the answers are the same, *pace* Schofield (1980a), pp. 106–107 and ff.

26. 187a29, b1: Anaxagoras. The shift from singular to plural is a little puzzling, but the claims mentioned in a29–30 ("all things were together") and b1 ("everything is mixed into everything") are specific to Anaxagoras (although Bonitz [1870], 467b26, takes the plural here to refer to both Anaxagoras and Empedocles). On a30 see note 27.

27. 187a30 καθέστηκεν: Charlton (1970) translates "and that he makes the coming to be of a thing of a certain sort an alteration"; this makes

the sequence of references to Anaxagoras even more puzzling (see n. 26). But the verb is really part of what is being ascribed to Anaxagoras, as *De generatione et corruptione* A 1. 314a13–15 shows: "But Anaxagoras himself didn't understand his own utterance: he says that coming-to-be and perishing consist in the same thing as being-altered" (καίτοι 'Αναξαγόρας γε τὴν οἰκείαν φωνὴν ἠγνόησεν· λέγει γοῦν ὡς τὸ γίγνεσθαι καὶ ἀπόλλυσθαι ταὐτὸν καθέστηκε τῷ ἀλλοιοῦσθαι). (187a30 is maltreated in several translations: Carteron [1926], p. 35 apparently fails to notice that καθέστηκεν is singular, and Apostle [1969], p. 14, translates καὶ . . . καθέστηκεν "and some regard," explaining on p. 194, n. 11, that it is monists who are being referred to.) DK ii 20.17 take the reference in both passages to be to Anaxagoras fr. 17, but that fragment says (DK ii 41.13–14) it would be right to call coming-to-be 'commingling' (συμμίσγεσθαι) and perishing 'disconnecting' (διακρίνεσθαι). Ross (1936), p. 484 *ad* a29–30 seems to think Aristotle has another passage from Anaxagoras in mind; Joachim (1922), p. 64 *ad* 314a13–15 takes Aristotle to be interpreting fr. 17: "Aristotle's interpretation is justified by the peculiar character of τὰ ἐόντα χρήματα ('the things that are') in Anaxagoras' system, which gives a special meaning to σύμμιξις ('commixture') and διάκρισις ('disconnection')." I suspect something like this is right, but it would be nice to have an explanation of the 'special meaning' given to *mixture* and *separation*.

According to Wagner (1967), pp. 414 *ad* 14, 13 ff., Aristotle is saying that Anaxagoras, because he recognizes only one type of change, namely separation, is unable to distinguish coming-to-be from alteration. I hope this is wrong. A philosopher who denies that anything ever comes-to-be and also denies that anything ever alters is still in a position to distinguish the two, that is, to say what these two sorts of change would be like if they ever occurred. And it would be more than just unfair to say of such a philosopher that he *identified* the two.

See also next note.

28. "οἱ δέ refers primarily to Empedocles, whose doctrine Aristotle often refers to as identifying γένεσις with σύγκρισις καὶ διάκρισις, though this is equally true of, and is ascribed by Aristotle elsewhere to, Anaxagoras" (Ross [1936], pp. 484–485). Anaxagoras fr. 17 makes the identification (n. 27 above); but the only passage in Aristotle that Ross (pp. 484 *ad* 29–30) cites (*De generatione et corruptione* 314a13) makes Anaxagoras identify γένεσις with ἀλλοίωσις, as here in 187a30. Perhaps he has in mind *Physics* Γ 4. 203a27–30, where διάκρισις and γένεσις seem to be interchangeable.

29. ἐνυπάρχειν: cf. ἐν . . . ὑπάρχον *Categories* 2. 1a24–25.

30. Following Furley (1976), pp. 64, 68 n. 18 (Anton and Preus [1983], pp. 72, 75, 88 n. 18). Schofield (1980a), p. 167, n. 67 says "this

seems improbable in the light of 187a32 ff.": I do not see what it is about 187a32 ff. that renders it improbable.

31. So I am inclined to think, with Philoponus *in Physica* (Vitelli [1887–88]) 397.26–27, 396.27, Simplicius *in Physica* (Diels [1882]) 460.12, Hardie and Gaye (1930), and Carteron (1926), p. 96. But Schofield (1980a), p. 153, n. 34, denies this, and other recent translators and commentators take it differently: Wagner (1967), p. 66, Hussey (1983), pp. 7, 75.

32. The "Principle of Predominance": Kerferd (1969), in Mourelatos (1974), p. 491 (as in n. 24 above).

33. So also Furley (1976), p. 81 (Anton and Preus [1983], p. 84). But Furley's commentary is different from mine.

34. Perhaps when Aristotle says, in 187a25–26, that Anaxagoras makes the underlying bodies "the homoeomers and the contraries" (τά τε ὁμοιομερῆ καὶ τἀναντία), we should translate "the homoeomers, that is, the contraries."

35. I am not convinced by Schofield's assaults on him (Schofield [1975], pp. 14–24 and [1980a], pp. 135 ff). Schofield's skepticism is shared, to some degree, by Furley (1976), pp. 66–67 (Anton and Preus [1983], pp. 74–75).

36. Ross's survey of Plato's language about the theory of forms (Ross [1951], pp. 228–230) is a useful place to start, but so selective that his claim (p. 228) that "it is near enough to being complete to furnish a true indication of Plato's usage" (or the claim in Brentlinger [1972], p. 68, n. 9, that it covers "all the important dialogues") is seriously misleading. Among my complaints are that he takes no note of the immanentist language in the *Phaedo*, and he makes no reference whatever to the *Charmides* (the latter complaint is also voiced by Sprague [1973], p. 65, n. 22). For others, see Owen [1953], reprinted in Allen [1965], p. 321, n. 2; Cherniss (1957), pp. 250–251 = Allen (1965), p. 363 = Cherniss (1977), pp. 323–324; Allen (1970), p. 146, n. 2. According to Allen, Ross fails to cite idioms, which Allen takes to "indicate 'transcendence' in the early dialogues."

Fujisawa (1974), p. 42 provides a different list, but I have some reservations about that one as well. For one thing, numerous occurrences of μετέχειν in the *Protagoras* and elsewhere are ignored, presumably because the context is not one in which Socrates is seeking a definition. See also below, nn. 42, 45.

This is one of the many points at which either Brandwood (1976) or computer access to the text is indispensable. (I have used the former.)

37. Notably, by Ross (1951), pp. 21, 228–230.

38. So also Allen (1970), p. 155, on the 'first friend' of *Lysis* 219cd. But Allen seems to me to use this device only when it suits him: cf. next note.

39. So I find myself in disagreement not only with Ross but with Allen (1970) (see also [1971]), who sees in the early dialogues a metaphysics of separate (as opposed to immanent) forms. Prauss (1966), p. 17–22, speaks of 'the existence of the universal' ("die Existenz des Allgemeinen") as simply self-evident to Socrates and the early Plato (see p. 18), and even this seems to me to go too far. On the other hand, I find myself in virtually complete agreement with Woodruff (1982), p. 161 et passim.

The present section is not supposed to be a complete coverage of the immanentist language of the early dialogues: I hope to come a little closer to completeness in a forthcoming book on the development of Plato's theory of forms.

40. I am, then, inclined against as moderate a position as that of Malcolm (1968). See Woodruff (1978), pp. 103–109; (1982), pp. 45 n. 56, 163–164.

41. Ross (1951), p. 228; Brentlinger (1972), p. 66.

42. The first of these is missing from the list in Fujisawa (1974), p. 42, although, as far as I can tell, it meets his standards of significance.

43. *Pace* Tarrant (1928), etc. See Woodruff (1982), pp. 93–103 et passim. Most recently, Kahn (1985), pp. 267–273, has weighed in on the side of the athetizers. He says (p. 268): "I am inclined to assert . . . that anyone who takes the *Hippias Major* for a work of Plato's has no sense for the art of the greatest prose writer of antiquity. . . . The grounds for my judgment are very much those expressed by Wilamowitz . . . : 'it has no Socratic *ethos*; it lacks Platonic wit and Platonic charm'. (To which I will add: and it makes no contribution to our understanding of Plato. . .)." I fear I must lack the sense Kahn refers to; I think the dialogue to be actually quite funny, and I think it has a great deal to tell us about Plato's philosophy. For this last, I must defer discussion: see n. 39 above *ad fin*.

44. It occurs more times in that dialogue than in any other, including the monsters, *Republic* and *Laws*.

45. This also is unaccountably missing from Fujisawa (1974), p. 42 (see n. 42 above).

46. Well, almost no one: there is always Shorey (1903), pp. 31–32, with n. 201. But see Dodds (1959), pp. 20–21, esp. p. 21 n. 1, 314 *ad* 497e1; Irwin (1979), pp. 202–203 *ad* 497e; Kahn (1988), p. 87.

47. Sprague (1962), pp. 25–30, and, more briefly, Sprague (1965), pp.

55–57 nn. 95–96, sees here an attack on the theory of forms. The objection, she thinks, is, or is very like, that of *Parmenides* 130e5–131c11 (Sprague [1967], pp. 95–98; see also Davies [1897], p. 10). Gifford (1905), p. 59 *ad* 301a1, by contrast, follows Stallbaum in seeing "only the *logical* doctrine of universals as held by Socrates, upon which Plato afterwards founded his *metaphysical* doctrine of 'Ideas'." I do not know whether to agree with this or not; it depends on how much is incorporated in 'the logical doctrine of universals.'

48. παρεῖναι was used earlier in the dialogue in the same way: 280b2, b7.

49. This is the way Gifford (1905), p. 60 *ad* a8 construes the question; so also Guthrie (1975), p. 278 with n. 2.

50. This is my own preferred way of reading it.

Sprague (1962), pp. 26–27, and (1965), note on p. 56, construes it quite differently, as introducing a fallacious argument to the effect that the beautiful is the same as the beautiful things, because both are different: we are supposed to understand Dionysodorus as relying on the idea that if x and y are both F, e.g. different, x = y. This seems to me a lot to supply. (See also Guthrie [1975], p. 278, n. 2).

Mohr (1984), p. 298, construes Dionysodorus' question so that it encapsulates a reductio ad absurdum against immanentism, establishing "the transcendence of the form." His version of the question is: "Well, Socrates, you have claimed that the beautiful is different from the beautiful things (301a3), but if the beautiful (the one thing, ἑτέρου) is exclusively immanent in the beautiful particulars (the other thing, ἑτέρῳ), how can you consistently maintain that the beautiful (τὸ ἕτερον) is in fact different (ἕτερον) from the other things you claim it is different from, namely, the many beautiful things?" We are supposed to supply the following argument: if the form is not transcendent, it is 'exclusively immanent' in the particulars; if it is 'exclusively immanent' in the particulars, it is not different from them. Apart from the inherent implausibility of importing all that into the text, the argument, in the absence of any independent explanation of 'exclusive immanence,' is a terrible one.

51. 217d2 ψιμυθίῳ: more commonly, and correctly, translated as 'white lead,' but there is no part of the original Greek word that corresponds to *white*: it is no sort of tautology that ψιμύθιον is white.

52. Cf. Becker (1936), pp. 394–395.

53. See von Arnim (1914), p. 51; Guthrie (1975), pp. 150–151.

54. Contrast Allen (1970), pp. 122–123, and see n. 38 above.

55. As Allen (1970), p. 146, n. 1, points out.

56. See also *Republic* i 331a2.

57. Bluck (1955), pp. 17–18, 118.

58. Hackforth (1955), p. 147 et passim; Vlastos (1969a), p. 298 = Vlastos (1973a), pp. 84–85 = Vlastos (1971), pp. 140–141.

59. Hackforth (1955), p. 162; Keyt (1963), p. 168.

60. Nehamas (1972–73), p. 475; Fujisawa (1974), p. 45; Gallop (1975), p. 195. For further references see Gallop; more recent additions are D. Frede (1978), p. 28; Matthen (1984), p. 281. There are a few denials: Verdenius (1958), p. 232–233; O'Brien (1967), pp. 201–203; Guthrie (1975), pp. 353–356.

61. 100d6 προσγενομένη: apart from the disagreement in case and gender between this and its purported subject ἐκείνου τοῦ καλοῦ (d5), which might be explained by (an ungrammatical) assimilation (so Bluck [1955], p. 115, n. 1, followed by Gallop [1975], pp. 234–235, n. 63), it seems to me peculiar that προσγίγνεσθαι should be treated as the general relation of which παρουσία and κοινωνία are examples. But none of the proposed emendations (see, e.g., Stallbaum [1885], p. 187, Archer-Hind [1894], p. 100, Burnet [1911], p. 111) is particularly attractive. Fortunately, it makes little difference to the general sense.

Perhaps, if the word is retained, προσ- should be construed as vaguely as possible: "however and in whatever way it comes-to-be-related-to [them]."

62. (1) was his first 'hypothesis,' and (2) is the first thing he 'posits' as agreeing with it: see 100a3–5.

63. See n. 62: here Socrates is applying the negative part of his method (100a6–7).

64. Assuming that προσγενομένη is kept in 100d6, see n. 61.

65. Cf. Aristotle, *Metaphysics* A 6. 987b13–14.

66. *Pace* Fine (1986), pp. 73–80: she saddles Socrates with a theory to the effect that Forms have parts that are in things in the sense "that they are where those things are," which she then explains as meaning that they are "properties of things" (p. 79). Apart from ignoring Socrates' own diffidence on this question, this explains the obscure in terms that are, at least to me, equally obscure: I cannot see what it means to say that the properties of a thing are where it is.

67. Fine (1986), p. 90 cites 211b4–5 as showing that Plato took the forms to be 'impassive', but on p. 79, n. 16, dismisses 211ab along with *Timaeus* 52: either, she thinks, these passages do not deny the sort of imma-

nence she takes to be operative in the *Phaedo*, or, "even if they do, that does not show that in the *Ph.* Plato did not flirt with immanence." But (a) the immanence she sees in the *Phaedo* has the forms 'where' their participants are, and *Symposium* 211a8 plainly *does* deny that; (b) there is no question of Plato 'flirting' with immanence in the *Phaedo*: according to Fine, the theory of the *Phaedo* is that there are immanent characters in things and those immanent characters are parts of forms, and Aristotle in objecting against Eudoxus is actually objecting against this theory; (c) the claims of the *Symposium* are made on the basis of the argument of *Phaedo* 74: the *Symposium* cannot be prized apart from the *Phaedo* on this score. (Here (c) of course requires further discussion, which I hope to provide shortly in a book on *Plato's Metaphysics*, but I do not think many will find the claim surprising.)

68. 102d7 τὸ ἐν ἡμῖν μέγεθος: the normal translation, 'the tallness in us,' conduces to the idea that there is one tallness upstairs and another down here; but abstract nouns in Greek normally have the definite article, as did 'tallness itself', αὐτὸ τὸ μέγεθος, in d6.

69. Bluck (1955), p. 17; Gallop (1975), p. 236, n. 69.

70. 103a6 αὐτὸ τὸ ἐναντίον: 'the contrary itself' in Socrates' next speech.

71. τὸ ἐναντίον πρᾶγμα: here there is a word for 'thing.'

72. αὐτὸ τὸ ἐναντίον: notice that this does not mean "the form of contrary."

73. ἅ subject for ἀναγκάζει, ὅτι object of κατάσχῃ: so O'Brien (1967), p. 214 (in the translation; on p. 215 he curiously says "We translate ἅ as subject of κατάσχηι and ὅτι as object"), and others. Differently, Grube (1931), p. 198, Gallop (1975), pp. 235–236, n. 70, take ἅ as object of κατάσχῃ, ὅτι as subject, giving "which whatever occupies them forces [them] to have." Perhaps what Socrates says in 104d5–7 by way of clarifying his remark favors this, but see O'Brien (1967), p. 216. I cannot agree with Gallop that "much hinges on the grammar and text at 104d1–3": the theory is perfectly clear from the examples, whatever we do with this sentence.

74. Taking αὐτό to refer to ἅ. So Burnet (1911), p. 119 *ad* d2: "There is nothing abnormal in the shift from plural (ἅ) to singular in a case like this. After an indefinite plural some such subject as 'any one of them' is often to be supplied"; he cites 70e5 (ὅσοις . . . αὐτό), *Laws* ii 667b5–6 (ἅπασιν ὅσοις . . . αὐτοῦ) as parallel. So also O'Brien (1967) loc. cit., followed by Burger (1984), pp. 168–169. Archer-Hind (1894), p. 112 *ad* 11) objects: "To say nothing of the grammar, this makes sheer nonsense, representing the idea as the idea of itself." But Socrates has not said that the occupier has to be an idea, and, anyway, I fail to see the nonsense: if the occupier is an idea (as it

may be in the case of the number three, say), "there is really nothing extraordinary in speaking of the triad, or any other transcendental 'form' impressing its own form upon a particular" (Grube [1931], p. 198 *ad* 'ii)'). (Archer-Hind takes αὐτοῦ to refer to ὅτι, as do, to judge from their translations, Bluck [1955], p. 123, and Hackforth [1955], p. 151. Against this, see O'Brien [1967].)

75. αὐτῷ secl. Stallbaum (1885), p. 201; Ross (1951), p. 132; Hackforth (1955), p. 194 *ad* 104d3; Gallop (1975), p. 234, n. 71. Grube (1931), p. 199, thinks it can be kept as a 'dative of advantage.'

76. Here I follow Burnet (1911), p. 119 *ad* d1.

Vlastos (1956), p. 93, n. 14 (= Allen [1965], p. 290, n. 2) says "I take it for certain that Plato assumes that" the intermediates are forms. He offers no argument for this, but merely refers to 102b1–2, which is not relevant.

Keyt (1963), p. 168, n. 2, offers three considerations: (1) the tallness in us either withdraws or perishes, and so do fire and snow; (2) 103e5–6 speaks of the intermediate importing its own form, so there must be a form for fire; (3) Socrates' examples include fire, snow, disease, two, and three, so, because the last are ideas, the others ought to be. (So also O'Brien [1967], pp. 220–221] thinks that by 104e7–105b3 fire is "thought of to some extent as a form," because it is there listed with three and two (or rather, with ἡ τριάς and ἡ δυάς, which O'Brien thinks are to be distinguished from τὰ τρία and τὰ δύο: see ibid., pp. 212, 218–219].)

(1) and (3) are of the same type; anyone who, like myself, finds it plausible to think that some of the intermediates might be forms and others not will be unmoved. As for (2), plainly to speak of an intermediate as importing its own form is not to imply that it *is* that form (contrast Archer-Hind, quoted in n. 74).

77. Again, see Burnet (1911), p. 123 *ad* d3.

78. Hackforth (1955), pp. 163, 165, thought the soul had to be a form in this argument, but an 'immanent form'; he is half-followed in this by Keyt (1963), p. 169: "Plato treats the soul *as if* it were an immanent form." Schiller (1967) correctly rejects the idea that anything in the final argument requires thinking of the soul as a form, or even thinking of it as if it were a form, but retains the apparatus of 'immanent forms.'

79. Nor should we rely too much on the facts (1) that the narrator of the *Parmenides* is Cephalus of Clazomenae, who represents himself as on a philosophical pilgrimage to Athens with others from Clazomenae in order to hear a recitation of the dialogue, and (2) that Anaxagoras was from Clazomenae. Brumbaugh (1961) passim (see esp. pp. 28–29, 19–20 n. 2, 25–26) makes much of this; Schofield (1973), pp. 3–4 is more skeptical, but still thinks it "reasonable to suppose that we are meant to think of" Cephalus and

his compatriots "as followers of Anaxagoras"; Allen (1983), p. 63 is completely skeptical, perhaps rightly.

80. Although Cherniss (1945) thought so. Oddly, something like this seems to be presupposed by Allen (1960), p. 143.

81. See Dancy (1984), esp. pp. 180–181.

82. Cherniss (1944), p. 536: "At any rate, it is a conception of ideas as immanent that is there attacked . . . , so that there must have been such a notion current, and we have no reason to doubt Aristotle's ascription of it to Eudoxus." The clause "so that . . . " is a non sequitur (see also Allen [1960], pp. 143–144, Schofield [1973], pp. 1–3).

That Eudoxus at least was in the background of Plato's objection in 130e–131e would be entailed by the interesting thesis that the *Parmenides* was written after Aristotle's *On Ideas*. This thesis is to be found in Philippson (1936), pp. 120–125; Düring (1966), pp. 49 (cf. pp. 7–8), 253; D. Frank (1984), pp. 9–10, 122 (on which see Barnes [1985], p. 103). There is no reason to think it true: it once more portrays the Academics as communicating with each other by publishing. But Cherniss (1944), pp. 538–539, provides no reason for thinking it false, either (*pace* Leszl [1975], p. 79): his claims are entirely dependent on his 'unitarian' conception of Plato's intellectual life. Rist (1989), p. 14 would have *On Ideas* come "at some point near the time of Plato's death". I am not quite sure I see why.

83. This would have to be true if Allen (1960), p. 143, were right.

84. On the force of this claim, see Vlastos (1987), pp. 187–194, *contra* Fine (1984), pp. 56–59.

85. If Schofield (1973), p. 15, n. 59, were right, the denial of immanence here could also be found in *Phaedo* 74a–c. But there is nothing so explicit there.

86. I cannot see in the arguments of 130e–132d the "sequence of increasingly more sensible attempts to explain the idea" that things participate in Forms discerned by Schofield (1973), p. 2. On the other hand, neither can I see the position Socrates espouses here as one Plato never really put any stock in, as Allen (1983), pp. 110–111 and Fine (1984), pp. 58–59 seem to think.

87. Whose relevance to the Eudoxus issue has been pointed out by Schofield (1973), pp. 14–19; he believes it to be an attack on Eudoxus.

88. Actually, there is some conflict between the premises for the argument over largeness and those of the argument over smallness: see Schofield (1973), p. 17.

89. So Schofield (1973), pp. 18–19.

90. See the *scholium* to Euclid v, Heiberg and Stamatis (1969–77) Vol. 5, 1 211.7–8, translated in Heath (1926), Vol. 2, p. 112. But see also Knorr (1986), pp. 79–80, (1978).

91. Heiberg and Stamatis (1969–77), Vol.2, 1.10–15, with Heath's translation and note (Heath [1926], Vol. 2, pp. 114, 120 ff., esp. 120–121 on the historical question).

92. This was suggested to Ryle (1966), pp. 286–295 by the shift from indirect to direct discourse at 137c4 (the last "he said" of the dialogue). Without endorsing any of Ryle's proposals, we must at least consider this possibility.

93. This text, as printed in Ross (1924) or Jaeger (1957), is a doublet of that in M 5. 1079b12–26, with one trivial (τἆλλα 991a21, τὰ ἄλλα 1079b25) and one interesting difference: on the latter, see below pp. 27–28.

94. a13 ἐν τούτοις γὰρ ἂν ἦν, a14 ἐνυπάρχοντα: cf. ἐν . . . ὑπάρχον *Categories* 1a24–25; see also the texts marked earlier with note number 29.

95. The mss support for the standard reading ὡς in 991a15 (and in 1079b19) is shaky, as the apparatus in either Ross (1924) or Jaeger (1957) ad loc. shows and Becker (1936), p. 391, n. 8, points out. Without it, we should have to read αἰτία instead of αἴτια (as Becker says) and translate "for then the white might perhaps be considered a cause by being mixed into the white [thing]" or "a cause for the white [thing] by being mixed [into it]" (*pace* Becker, on whose emendation see the next note, which also discusses the different possible translations).

96. Ross (1924), Vol. 1, p. 198 paraphrases a15–16 ὡς . . . λευκῷ "as white is the cause of whiteness to the white thing by being mixed in it." He does nothing to sort this paraphrase out into the Greek. One possibility is: "in the way that the white [is a cause] for the white [thing, of its being white], by being mixed in it"; another is: "in the way that the white [is a cause of something's being white], by being mixed in the white [thing]". I have preferred the latter, as does Apostle (1966), p. 30; most others (Ross [1928]; Barnes [1984], Vol. 2, p. 1566 and, differently, p. 1707 at 1079b19; Annas [1976], p. 99 at 1079b19; Fine [1986], p. 72) seem to prefer the former. Alexander, *in Metaphysica* 97.2–8 (and cf. further paraphrases in 97.8 ff.), explains the passage in a way that does not commit him on this question: he uses double datives, one constructed with αἴτιον/αἴτια and the other with μεμῖχθαι etc.; e.g. 97.2–4: "For if it were by being mixed into these [things] [*sc*. things here below] that they [*sc*. the forms] were causes for their being, it would be as if the white were said to be a cause for the white body of its being white, through being mixed into it" (εἰ γὰρ ἦν τῷ μεμῖχθαι τούτοις αἴτια

αὐτοῖς τοῦ εἶναι, οὕτως ἂν ἦν ὡς εἰ τὸ λευκὸν λέγοιτο αἴτιον εἶναι τῷ λευκῷ σώματι τοῦ λευκῷ εἶναι διὰ τὸ μεμῖχθαι αὐτῷ). I doubt that there is much of an issue here, but my way seems to me in some sense more economical.

97. We know nothing about who these might be. Leszl (1975), p. 336, says that they are probably not Academics, or Aristotle would have said so; this is surely unsound.

98. 991a18 συναγαγεῖν: alternatively, 'to infer': this would refer more directly to the fact that the arguments are reductiones ad absurdum.

99. Ross (1924), Vol. 1 punctuates the text so that this clause (a19–20) attaches to the preceding but paraphrases it (p. 189) as introducing the sequel. He translated it in the latter way in Ross (1928), and is followed in this by Barnes (1984), Vol. 2, p. 1566. It seems to me better taken the former way: see below.

Alexander *in Metaphysica* 99.3ff., esp. 100.22–101.10, gives two ways of reading the comment: either Aristotle means the other things are not composed of forms in any of the customary ways of speaking of things being 'composed of' (ἐκ) things (and Alexander, 99.9–100.22, dutifully reviews the ways he finds in *Metaphysics* α 2. 994a22–24 and Δ 24), or he means the other things are not composed of forms in any of the ways Platonists customarily speak of the relationship between the forms and the other things: in particular, the others are not composed of forms in the way Eudoxus conceives forms, nor in the way the paradigm-mongers who are about to be discussed conceive them. Ross (1924), Vol. 1, p. 198 *ad* 20 prefers the former reading, on the ground that Aristotle has already (A 6. 987b13–14) said that the Platonists "did not specify the relation between particulars and Ideas." That is inadequate to decide the issue: here in A 9 Aristotle is discussing various ways the relationship *might* be specified, and he could perfectly well be saying that none of the ways standardly discussed makes the other things composed of forms. Still, I think Ross is right, and that this fits with taking the clause as attached to the preceding: again, see below.

100. See here Plato, *Parmenides* 133a–134e. Ross (1924), Vol. 1, p. 198 *ad* 12, 13 says: "This argument is met by Plato in *Parm.* 134D", but even if it is the same argument (which is not clear to me), it is not *met* there.

101. Joachim (1922), p. 249.

102. Annas (1972), p. 326, cleverly connects these last two passages with the requirement in the *Phaedo* (see immediately below for the relevance of this) that the cause of something not also be the cause of its contrary. Perhaps too cleverly: it is not clear to me that Aristotle's point is so precise.

103. See Cherniss (1944), pp. 450–452, Vlastos (1969a), pp. 303–305 = Vlastos (1970), pp. 144–146 = Vlastos (1973a), pp. 88–90.

104. According to Vlastos (1969a) in Vlastos (1970), p. 144, n. 39 = Vlastos (1973a), pp. 88–89, n. 39 (not in the original of 1969), in this passage "the *aitia* of a thing's coming to be *F* is not (i) the form but (ii) *the thing's coming to participate in that form*." In part this claim depends on a faulty reading of a distinction Cornford (1939), p. 69, n. 1, thought he saw between 'participating' (μεταλαμβάνειν) and 'partaking' (μετέχειν): the former "means '*beginning* to partake when the thing *becomes*" F, whereas the latter "is used of *having* a share and corresponds to *being*" F. Cornford thought he saw this distinction operating in *Parmenides* 129aff., 155e11–156a1, and, somehow, in *Phaedo* 101c. It is difficult to see how, as the only verb in that passage is μετέχειν, but Cornford blandly puts the noun μετάσχεσις (101c5) on the side of the verb μεταλαμβάνειν, where it in fact comes from μετέχειν. Nonetheless, Vlastos (1969a), p. 302, n. 32 = Vlastos (1970), pp. 142–143, n. 32 (with some unfortunate omissions) = Vlastos (1973), p. 87, n. 32 (with the omitted material restored), cites Cornford's note as showing that the cause of something's coming to be F in 101c is its coming to partake of the form for F things.

Cornford's actual strategy for this passage becomes clear only a little later (Cornford [1939], p. 79): "Just as a thing's *being* beautiful is due to its *having a share* (μετέχειν) in Beauty, so its *becoming* beautiful means that it *comes to partake* of Beauty (μετασχεῖν, ingressive aorist, from which the noun μετάσχεσις, here only, is formed for 'acquiring a share', 101C)." So the distinction between the two verbs is quite irrelevant. I suppose Cornford is right about the 'ingressive aorist' (for which see Goodwin [1889], p. 16, § 55 or Kühner-Gerth i 155–156 § 386.5). Whether that determines the sense of μετάσχεσις in this passage is less clear. And it remains true that something *other* than the form is required to bring it about that something comes-to-partake of the beautiful: this Cornford (1939), p. 79, n. 1 concedes.

105. See Annas (1974), esp. pp. 323–326.

106. Here the term *F* (or *f*) need not be a term in what is sometimes called the 'category of substance': white(ness) could be conceived as the substance of white things just as much as *man* is the substance of a man.

107. See here Z 6. 1031b6–7, b20–22 (so Cherniss [1944], p. 377). But this goes from the obscure to the yet more obscure.

108. *Pace* Fine (1986), pp. 72–73, who gets off on the wrong foot, I think, in seeing the immanence discussed in 991a12–13 as the object of Aristotle's subsequent attack.

109. At least, so I understand him. There was some justice in Becker's finding a15–16, ὥς τὸ λευκὸν μεμιγμένον τῷ λευκῷ, difficult to understand (Becker [1936], pp. 389–391), even if there is no justifying his emending it to "ὥς τὸ λευκὸν μεμιγμένῳ τῷ λευκῷ (scil. αἴτιόν ἐστιν)" (p. 391); he wanted this to mean something like "the forms might perhaps be considered causes in the way that [pure] white [i.e., the form] is a cause for the mixed white." Becker is attacked by Cherniss (1944), pp. 532–534, with his usual vigor; the only part of this attack I feel comfortable with is that concerned with the text (pp. 532–533). Because it is not really unintelligible (and is not really any more intelligible after Becker's emendation; Lasserre (1966), p. 149, in addition, finds the word order odd), emendation is unnecessary.

110. Leszl (1975) Ch. 21, pp. 331–349. I am not impressed by Leszl's attempt to show that a hedonist could not have a theory of forms (pp. 337–339) or by his attempt to show that Eudoxus was too young to have had anything to do with the Academy (pp. 339–340). And he conceives the theory of forms as monolithic: he speaks of the 'typical doctrines of this school,' that is, the Academy (p. 337), and means high Platonism.

111. Cherniss (1944), p. 534 asserts, without argument: "The identification of Eudoxus' notion and the theory of Anaxagoras is due to Aristotle himself." But the structural similarity is there, and it would be surprising if Aristotle was the first to have seen it. Here, too, I am on Becker's side (see n. 109, and see also Schofield [1973], p. 3, n. 11).

112. Cherniss (1944), p. 537.

113. This is not exactly to deny the remarks of Düring (1960), p. 54 (Eudoxus' theory "probably sent a shudder down Plato's spine") or Robin (as reported by Allan (1960), p. 143: "une interprétation tout à fait scandaleuse de la théorie des Idées"). But perhaps Rist (1989), p. 59, understates the case when he speaks of Aristotle as referring to Eudoxus as "a 'corrector' of Plato's theory" (I do not know what passage Rist here has in mind).

114. Fr. 30 in Heinze (1892), 170.1–4.

115. But Speusippus too refers to the number 10 as an εἶδος and even as a παράδειγμα used by god in framing the universe: see below, pp. 105–106.

116. Both texts are included in fr. 34, Heinze (1892), 171.1–4, 5–6.

117. Contrast Cherniss (1945), p. 85 (Plato "probably felt . . . that he had . . . expressed his meaning as clearly as words, spoken or written, can ever mirror the eternal truth") with Plato, *Phaedrus* 277d ("if Lysias or anyone else ever wrote or writes . . . thinking that there is any great clarity of firmness in it, that is a disgrace for the writer"; Ross (1951), p. 142, also cites

this passage against Cherniss). But there is nothing to drive us to the opposite extreme: to the view that there were secret doctrines in the Academy.

118. E.g., von Fritz (1926–27), p. 19; Lasserre (1966), p. 149.

119. Philippson (1925), p. 2; von Fritz (1926–27), loc. cit.; Karpp (1933), p. 5; von Fritz (1935), p. 413 ad fin. On the other hand, in Becker (1936) it is a full-scale theory of color, and so it is in Gaiser (1965), p. 198. According to Lasserre (1966), p. 270, Gaiser's arguments only make this a possibility.

120. An idea of Karpp's (Karpp [1933], p. 34 n. 12), but often forgotten or muddled (see n. 122).

121. Fully: ὃν 'Αναξαγόρας μὲν πρῶτος Εὔδοξος δ' ὕστερον καὶ ἄλλοι τινὲς ἔλεγον (991a17–18), ὃν 'Αναξαγόρας μὲν πρότερος Εὔδοξος δ' ὕστερος ἔλεγε διαπορῶν καὶ ἕτεροί τινες (1079b20–22).

122. Cherniss (1944), p. 525, notes the difference, and interprets it so (p. 539): "it was just in the "separation" [*sc.* of the forms] that he [Eudoxus] found difficulty (διαπορῶν, *Metaphysics* 1079B21)." He does not explain how he manages to pin this down so precisely. Lasserre (1966) prints 991a14–19 as D 1, p. 12; he does not note the discrepancy (indeed, he says "= 1079b18–23"). Guthrie (1978), p. 453 comments on διαπορῶν but acts as if it is to be found in book A (see also p. 452).

123. Syrianus' report on M speaks of "the problems raised by Eudoxus about such things" (*in Metaphysica*, Kroll [1902], 117.3–4: τὰ Εὐδόξῳ περί τινων τοιούτων ἠπορημένα), but this is of no independent evidential value.

124. Ross (1924), Vol. 1, p. 198 *ad* 9 gives 'to raise a difficulty,' 'to work through the difficulties,' and 'to establish by discussion of the difficulties' as possible paraphrases for different occurrences of διαπορεῖν. The question is whether Eudoxus would fall under the first or the third of these senses; Ross himself classifies the occurrence in 1079b21 under the first head (loc. cit.; he has no comment on it ad loc.). But this is hard to see: the idea that a form is a physical ingredient is not by itself an objection against anything.

125. By Cherniss (1944), p. 525.

126. Becker (1936), p. 390, insists that these paraphrases are Alexander's own and not Aristotle's; it is not at all clear why. But neither is there a case for supposing them to be Aristotle's.

127. See 59B6 at DK ii 35.14–16, 59B11 = DK ii 37.12–14, 59B12 at DK ii 37.22–23; Aristotle, *Physics* A 4. 187b1 (below).

128. See 59B12 at DK ii 39.6–7; Aristotle, *Physics* A 4. 187b2–7 (below).

129. None of Ross (1955a), Leszl (1975), or Gigon (1987) prints 97.17–19 as a fragment from *On Ideas* (although Leszl, p. 49 translates it and refers it to Ross's fr. 5, where it does not occur, and all of 97.17–21 is included in Lasserre (1966) 12 [D 2]).

130. The phrase τὰ πρὸς αὐτὰς τὸ εἶναι ἔχοντα should not be taken to refer to any sort of 'material principle' (*pace* Düring [1966] p. 253, n. 54). See von Fritz (1926–27), p. 7 with n. 11: Düring's view is presumably based on the considerations adduced by von Fritz on pp. 7–10; but the most that von Fritz shows is that the things that have their being relative to the Ideas are bodies, that is, physical objects (not a "Stoffprinzip").

131. E.g. 97.10–11.

132. L and F, which, however, in books A and α depart considerably from the others and are not in general to be trusted: see Hayduck (1891), pp. vii–ix; Wilpert (1949), p. 42 (note from p. 41), Harlfinger in Leszl (1975), p. 17–18. These mss are apparently a later reworking of Alexander's commentary.

133. That is, in what he just said a couple of pages ago: A 8. 989a33-b4, quoted later. See also the phrasing in Alexander's own paraphrase of this passage, 68.15–23.

134. Cf. *Metaphysics* A 8. 989b1–2 and N 5. 1092a24–26 (quoted later, p. 46), *De generatione et corruptione* A 10. 327b20–22.

135. Cf. *De generatione et corruptione* A 10. 327b20–22 and *Metaphysics* A 8. 989a33–b4 (the latter is quoted in the text later).

136. *Physics* A 4.

137. = Rose (1886), pp. 151–152 (fr. 189); Ross (1952), pp. 132–133 (trans.); Ross (1955a), pp. 128–129 (Greek); Leszl (1975), pp. 36–38 (text by Harlfinger), pp. 49–50 (trans.); Barnes and Lawrence (1984), pp. 2440–2441 (trans.).

138. So also Leszl (1975), p. 49; not "by mixture with the ideas" (Barnes and Lawrence [1984], p. 2440).

139. Cherniss (1944), pp. 525–526, retains the enumeration of the arguments assumed by von Fritz (1926–27), p. 8 (et passim) and Karpp (1933), p. 30, etc., in which (3b1) and (3b2) are the fourth and fifth objections, although his own discussion of this argument would dictate an enumeration as above. There is one substantive point that turns on this question: see later, text at n. 157.

140. 98.3 ἐν πλείοσι: this could as legitimately be translated "in many places".

141. 98.4: reading μέρους, von Fritz' emendation for μέρος (von Fritz [1926–27], p. 15), with Ross (1955a), 129.2, Harlfinger (in Leszl [1975], p. 36) et al. This has the support of L (see Harlfinger's apparatus: this is not to be found in Hayduck [1891]). The alternative reading (preserved in Lasserre [1966], 12.20; Gigon [1987], 383b16) would translate: "but if as a part, the part which partakes of the man-itself, not that which partakes of the whole of the man-itself, will be a man." This plainly makes less sense.

142. This is another consequence of (3b) rather than a new argument: as von Fritz (1926–27), p. 15, remarks, one expects ἔτι οὕτω rather than just ἔτι.

143. Düring (1966), p. 253, n. 55, counts this as two objections.

144. The reference is to *Metaphysics* A 9. 991a27–b1 = M 5. 1079b31–35, quoted below.

145. This is ambiguous between "the *idea* of man is both an animal and a man" and "any given individual man is both an animal and a man". The latter seems preferable, since Alexander goes on in the next sentence to claim that the Idea of man is an animal.

146. Düring (1966), p. 253, n. 55, counts (4) as three objections, and refers for all to *Topics* Z 6. 143b23, which is not relevant.

147. Karpp (1933), p. 30, Cherniss (1944), p. 526, Düring (1966), p. 253, n. 55, and Lasserre (1966), p. 13, count this as two objections. The lack of a connective makes it harder to read as one objection, but not, I think, impossible. I am here in agreement with Leszl (1975), p. 50.

148. Cherniss (1944), p. 526, quotes 98.21–24 and states "This of itself would indicate that he drew his whole list from that work of Aristotle's"; surely, that is to place too much weight on the words. But apparently this inspires Lasserre's outrageous exaggeration to the effect that Karpp's view that the first seven objections (the first five in my enumeration) are Alexander's own and not Aristotle's "widerspricht offen der Überlieferung" (Lasserre [1966], p. 150). Even the more moderate view (Karpp [1933], p. 30) that the words indicate that the immediately preceding objection(s) come from the Περὶ ἰδεῶν is wrong. Speaking of "these and all the other apples in the basket" does not presuppose either that these apples are in the basket, or that they are not in the basket. And we shall see that this is true of Alexander's use of ὅσα ἄλλα as well: see later, p. 34.

149. von Fritz (1926–27), pp. 2–6.

150. Cherniss (1944), p. 530.

151. He kept them apart in 68.18–20, 20–23; he is just being careless here. It is faintly possible to read 97.22–24, 24–25 as two objections, but there would be considerable overlap between the two.

152. As Cherniss (1944), p. 527, prefers.

153. Karpp (1933), pp. 29–30, thought that, all the way up to this point, Alexander was providing objections of his own.

154. It is common to evade it, so Fine (1986), p. 87 n. 23, "assumes without argument" that the objections are all from *On Ideas*, and says: "Although Aristotle's arguments here are ostensibly aimed against Eudoxus, not Plato, I assume Eudoxus held a theory of immanent Platonic Forms; for the sake of simplicity, I shall write as though Aristotle is criticizing Plato directly." This is a lot of assuming, and there is more than simplicity at stake. In fact, Fine believes these are arguments that apply against the Theory of Forms as it appears in the *Phaedo* (Fine [1986], pp. 73–80), so the phrase "immanent Platonic forms" is, in her usage, pleonastic. See note 108.

155. I think this may have been first pointed out to me, years ago, by G. E. L. Owen.

156. The only difference is that the last two objections he counts as three.

157. This is the substantive point mentioned earlier in n. 139.

158. So also Cherniss (1944), p. 530; Berti (1962), p. 236; Leszl (1975), p. 50; see n. 139.

159. According to Fine (1986), p. 89, the first and third consequences in the second part, (b1) and (b3) "constitute a dilemma . . . anticipated in the *Parmenides*. Either the parts of Forms are (a) anhomoeomerous or (c) homoeomerous. If they are anhomoeomerous, they cannot do their explanatory work. But if they are homoeomerous, the resultant conception of forms is incoherent." Nothing in the text indicates that the author of this objection saw it this way: the first consequence is introduced with *but*, the second with *again*, and the third with *next* (δέ 98.4, ἔτι, ἔπειτα 98.6). Worse, (b3) does not argue *from the assumption* that the forms are homoeomerous but *to the conclusion* that they are, and then that this is absurd.

As for the *Parmenides*, it is far from clear that it 'anticipates' this. Fine (1986), pp. 82–83, takes Parmenides in 131cd to be saying that the form largeness is one that cannot be homoeomerous, because parts of it will be smaller than it. I do not see that the argument requires anything of the sort.

160. Especially if Burnet's brackets around ἓν εἶναι in a10–11 are ignored; see Dancy (1984), p. 180.

161. If we adopted the alternative translation "in many places" (see n. 140), there would be another intermediate step and the conclusion would read slightly differently. The correspondence with *Parmenides* 131b1 suggests we should stick with "in many things."

162. For the text at 98.4, see n. 141.

163. The best case is made by Fine (1986), p. 89: as she sees it, the parts of a man would be, say, arms and legs, and so these would be parts of the man-itself; so someone who had the man-itself's arm would have to be a man. But this is contradicted by the third consequence, that the forms would have to be homoeomerous.

164. = DK 59B12, ii 37.18–19; Kirk and Raven (1957), p. 372 t503; Kirk, Raven, and Schofield (1973), p. 362 t476.

165. Hicks (1907), p. 236 *ad* b19 argues that the term ἀπαθής does not stem from Anaxagoras. I do not mean to be suggesting that it does.

166. Cherniss (1944), p. 531, says, commenting on this objection: "for Aristotle's use of the term ὁμοιομερές against the Platonists cf. *Metaphysics* 992A6–7, and for its connection with μῖξις cf. *De Generatione* 328A10–12." Neither reference is germane.

In *Metaphysics* A 9. 992a, Aristotle is arguing against the identification of Forms with numbers, and says in a6–7 that the identifiers treat the One as a homoeomer. The argument is quite obscure, but a2–6 shows that what he means is that every instance of the One, every unit of which the Form-numbers are composed, is materially of the same sort as every other, just as every instance of water, regardless of its size and shape, is still water. This has nothing to do with Alexander's argument.

In *De generatione et corruptione* A 10. 328a10–12, Aristotle claims that every *mixture* must be homoeomerous, and this, too, is completely irrelevant to Alexander's argument.

167. Fine (1986), p. 89, says nothing about this clause: see n. 159.

168. These 'Transmission Theories of Causality' are discussed in more detail in the second of these studies.

169. Cherniss (1944), p. 528, rightly points out that Karpp (1933), p. 33, is in error in supposing that Alexander makes the Idea of man prior to that of animal: see Alexander *in Met.* 105.7–8.

170. 991a30: only late mss appear to have τῶν ἰδεῶν; it is printed in Bekker but not in either Ross (1924) or Jaeger (1957). (There are no reported mss for 1079b34 that have this.)

171. 991a30–31 οἷον τὸ γένος, ὡς γένος εἰδῶν: 1079b34–35 read

οἷον τὸ γένος τῶν ὡς γένους εἰδῶν, "e.g. the kind [will be a paradigm] of the forms as of kind," i.e., the 'forms' in the sense of species of a genus. See Ross (1924), Vol. 1, p. 199 *ad* 31.

172. von Fritz (1926–27), pp. 9–10, followed by Cherniss (1944), p. 525; Lasserre (1966), p. 150; Leszl (1975), pp. 341–342; Isnardi Parente (1979), p. 135. But von Fritz looks to *Physics* A 5–6 to explain how mixture requires contrariety, which is wrong; he does not seem to realize that the passage that has to be looked at is in *De generatione et corruptione* A 10.

173. von Fritz (1926–27), p. 10, makes light of this. It is true that the feminine ἀλλήλας might have come by attraction, but the intervening objection seems to me to make it almost impossible to read the subject as "the Ideas and the other things."

174. Fine (1986), p. 87, apparently takes the conclusion to be (C2); she says nothing about the alternative reading, and does not mention the underlying premise that things that mix have to be contraries. She takes the absurdity to be that there are forms of contraries; she thinks Aristotle (wrongly) ascribes to Plato the view that there are no forms for contraries. Her basis for this claim is apparently just the present passage and Alexander *in Met.* 83.28–30 (which does not say that any more than the present passage).

175. But it is a part of Aristotle's theory, *contra* Isnardi Parente (1979), p. 135, n. 191.

176. See Joachim (1903) (for the contrariety condition, see pp. 79–80); Partington (1961) (who seems not to mention the contrariety condition); Bolzan (1976) (see p. 136); Bogaard (1979) (see p. 19). Williams (1982), p. 150, comments on *De generatione et corruptione* 328a23–33 without mentioning the contrariety condition.

177. At any rate, this is the only passage I know of, and only it and the presumed fragment from the Περὶ ἰδεῶν are mentioned in Bonitz (1870), 469b41–42.

178. For further references, see Dancy (1978), p. 386.

179. See *De mixtione* 229.9–11 and the subsequent discussion to the end of Ch. 13; Karpp (1933), p. 32.

180. Karpp (1933), pp. 33–34, also (see n. 153) rejected this as a formulation of Alexander's.

181. μέν in a16 is picked up by οὐδέ a19, and there is another μέν/δέ pair at the middle of it all, a17.

182. Cherniss (1944), p. 535, cites the two passages from the *De caelo*;

Düring (1966), p. 253, n. 54, cites the first one without, apparently, understanding its significance.

183. On which see Sorabji (1972).

184. Ross (1924), Vol. 2, p. 490 *ad* 24, followed by Cherniss (1944), p. 530.

185. The second is to the effect that when a mixture has taken place, the result is new, and the ingredients are no longer there in actuality, but only in potentiality (Ross loc. cit.). This may be relevant later.

186. As Cherniss (loc. cit.) thinks.

187. See Cherniss (1944), p. 532.

188. See also Z 10. 148a14–22, *Metaphysics* B 2. 998a14–15.

189. In *Metaphysics* A 6. 987a29–b14, M 4. 1078b12–32 (a doublet of the first passage), M 9. 1086a24–b4.

190. Cf. *Metaphysics* K 7. 1067b9–11.

191. See Owen (1968), pp. 110–111 = Owen (1986), pp. 226–227.

192. In fact, this is the last of three possible replies in Owen (1968), p. 111 = Owen (1986), p. 227. But he himself argues against the first one, and I do not understand the second.

193. See, e.g., Todd (1976), p. 50.

194. The text here is that of Ross (1936) (μέμικται in a7 instead of Bekker's ἐμέμικτο, καὶ in a8 instead of Bekker's ἢ).

195. See Anaxagoras 59B6 at DK 35.15, 16–17, 59B8 at 36.4–6, and 59B12 at 39.2–4 (the latter two are cited by Simplicius in his commentary at this point, *in Physica* 175.11–14; all are quoted earlier, pp. 5–6).

196. ἀχώριστα.

197. See here Anaxagoras fr. 13 (Simplicius *in Physica* 300.31–301.1 = DK ii 39.13–17): "And when mind began to move [things], [it] was unjoined from everything that was being moved, and whatever mind moved was disjoined; while things were being moved and disjoined, the rotation was making [them] disjoin much more." (καὶ ἐπεὶ ἤρξατο ὁ νοῦς κινεῖν, ἀπὸ τοῦ κινουμένου παντὸς ἀπεκρίνετο, καὶ ὅσον ἐκίνησεν ὁ νοῦς, πᾶν τοῦτο διεκρίθη· κινουμένων δὲ καὶ διακρινομένων ἡ περχώρησις πολλῷ μᾶλλον ἐποίει διακρίνεσθαι). The second clause might also be translated "there was an unjoining from all that was moved," where the subject is not mind. Kirk and Raven (1957), p. 373 t504, have the latter, as

does Schofield (1980a), p. 154, n. 45. But in Kirk, Raven, and Schofield (1983), p. 364 t477, it is translated as here. Cleve (1949), p. 43 (repeated on p. 55), has "on the part [ἀπό] of the whole moved [district] severance took place."

198. One can imagine a response to this on Anaxagoras' behalf: it is the unlimited smallness of the ingredients that ensures that you cannot get at them to extract them. But I shall not pursue this here.

199. Adopting Ross' emendation παντὶ for the mss' πάντῃ (see Ross [1955b], p. 289).

200. Plato here refers to the battle as a 'gigantomachy' (γιγαντομαχία); the identification of the rivals as gods and giants is an obvious, and standard, interpretation.

201. 246a8 πέτρας καὶ δρῦς: on this proverbial phrase see the extensive note *ad* Hesiod, *Theogony* 35 in West (1966), pp. 167–169; the present occurrence would fit under his classification (2), "Oak and rock as symbols of insensibility, solidity, etc." (p. 167).

202. Cherniss (1944), pp. 439–440, n. 376.

203. For a list of nominations for the giants, see Cornford (1935), p. 231 n. 2. Unfortunately, Cornford provides no references.

204. Taylor (1961), p. 18.

205. The potential significance of this is that Eudoxus seems to have carried on the mathematical work of Theaetetus; see Knorr (1975), pp. 273ff. Of course, it has almost no weight as evidence for the claim that the *Sophist* is here referring to Eudoxus.

206. Aristotle, *Nicomachean Ethics* K 2. 1172b9ff.

207. Barnes (1979), Vol. 2, p. 21 = Barnes (1982), p. 323, also makes this point.

208. The two occurrences of the noun *things* in this translation represent a word in the original (χρήματα).

209. Or, possibly, 'looks' or 'aspects' (ἰδέαι); I follow Vlastos (1950), p. 32, with n. 7 (= Mourelatos [1974], p. 461 with n. 7, Furley and Allen (1975), p. 324 with 342 n. 7) and Schofield (1980a), p. 102 in translating it 'forms' (as we are no longer discussing Plato: see n. 14). In any case, not 'shapes' (so Cornford [1930], p. 28 = Furley and Allen [1975], p. 294, Raven in Kirk and Raven [1957], p. 378 = Kirk, Raven, and Schofield [1983], p. 369), at least, not if the rest of this appendix is right.

210. Simplicius omits part of fr. 4, namely DK ii 34.8–16 and the final sentence. Fränkel (1960), p. 287 n. 1, thinks fr. 4 is a composite of three texts. One might be tempted to go one step further and suppose that ll. 5–8 and ll. 8–16 were originally distinct; l. 8 does come on with "curious abruptness" (Guthrie [1965], p. 314). But the continuity of the fragment in the text Simplicius used is supported not only by the citations in *in Physica* 34.28–35.9 and 157.9–16, as DK note, but also by one in *in De caelo* 609.5–11. (So I do not think the division of the fragment into three in Barnes [1979], Vol. 2, pp. 17, 294–295, n. 5 [= Barnes (1982), pp. 319, 624–625 n. 5], p. can claim to represent Anaxagoras, if it is supposed to.) In any event, the passage just quoted is convenient for my purposes, as it was for those of Cornford (1930), p. 28 = Furley and Allen [1975], p. 294) just because it leaves out the irrelevant lines 8–16.

211. Reading πλήθους in 156.8 with Diels (1882) (and the mss; see also Cornford [1930], p. 28 = Furley and Allen [1975), p. 294 and 320, n. 55) rather than πλῆθος with DK ii 35.2, Schofield (1980a), p. 122. It makes precious little difference: the latter would translate "and seeds unlimited in plurality".

212. Contrast Cornford (1930), p. 29 = Furley and Allen (1975), p. 296.

213. See Cornford (1930), p. 28, n. 3 = Furley and Allen (1975), p. 320, n. 56.

214. Stocks (1930) unaccountably has "earth and fire" here, and this has gone uncorrected in Barnes (1984), Vol. 1, p. 495.

215. Reading μίγματα with Allan (1936) and some mss.

216. 302b3 ἠθροισμένων: Allan (1936) prints ἠθροισμένον with M: "each . . . is collected from all the invisible homoeomers."

217. See Ross (1936), p. 483 ad loc.

218. DK ii 32.12–16.

219. Steven Strange has suggested to me that κατεῖχεν here is a military metaphor, as it is in *Phaedo* 104d1 and d6 (see earlier, p. 19); then there is another small point of contact between the language of Anaxagoras and that of the theory of forms.

220. Although, in fact, the text at this point is just a bit shaky. But nothing indicates that Aristotle's original confined itself to fire and air.

221. *Pace* Cornford (1930), p. 17 with n. 1 and p. 28 (= Furley and Allen [1975), p. 279 with 316 n. 11 and p. 296); Raven, in Kirk and Raven

(1957), p. 383 = Kirk, Raven, and Schofield (1983), p. 373; Guthrie (1965), pp. 292–294. Contrast Barnes (1979), Vol. 2, pp. 24–25 = Barnes (1982), pp. 326–327.

222. Lloyd (1966), p. 246, mentions it but rejects it, as far as I can tell, for two reasons. First, "while the term μοῖρα may perhaps be used of simple portions of substances . . . the term σπέρμα does not appear to have been used either as a synonym for μοῖρα or for the μοῖραι of natural substances." But the hypothesis is that the hot is one seed, the cold another, and so on. Anaxagoras' claim that everything has in it a portion (μοῖρα) of everything means that everything has in it a portion of the hot. Plainly this does not require 'portion' and 'seed' to be synonyms.

Second (246 n. 1), "According to the first part of Fr. 4, the seeds are not *of* all sorts of forms and colours and tastes, they *have* these: as KR [Kirk and Raven (1957)] 380 [= Kirk, Raven, and Schofield (1983), p. 370] point out, then, some at least of the opposites (e.g. bright and dark) are actually ingredients in the seeds." I do not see that the word *having* (ἔχοντα) in fr. 4 has to bear that much weight: it certainly need not mean 'has as an ingredient.'

223. Ross (1924), Vol. 1, p. 132 *ad* 984a14 may have been the last to accept it. It makes fleeting appearances in Schofield (1980a), pp. 121ff., esp. pp. 128–132, and p. 164, n. 38, where it is dismissed as "not incompatible with" the view Schofield himself advocates. I cannot see this, and Schofield does not, as far as I can tell, explain the remark.

224. Guthrie [1965], p. 325.

225. Ibid., p. 300; so also, e.g., Reeve (1981), p. 99.

II. ANCIENT NON-BEINGS

1. Meinong (1904); Meinong (1971), p. 486; translation by I. Levi, D. B. Terrell, and R. M. Chisholm, in Chisholm (1960), p. 79.

2. Meinong (1971), p. 486; Chisholm (1960), p. 79 (translation slightly modified).

3. See, e.g., Parsons (1980), Routley (1980), Lambert (1983).

4. "Das Vorurteil zugunsten des Wirklichen," Meinong (1971), p. 485.

5. The only alternative that seems natural, 'Existentialism,' has become entrenched in a rather different sense.

6. The term also used by Cargile (1979), p. 169 ff.

7. Meinong's own label for his theory.

8. Routley (1980).

9. Cargile (1979), p. xiii, says of Meinongianism, with reference to a formulation like the above, that it "is close to contradictory and is unnecessary." Perhaps it is unnecessary. But when it comes to contradiction, close does not count.

10. i 231. Lines 1–6 are from Proclus, Diehl (1903), i 345.18; lines 3–8 from Simplicius *in Physica*, Diels (1882, 1895), 116.25–117.1.

11. 2.1 κόμισαι δὲ δὺ μῦθον ἀκούσας: alternatively, "and you attend to the story you've heard."

12. 4 'Αληθείηι γὰρ ὀπηδεῖ: in the mss of Simplicius and Proclus this appears as 'Αληθείη γὰρ ὀπηδεῖ, "for truth follows [it]"; 'Αληθείηι is an emendation of Bywater's, universally accepted.

13. See esp. Gorgias *apud* Sextus Empiricus vii. 80 (= DK 82B3, ii 282.5–6). Ebbesen (1986), pp. 115–116, doubts that the example actually occurred in Gorgias, but its absence from the corresponding account in *De Melisso, Xenophane et Gorgia* is not much ground for doubt: the *MXG* is very sketchy.

14. See, e.g., Owen (1960), Mourelatos (1970), pp. 90–93, 94ff., Furth (1971), Gallop (1984), pp. 7ff., Austin (1986), pp. 4–6.

15. See the discussion of the inference pattern 'S is P, ∴ S is' in Dancy (1983), pp. 412–415 (reprint pp. 52–54).

16. The passage is variously excerpted and discussed in texts on the Presocratics. 324b35–325a6, 325a23–325b11, 325b24–33 = DK 67A7; 325a2–6, 13–16, 23–32 = Robinson (1968), pp. 195–196, t10.1; 325a2–13, 23–b5 = Kirk, Raven, and Schofield (1983), pp. 406–408, t545; Furley (1967), pp. 79–81, quotes and translates 324b32–325a12, 325a23–32.

17. See also *Physics* Δ 6. 213b4–14. The claim that there can be no motion without a void is one Aristotle, of course, rejects: Δ 7. 214a28–32.

18. Or 'since it is, all alike' (ἔστι instead of ἐστι): see Owen (1960), pp. 92–93 = p. 62 of the (1975) reprint (this latter pagination appears in the margin of the 1986 reprint).

19. As by Bicknell (1967); see Kirk and Stokes (1960), to which Bicknell is objecting.

20. See Owen (1960), pp. 61ff. of 1975 reprint.

21. i 272.3–8.

22. See Furley (1987), pp. 112–113.

23. There is an unfortunate typographical error in the translation of this in Robinson (1968), p. 196: it should not read 'Those he conceded to be appearances,' but 'Those he conceded to appearances'; that is, he conceded that there really were such things.

24. Reading, in a27, οὔτε with the majority of mss (and Bekker, followed by Williams [1982], p. 27) instead of οὐκ, which appears only in E (followed by DK ii 73.5 and Joachim (1922), pp. 28). The latter text would translate: "[he agrees] with those who establish the one on there not being change without a void, and says that the void [is] not a being and that nothing of being is not a being." This would make a slight difference to the logical relationships among the propositions laid out later; see next note.

25. See n. 24; with the alternative text, (2) and (3) would be more closely related; Leucippus would be conceding (1) to the Eleatics, and adding (according to Joachim [1922], p. 162, still in agreement with the Eleatics) (2) and (3). Perhaps (2) and (3) should then be thought of as alternative ways of saying the same thing. I find this slightly more difficult than the paraphrase I have given in the text.

26. 325a28. Philoponus paraphrases: "each of the beings is strictly a being, but in the being nothing is not a being" (Vitelli [1897], 158.22–23: ἔστιν ἕκαστον τῶν ὄντων κυρίως ὄν, ἐν δὲ τῷ ὄντι οὐδέν ἐστιν οὐκ ὄν). Guthrie (1965), p. 396, thinks that this "suggests . . . that it was to 'father' Parmenides rather than to his followers Zeno and Melissus that Leucippus looked for his arguments." The suggestion, if it were of any significance (which I doubt), would be extremely weak: compare Melissus fr. 7.7, quoted on pp. 66–67.

27. Or by using some other permutation of the words 'is,' 'real,' and 'exist.' Cf., e.g., Joachim (1922), p. 162 *ad* 325a26–32: "the Void exists, though it is not a 'real'"; so also Bailey (1928), pp. 75–76. Furley (1987), p. 120 says: "Leucippus and Democritus denied that the void, being nothing, must be non-existent." Here I am not clear as to the force of 'non-existent.' It may be that Furley is thinking of a way of cutting down on the strangeness of the position that might be derived from Mourelatos (1970), pp. 74ff.; see also Mourelatos (1976), Mourelatos (1979). (But Furley [1973], pp. 11–12, objects to this line, at least for the interpretation of Parmenides.) In fact, I should be sympathetic toward this maneuver: it involves construing the 'is' in these claims elliptically, as I have tried to do in connection with Aristotle in Dancy (1983). But no one has worked it out for Leucippus and Democritus. And I do not think it conflicts with the claims I make here.

28. I here agree with Williams (1982), p. 129. But I do not understand him when he says: "That Leucippus' doctrine is prompted by some dim

awareness of the logical differences between the verb *be* and other verbs and between the noun *vacuum* and other nouns goes without saying."

Barnes (1979), Vol. 2, p. 101 (= Barnes [1982], p. 403) roundly says: "If we are to take seriously the assertion that 'the non-existent exists', we must make it something more than a simple self-contradiction; and the only way of doing that is to posit two different senses for 'exist'." (Asmis [1984], p. 248, approves of this, and ascribes the ambiguity to two different ways in which sense-perception works to show us things.) Sedley (1982), pp. 181–182, finds it unlikely that there are different senses for *exist*, but opts instead (pp. 182–183) for a distinction between two different respects in which the void might be said to exist: Democritus would be telling us that it exists inasmuch as it occupies a place, but as it has nothing in it, "insofar as the occupant is nothing it does not exist" (p. 183). This latter seems to me an equivocation: what is the referent of the pronoun 'it' in 'it does not exist'? (See also Furley [1987], p. 112, n. 10.)

29. = DK 67A6, ii 72.13–17; Kirk, Raven, and Schofield (1983), p. 413, t555; Robinson (1968), p. 196, t10.2.

30. The text in b9, τοῦ κενοῦ τὸ σῶμα, is that of Ross; all the mss have τὸ κενὸν τοῦ σώματος, which is backwards. DK ii 72.16 and Kirk, Raven, and Schofield (1983), p. 413, follow Zeller's emendation, τὸ κενὸν ⟨ἔλαττον⟩ τοῦ σώματος. See Ross (1924), Vol. 1, 139 ad loc for other options.

31. DK 68B156 (= Robinson [1968], p. 197, t10.4); cf. 68A49.

32. The Greek δέν was, I think, simply nonsense: its use in Alcaeus may be as a shortened form for οὐδείς (so LSJ s.v. δείς; but Barnes [1979], Vol. 2, p. 101 with n. 11, p. 303 [= Barnes (1982), p. 403 with n. 11, p. 633], thinks otherwise; Moorhouse (1962) argues that it must mean 'thing,' as in Democritus, but then is unable to say what the Alcaeus-fragment means—which is no argument against his claim). On the Atomists' 'hing,' see Furley (1987), pp. 119–120.

33. Aristotle does not here name the atomists, but it is clear that they are the people in question (cf. Ross [1936], pp. 480–481 ad loc.; Furley [1967], pp. 81–82; Kirk, Raven, and Schofield [1983], p. 409 n. 1).

34. Bailey (1928), pp. 118–119 thinks that Democritus distinguished the negatives οὐκ and μὴ so as to say that whereas the void "was not 'the real' (ὄν), not body, neither was it the 'not-real' (μὴ ὄν), that which does not exist at all, but only 'unreal' (οὐκ ὄν)." The evidence for this is that "Aristotle seems so careful in his use of the negative (οὐ)". This is strange: of the passages cited, only 187a2 characterizes the void as οὐκ ὄν; the rest have μὴ ὄν.

35. DK 68A37 = Robinson (1968), p. 197, t10.3.

36. 246a8 πέτρας καὶ δρῦς: see n. 201 of the first study.

37. 247e3–4 τίθεμαι γὰρ ὅρον ὁρίζειν τὰ ὄντα ὡς ἔστιν οὐκ ἄλλο τι πλὴν δύναμις. According to the apparatus in Burnet (1900–07), *ad* e3, Ast bracketed ὁρίζειν (Burnet follows this, as now do Long and Sedley [1987], Vol. 2, p. 269, t44h.3) and Badham eliminated ὁρίζειν τὰ ὄντα. There is no reason for emendation: the translation here is closer to the second of the two Cornford (1935), p. 234, n. 1, lists as unacceptable, but follows Owen (1970), p. 230 (in n. 14 from p. 229) = Owen (1986), p. 109, n. 13 in taking the understood subject as 'the things that are.'

On the translation of ὁρίζειν as 'delimit,' see later; the translation does not signal any agreement on my part with Cornford and others that we are not here dealing with a definition.

38. The term ὅρος is used of it in 247e3 and 248c4; by itself, this is no guarantee that we should understand the thing as a definition. (On the terms ὅρος, ὁρίζειν, see Runciman [1959], pp. 178–179.) According to Cornford (1935), p. 238, n. 3, "it is a mark, not a definition"; but he gives no reason for this. Runciman (1962), p. 77, agrees with Cornford ("As Cornford rightly points out, it is in any case something more like a symptom than a definition that seems to be meant"), but again offers no reason. Bluck (1975), p. 93, follows suit. But see Owen (1970), p. 230, in n. 14 (from p. 229) = Owen (1986), p. 109, n. 13. No one has given any reason against understanding it as a definition. In *Topics* E 9. 139a4–8, Aristotle envisages someone offering it as a *proprium* of being, but then in Z 7. 146a21–23, he has someone offering it as a definition (ὁρισμός). There is, then, nothing formally in the way of treating it as a definition, and there is not a shred of evidence to the effect that it is not.

39. Whose existence he may have denied: Diogenes Laertius (hereafter DL) x 13 (Long [1964], Vol. 2, p. 500.3–4; Usener (1887), pp. 365.21–366.1 and fr. 232, pp. 173.23–174.1; Arrighetti [1973] [1] 13.4–5 [p. 11].

40. = Long (1964), Vol. 2, 513.15; Usener (1887), p. 6.5–6; Arrighetti (1973), p. [2], 39.9; Long and Sedley (1987), Vol. 1, p. 27, t5A(2); Vol. 2, p. 20, t5A.1–2.

41. = Long (1964), Vol. 2, p. 514.4; Usener (1887), p. 6.16; Arrighetti (1973), [2], 41.1 (p. 39); Long and Sedley (1987), Vol. 1, p. 17 t8A(2); Vol. 2, p. 30, t8A.2.

42. According to Arrighetti (1973), p. 494, the only Epicurean ground. But how does he know that Lucretius i 384–390 (Long and Sedley [1987], Vol. 1, p. 32, t6A(5); Vol. 2, p. 24) does not come from Epicurus? Perhaps he

thinks this is the same argument, as it tells us that a certain motion is not possible without a void. (The argument is to the effect that when two broad, flat bodies are separated, the air cannot fill the space between them instantaneously, so there must be a momentary void at the center as the air rushes toward it.) But it is not. (Nor is it, as far as I can tell, "a proof . . . of the *possibility* of a void, in refutation of those from Melissus onward who had argued that void was a logically incoherent notion," *pace* Sedley, in Long and Sedley (1987), Vol. 1, p. 32. Melissus would hardly have been impressed by an argument for the possibility of a void that presupposed the possibility of motion.)

43. Long (1964), Vol. 2, 513.17–18; Usener (1887), p. 6.8–9; Arrighetti (1973) [2], 40.1–2 (p. 39); Long and Sedley (1987), Vol. 1, p. 27, t5A(2); Vol. 2, p. 20, t5A.3–4. The text just cited follows Long and Arrighetti rather than Usener and Long and Sedley. Hicks (1925), Vol. 2, p. 569, appears to translate Usener's text, but prints (p. 568) a text closer to the other (but he simply drops the words 'ὥσπερ προεῖπον τὸ πρόσθεν' from the end of the preceding clause). Sedley (1982), pp. 183–184 argues for Usener. The point is not of importance here.

44. Long (1964), Vol. 2, p. 513.18–19; Usener (1887), p. 6.9–11; Arrighetti (1973), p. [2], 40.2–4 (p. 39); Long and Sedley (1987), Vol. 1, p. 27, t5A(3); Vol. 2, p. 20 t5A.4–5. There are possibly two distinguishable grounds here: see Sedley (1982), p. 189.

45. Long (1964), Vol. 2, p. 513.21; Usener (1887), p. 6.13; Arrighetti (1973) [2], p. 40.5; Long and Sedley (1987), Vol. 1, p. 28, in t5A(4) ("as completely substantial things"); Vol. 2, p. 20 t5A.7.

46. Long (1964), Vol. 2, pp. 525.19–526.8; Usener (1887), pp. 21.14–22.8; Arrighetti (1973) [2] 66.4–5 (p. 59) and 67.1–9 (p. 61); Long and Sedley (1987), Vol. 1, p. 66, t14A(6); Vol. 65, t5A.28–35.

47. See Sedley (1982), pp. 189–190.

48. Long and Sedley (1987), Vol. 1, p. 28, t5B(8): Vol. 2, p. 21.

49. "fungi = παθεῖν in *Ep. ad Hdt.*, 67" (see above, 526.6): Bailey (1947), Vol. 2, p. 669 *ad* l. 441.

50. Hahm (1977), pp. 11–12, ignores this expansion, and has both the Epicureans and the Stoics accepting the Stranger's gift unmodified.

51. On one account of the matter, the Stoics' acceptance of the definition of 'being' from the *Sophist* is no accident: on this account, the *Sophist* is at this point attacking Antisthenes, who accepts the definition and retains his crude materialism, which he then transmits to the Cynic 'school,' from which

the Stoics got it in turn. See Ueberweg/Praechter p. 162; Bréhier (1962), pp. 6–7; Gould (1970), pp. 108–109. I doubt that this is right.

52. This passage is not in *SVF*.

53. So, e.g., Einarson and De Lacey (1967), p. 242 n. a–b, etc.

54. See Hadot (1969), Goldschmidt (1972).

55. And sometimes the correct translation is more like 'be so', e.g. *Phaedo* 78a10, *Timaeus* 30c2.

56. In *Laws* vi 751e1 and *Philebus* 19a7 it means something like 'undertake,' and, for what it is worth, in *Alcibiades* II 141b2, 3 it means 'promise.'

57. So also Dörrie (1955a), p. 36 n. 130 in Dörrie (1976).

58. Hayduck (1891), p. 83.25 καθ' αὑτὰς ὑφεστάναι.

59. See Dörrie (1976), p. 37.

60. KΔ 22 (Diogenes Laertius x 146: Long [1964], Vol. 2, p. 562.15, Usener [1887], p. 76.5; Arrighetti [1973], p. 129 at 146.5: oddly, not in Arrighetti's index), to which perhaps DL x 32 (Long [1964], Vol. 2, p. 510.4, 5; Usener [1887], p. 105.20, 21; Arrighetti [1973], p. 23 at 32.5–6, 6) and DL x 139 (Long [1964], Vol. 2, p. 559.6; Usener [1887], p. 71.9; Arrighetti [1973], p. 121 at 139.6: part of a gloss) should be added: but these occurrences could easily be paraphrase rather than quotation. (So Dörrie [1955a], p. 41, in Dörrie [1976]: but he does not comment on the occurrence in KΔ 22, which ought to have given him at least as much trouble.)

61. Plutarch, *De Communibus Notitiis adversus Stoicos* 1081f (= Long and Sedley (1987), Vol. 1, p. 305, t51C(5); Vol. 2, p. 302, t51C.16–19) and Stobaeus (*SVF* ii fr. 509 p. 164.26–30, Long and Sedley [1987], Vol. 1, p. 304, t51B(4); Vol. 2, pp. 301–302, t51B.11–15). See Long (1971a), pp. 89–90; Sorabji (1983), pp. 22–26; Long and Sedley (1987), Vol. 1, pp. 307–308; Vol. 2, p. 303 *ad* 16–21.

62. This latter division Plutarch works up with various Platonic materials and hands to Plato himself; in 1115d he says: "To Plato 'not to be' and 'to be not [a] being' seemed to differ extraordinarily; for by the one [the] denial of all being was signified, and by the other [the] otherness of the partakable and what partakes [of it]." This allows him to deny (in Plato's name) being to things here below: these are not beings, which is not to say that they are not (1115d); they are images as opposed to originals (1115ef); they are things that come-to-be, not beings (1115f–1116b). Then, in the passage quoted, he introduces the Stoic distinction between 'beings' and 'somethings' as a more recent

variant of the same distinction. But, as we shall see, he wants to reject the Stoic stuff as nonsense, and this leads him back in the direction of Actualism.

63. *SVF* ii 331 (p. 117); Long and Sedley (1987), Vol. 1, p. 162, t27D; Vol. 2, p. 167, t27D.2–4.

64. Rist (1969), p. 152, n. 6 = Rist (1971), p. 55, n. 6 (to p. 38) cites it as if it did.

65. *SVF* ii 521 (p. 166); Long and Sedley (1987), Vol. 1, p. 305, t51F; Vol. 2, p. 304, t51F.1–6.

66. *SVF* ii 320, p. 115.17–18; cf. *Enneads* vi 1, 28.6–7 = *SVF* ii 319, p. 115.11. See also Anonymous, *Prolegomena* 9.2–4 (Westerink [1962], p. 19).

67. = *SVF* ii 329, p. 117.3–4, 5–6.

68. So also Long (1974), pp. 152–153; cf. Long and Sedley (1987), Vol. 2, p. 269, t44h with n. See also Bréhier (1962), p. 6–7.

69. *Common concept* is a Stoic technical term. For less roughness, see Sandbach (1930); Watson (1966), pp. 24–28; Gould (1970), pp. 60–65; Cherniss (1976), pp. 625–626; Schofield (1980b), pp. 284–289 (which emphasizes the common-sense character of the Stoic 'common concept', and can be misleading in isolation), and the texts and commentary in Long and Sedley (1987), Vol. 1, pp. 236–241; Vol. 2, pp. 238–243.

70. *SVF* ii 525, p. 167.19–20, 24–25. See also (with Cherniss [1976], p. 773, n. g) *CommNot* 1080f (not in *SVF*); Sextus, *Adversus Mathematicos* viii 263 (*SVF* ii 363; Long and Sedley [1987], Vol. 1, p. 272; Vol. 2, p. 269, t45B); Alexander *in De Sensu*, Wendland (1901), p. 73.19–20 (not in *SVF*); DL vii 55 (*SVF* ii 140; Long and Sedley [1987], Vol. 1, p. 197, t33H, Vol. 2, p. 199, t33H.5), Aëtius, *Placita* iv 20,2 (*DG*, 410a5–21; *SVF* ii 387, p. 128.3–11).

71. These brackets frame, not a supplement, but an actual emendation: see text later. The emendation is that of Cherniss (1976), p. 772.

72. Partially quoted in *SVF* i 90, p. 25.36–37; more fully in Long and Sedley (1987), Vol. 1, p. 272, t45A; Vol. 2, p. 269, t45A.4–5.

73. No doubt Cicero is here translating τὸ ποιοῦν καὶ τὸ πάσχον: see, e.g., DL vii 134 (Long [1964], p. 354.8–9 = *SVF* i 85, p. 24.6, Long and Sedley [1987], Vol. 2, p. 265, t45B.1), Aristocles *apud* Eusebius in *SVF* i 98, p. 27.13–14 = Long and Sedley (1987), Vol. 2, p. 270, t46G.2–3.

74. *SVF* i 137, p. 38.10–14.

75. Cleanthes: *SVF* i 518, p. 117.1–6 (Tertullian), 11–14 (Nemesius, but notice that at 117.11 von Arnim has supplied the name *Cleanthes* in the text of Nemesius: cf. Morani (1987), p. 21.6; still, the reference clearly should be to Cleanthes, see 20.14; also in Long and Sedley (1987), Vol. 1, p. 272, t45C, Vol. 2, pp. 269–270). Chrysippus: *SVF* ii 790, p. 219.24–28 = Long and Sedley (1987), Vol. 1, p. 272 t45D; Vol. 2, p. 270 (Morani [1987], p. 22.2–6). To connect this argument with the others, and with the Stranger's gift, we need the idea that to come into contact with or be separated from something is to act or be acted on. It is possible that Chrysippus was operating with a definition for 'body' that simply made contact (or perhaps contactibility) entail body (so, apparently, Hahm [1977], pp. 15–16), but it is equally possible that he was operating with the Stranger's gift and a mediating premise to get the conclusion that only bodies can make contact or be separated from each other. See here Lucretius i 432–442, 449–454, where the same question arises.

76. On this see, e.g., Reesor (1954), pp. 41–42, Reesor (1957), p. 65, Long and Sedley (1987), Vol. 1, p. 172, as well as references below.

77. *SVF* ii 797, p. 220.42–43, 221.1. See also Plutarch, *CommNot* 1084a (*SVF* ii 848, p. 230); Seneca, *Epistulae morales* 106.4–10 (Reynolds [1965], Vol. 2, pp. 445.23–447.8 = *SVF* iii 84, pp. 20.37–21.22; partially quoted later); Stobaeus ii 64.18 (*SVF* iii 305, p. 75). Further references in Cherniss (1976), pp. 854–855, n. d, Hahm (1977), pp. 17–18, 27, n. 45.

78. Reynolds (1965), Vol. 2, p. 445.23; *SVF* iii p. 20.37.

79. 107.9 *deducit*: so Reynolds (1965), p. 447.4, an emendation (for *adducit*) due to Gertz.

80. Reynolds (1965), Vol. 2, p. 447.2–7; *SVF* iii p. 21.17–21.

81. Reynolds (1965), Vol. 2, p. 495.3–6; not in *SVF*.

82. Reynolds (1965), Vol. 2, p. 473.11–14, *SVF* iii 307, p. 75.17–20.

83. Seneca is the only exception. But he has tremendous difficulties with this doctrine; see *Epistulae morales* 117.

84. It is hard for someone with Actualist leanings to keep this straight, as Plutarch shows. In *CommNot* 1074d (SVF ii 335): he first mentions Stoic Meinongianism—time, predicate, sayable, conditional, conjunction are not beings—and then protests—it is absurd to make what is true (a sayable) not be or obtain. But in this protest, he plainly no longer is sticking to Stoic vocabulary: his protest is directly contradicted by his own testimony in *Adversus Colotem* 1116bc (earlier, p. 72).

85. This suggestion is due to Dan Devereux.

86. E.g., Ross (1951), p. 152, "To Speusippus we may refer, in some cases with certainty and in others with high probability, the following passages"; Tarán (1981), p. 341, "If we compare this passage with F 42a, in which he is explicitly named, we can say with certainty that these lines refer to Speusippus." It may be said on Ross' behalf that two of the passages he lists are the ones in which Speusippus is named.

87. Or three: on *Nicomachean Ethics* A 6. 1096b5–7 see later, n. 103.

88. 1028b18–24 is fr. 33a in Lang (1911) (hereafter, = 33aL) and fr. 48 in Isnardi Parente (1980) (hereafter = 48IP); 1026b15–27 is fr. 29a in Tarán (1981) (hereafter, = 29aT).

89. See, e.g., Bonitz (1849), pp. 297–298; Ross (1924), Vol. 2, p. 162 *ad* 1028b16. The ascription of the view to Pythagoreans goes back at least to Asclepius *in Met.*, Hayduck (1888), p. 379.3–4.

90. For what it is worth, pseudo-Alexander says Aristotle is "speaking of Plato and those around him" (Hayduck [1891], p. 462.24: λέγων τόν τε Πλάτωνα καὶ τοὺς περὶ αὐτόν).

Frede and Patzig (1988), Vol. 2, pp. 29–30 argue that pseudo-Alexander's ascription is more likely to be right.

91. As Dan Devereux has pointed out to me, so might the early Aristotle. See Iamblichus' *Protrepticus* 38.10–14, printed in Aristotle, *Protrepticus* fr. 33, pp. 60–61 in Düring (1961) (Ross [1952], p. 32; Ross [1955a], p. 32; Gigon [1987], 304a30–35); *Topics* Z 4. 141b5–12, b19–29. Note also *Metaphysics* B 5. 1002a4–12.

92. These people could in fact be Pythagoreans, given what Aristotle says about Pythagoreans elsewhere (e.g., *Metaphysics* M 6. 1080b16–21, A 6. 987b27–29). So Tarán (1979), pp. 167–168; Tarán (1981), p. 299.

93. "Again, apart from the perceptibles, some think there is nothing of this kind" (ἔτι παρὰ τὰ αἰσθητὰ οἱ μὲν οὐκ οἴονται εἶναι οὐθὲν τοιοῦτον). Despite the gender, "nothing of this kind" must mean "nothing that counts as a substance" (Ross translates "do not think there is anything substantial").

Tarán (1979), p. 168, thinks "nothing of this kind" means "no such thing as surface, line, point, and monad." This seems wrong to me, given the continuation of the sentence: πλείω in b19 has to mean "more than one [substance]" (and it is so taken by Tarán, here and in Tarán [1981], p. 299).

94. b19 πλείω: Ross (1924), Vol. 2, p. 162 ad loc.: "πλείω may mean (1) more numerous than sensible substances (cf. A. 990b4) or (2) of more than one kind." He prefers (1). But it seems clear that (2) is required by the sequel: Plato believes, according to Aristotle, that there are *three* substances,

viz., forms, mathematicals, and perceptibles. (So also Cherniss (1944), n. 118 on p. 200, Tarán (1979), p. 170, n. 16; Frede and Patzig [1988], p. 31 *ad* b19.)

95. Alternatively, 'more so [beings]': Ross (1924), Vol. 2, pp. 162–163 prefers this, and he is followed in this by Tarán (1979), p. 170, n. 16. But this seems to me less likely: the question in b17–18 (quoted earlier) was whether surfaces, lines, etc. were more *substances* than the bodies they bound, and so here the Platonists are nominating candidates with a greater claim to the title *substance*. (I here concur with Frede and Patzig (1988), p. 31 *ad* b19.)

96. Here I concur with Tarán (1979), p. 170, n. 16; Frede and Patzig (1988), pp. 31–32 (although I do not think it is necessary, with Tarán (1979), pp. 167, 169 n. 6, Tarán [1981], pp. 142, 299 n. 84, actually to place a comma after μᾶλλον in b19).

97. 1028b22 ἀπὸ τοῦ ἑνὸς ἀρξάμενος: the translation 'taking off from the one as principle' suggests itself. Aristotle complains about Speusippus' theory, as we shall see, that it does not derive everything else from the One as principle; but the top realm of substances, the numbers, do derive from the One.

98. See n. 94.

99. E.g., *Metaphysics* A 9. 991b29.

100. See n. 97.

101. Nor is anything said in this text that implies that the One is the number one. Tarán (1981) thinks that, put alongside other texts, it does have this implication, but see later.

102. = 34aL, 42aT (for this form of reference, see n. 88). 1072b30–1073a1 = 53IP.

103. There is a passage in the *Nicomachean Ethics* that, if it pertains to Speusippus' metaphysics, is difficult to reconcile with this (cf. n. 87), viz. A 6. 1096b5–7 (= 37aL, 63IP, 47aT): "The Pythagoreans seem to speak more persuasively [sc. than the Platonists] about it [sc. the good], positing the one in the column of goods; and indeed, Speusippus seems to have followed them." I concur with Tarán (1981), p. 348, in finding the explanation offered by Merlan (1960a), pp. 110–111 (followed by Krämer [1963], p. 212, n. 55), that the One is in the column of goods but somehow not therefore strictly speaking good, unpalatable, but I do not understand his own attempt at reconciliation (Tarán [1981], pp. 349–350).

104. Tarán (1981), p. 28: "there is evidence that even in the case of his separately existing magnitudes . . . Speusippus asserted that the 'generation'

of them is only for the sake of knowledge, precisely because there can be no generation of eternally existing realities. If this is true of magnitudes, it must also be true of numbers." Tarán's position is somewhat ambiguous: earlier on p. 28 he makes it sound as if the language of generation is Aristotle's misinterpretation. But he does not say what it was that Aristotle was misinterpreting in that language, and I take it he concedes that talk of generation goes back to Speusippus, but wants to deny that it should be taken seriously.

105. See Vlastos (1939), Vlastos (1965), Tarán (1971), Mohr (1985), pp. 64–66.

106. = 54aL, 94IP, 61T; also in Heinze (1892) as a fragment of Xenocrates: 54a p. 179.24–28 (Isnardi Parente [1981] fr. 153, p. 112).

107. In Heinze (1892) fr. 54, p. 179.31–32; Isnardi Parente (1981) fr. 154, p. 113.

108. See the passages assembled as Xenocrates fr. 54 in Heinze (1892), pp. 179–180; Isnardi Parente (1981) frs. 155–157, pp. 113–114.

109. Brandis (1836), p. 489a9–12 = 54bL, 95IP, 61bT.

110. See Cherniss (1944), p. 423, n. 356, who favors the ascriptions in both cases, and Vlastos (1939) in Allen (1965) p. 383, n. 2 (the original, p. 73 n. 5, does not mention Speusippus), who is more suspicious. Stenzl (1929), p. 1660, and Isnardi Parente (1980), p. 335, accept the ascription to Speusippus without question; Tarán (1981), pp. 383–384 argues for it.

111. In Heinze (1892) fr. 68, p. 187.26, Isnardi Parente (1981) fr. 188, p. 121. For further references see Cherniss (1976), pp. 168–169, n. e, 170, n. a.

112. And it looks as if the same strategy is employed in *Metaphysics* N 4. 1091a23–29.

113. Whether it is a *good* argument is another question. The Xenocratean might respond: "well, in a geometrical construction, you start out with a blank expanse of sand and end up with a complex diagram; the antecedent state of disorder in my creation story is like the undisturbed sand, not like the first stages of the actual construction." But then are the first stages of the creation story compatible with the final outcome? It depends on the story. In the case of Plato's *Timaeus*, I think, there is some friction.

114. = 46L, 36IP, 72T.

115. Reading ταῦτα (Tannery) rather than ταὐτά (Friedlein), with Morrow (1970), p. 64, n. 67; Tarán (1981), p. 167. Lang (1911) reads ταὐτά p. 76.16); Isnardi Parente (1980) prints ταὐτά (p. 83) but translates 'queste' (p. 148).

116. There is a problem over Amphinomus: here he is said to have supposed *theorem* was to be preferred to *problem*, but Proclus later seems to ascribe to him a distinction among types of problems (220.7–12). Bowen (1983), p. 17, thinks Amphinomus went on using the term *problem* despite his reservations; an alternative is that Proclus is describing Amphinomus' position in his own terms.

117. If anybody; the locution 'x and those around him' (οἱ περὶ τινά, or οἱ ἀμφὶ τινά) can mean just 'x' by this time (LSJ *s.v.* περί C I 2). So Tarán (1981), p. 424 n. 239, Bowen (1983), p. 26, n. 14.

118. Archimedes seems to provide a good example of this. In the letter to Dositheus that precedes *On the Sphere and Cylinder*, he says, of the various things he is about to prove (Heiberg and Stamatis [1972] i 2.19–4.2; cf. 4.9–13): "These properties were beforehand present by nature in the figures mentioned, but were unknown by those who have dealt with geometry before us, none of whom has noticed that there is a commensurability of these figures" (ταῦτα δὲ τὰ συμπτώματα τῇ φύσει προυπῆρχεν περὶ τὰ εἰρημένα σχήματα, ἠγνοεῖτο δὲ ὑπὸ τῶν πρὸ ἡμῶν περὶ γεωμετρίαν ἀνεστραμμένων οὐδενὸς αὐτῶν ἐπινενοηκότος, ὅτι τούτων τῶν σχημάτων ἐστὶν συμμετρία). Accordingly, Archimedes frequently speaks of 'finding' lines rather than constructing them (e.g., i 14.4: cf. iii 358, the Index under 'εὑρίσκω'), but also frequently speaks the language of construction (e.g., i 18.21 περιγεγράφθω, 'let' a polygon 'be drawn around' a circle).

119. The question here has to do with how these people regarded constructions, not how in general mathematicians regarded them. Zeuthen (1896) claimed that Euclid, Apollonius, and others so regarded constructions, and this has been orthodoxy (see esp. Niebel [1959], pp. 7, 133–134, et passim) until recently (see Mueller [1981], pp. 14–15; Knorr [1983]). For present purposes, that is neither here nor there (see Knorr [1983], p. 141).

120. So Bowen (1983), pp. 18–21.

121. For this interpretation, see Adam (1902), Vol. 2, p. 118 *ad* 5; Shorey (1935), Vol. 2, pp. 170–171, n. b; Cherniss (1950–51), pp. 423–424 (= Cherniss [1977], pp. 250–251), Bowen (1983), pp. 19, 27, n. 30; and now Burnyeat (1987), pp. 218–219.

122. Which does not mean that Speusippus applied the device to the interpretation of the *Timaeus*.

123. Mueller (1980), p. 16, n. 14 (referring to *in Eucl.* 49.25): "The interpretation and translation of *logos* in the context at hand is very uncertain, I assume that *logoi* correspond to Platonic Forms as discursively understood (by the reason for Proclus) as opposed to those Forms as intuitively grasped

(by intellection for Proclus). There are, then, absolutely simple forms, from which are derived discursive forms, from which in turn are derived images."

124. Where I speak of 'propositions,' Proclus speaks of 'the things that follow from the principles', τὰ ἀπὸ τῶν ἀρχῶν (77.7). He has no single word for 'proposition'; when he is discussing Posidonius (80.21, 22–23, 24), he uses πρότασις in a way that lends itself to the translation 'proposition' (Morrow [1970], p. 66, so translates), but elsewhere he uses it for 'premise' (e.g. 193.18, 194.5, 6, 200.23, so translated by Morrow), and still later it becomes 'enunciation', a part of a Euclidean proposition (203.4, 5, 7, 18, etc., so translated by Morrow). In this last context, he uses 'problems and theorems' for the general term: see 203.1–2 (πᾶν δὲ πρόβλημα καὶ πᾶν θεώρημα). He gives as the 'parts' of a problem or theorem: 'enunciation' (πρότασις), 'exposition' (ἔκθεσις), 'determination' (διορισμός), 'construction' (κατασκευή), 'demonstration' (ἀπόδειξις), and 'conclusion' (συμπέρασμα). In other words, a 'problem or theorem' includes the claim being proved along with all the apparatus used in its proof. This is how I intend 'proposition' here.

It is impossible to tell from Proclus' report what language Speusippus, Amphinomus, and Menaechmus might have used. But the idea seems to be that each mathematical proposition, in this sense of 'proposition', should be regarded as a theorem (according to Speusippus and Amphinomus) or as a problem (according to Menaechmus). Bowen (1983), pp. 13–14, raises the question whether they are talking about what is proved or the argument used to prove it; I think this might be a false dichotomy.

125. So Barnes (1976), p. 285; less flamboyantly, Bowen (1983), pp. 15–16.

126. See Mueller (1980), pp. 15–17.

127. It looks as if the realism of Speusippus-Amphinomus and the constructivism of Menaechmus occasioned a parallel dispute over whether the first principles of mathematics should be called *axioms* (ἀξιώματα) or *postulates* (αἰτήματα), where the latter are fundamental constructions and the former fundamental statements (Proclus *in Eucl.* 181.4–182.4; cf. 47L, 37IP, 74T).

128. So also Morrow (1970), p. 158, n. 7.

129. Barnes (1976) might have availed himself of this passage in trying to show that the position of the 'circular demonstrators' on *Posterior Analytics* A 3 was one of Aristotle's own in an earlier period, but he does not.

130. In which case the reference might have been precisely to *Posterior Analytics* A 3.

131. See here Bowen (1983), p. 16 (and Bowen [1982], pp. 87–88). But Bowen obscures this point when he describes the difference between Speusippus-Amphinomus and Menaechmus by saying that the former "leave the geometer his constructions which are now understood as *rationes cognoscendi* rather than as *rationes essendi*" (Bowen [1983], pp. 16–17); on p. 19 he has Speusippus et al. saying "In short, construction-proofs do not constitute knowledge by producing new existents. So they cannot be construed as existence-proofs or *rationes essendi*; they must like pure deductions be *rationes cognoscendi*, means of discovering the eternally existent." The first of these claims is correct (as a characterization of Speusippus'position); the second does not follow from it, and is in fact false. The construction of the equilateral triangle, for example, would be construed, on this position, precisely as a proof of the (eternal) existence of an equilateral triangle, or as a proof demonstrating what was required for the existence of such a triangle.

132. *Pace* Tarán, who repeatedly (Tarán [1981] pp. 28, 29, 41, 105, 341) tells us that the eternity and separateness of Speusippus' numbers is incompatible with their derivation or generation, and cites Speusippus' reconstrual of the language of construction in mathematics as showing that Speusippus could not have generated his numbers (Tarán [1981], p. 426). (See also Dillon [1984], p. 328.) Tarán frequently resorts to taking talk of 'creation' in connection with Speusippus metaphorically (e.g. Tarán [1981] , pp. 47, 270, 272, 378, n. 190), but he never says what it is metaphorical *for*.

133. Kock fr. 11 = Athenaeus ii 59d–f; Gaiser (1963) nr. 6 (pp. 450–451); Tarán (1981) Testimonium 33 (pp. 127–128); there is a translation in Field (1930), pp. 38–39.

134. Tarán (1981), pp. 220–221 with n. 24, tries to discredit this fragment; what he is mainly concerned to do is support Cherniss's denial that it constitutes evidence for Plato's oral instruction in the Academy (see Cherniss [1945], pp. 62–63 with notes). The comments of Glucker (1978), pp. 163–164, esp. n. 10, p. 164, to which Tarán alludes with apparent disdain, are in fact very well taken. In any case, Cherniss concedes all I am concerned with here: "the parody testifies at most to the notoriety of the method of division and classification practiced by members of the Academy" (Cherniss [1945], p. 63).

135. 5–26L, 123–146IP, 6–27T.

136. ῥαφανίς, γογγυλίς: 23L, 143IP, 24T.

137. θύννος, θυννίς: 12L, 131IP, 13T.

138. This is discussed in Dancy (1981).

139. By Lloyd (1976), pp. 146 et passim.

140. Annas (1976), p. 213, takes Speusippus to have meant to say that goodness "did not apply to mathematical objects but only to items produced 'later.'" So also Tarán (1981), p. 335: "Since numbers and magnitudes are for Speusippus *eternal* and *separate* entities, and since there is no goodness or beauty in their ἀρχαί, there can be none in them either; for there is no development in numbers and magnitudes (as there is in plants or animals)." But the one long fragment we have from Speusippus' *Pythagorean Numbers* ([Iamblichus], *Theologoumena arithmeticae*, De Falco (1975), p. 83.6–23, with [Iamblichus'] introduction, 82.10–83.6 [= 53L, 122IP, 28T]; cited more extensively later, pp. 105–107) is an essay on the perfection or completeness (see τελεστικωτάτην 83.2, παντελέστατον 83.5, τέλειος and τέλειον 83.6, .10, .11, and τέλος 83.20, 84.14, .17, 85.21) of the number ten. Aristotle has Speusippus claiming that it is from indefinite, incomplete things that the more complete arise (1092a13–14, quoted immediately below). So it looks as if the number ten is something complete or perfect that has arisen from the One, which is not. So Speusippus no doubt did think there was beauty, if not goodness, in the number ten, which is something that arises as a result of some sort of 'development': out of the interaction of the One with Plurality. (See pp. 79–85 above on the temporal metaphors here.)

141. 1091a34–b3 is to be found in 34fL, 58IP, 44T; 1091b32–35 in 35aL, 46IP, 45aT; 1092a9 in 34e, 57IP. The most interesting of these is 1091b32–35, as it, together with Λ 10. 1075a34–37 (in 35dL, 46aT; in 66IP some crucial lines are omitted), suggests an argument that might have motivated Speusippus' denial that the One is good: if it is good, its opposite, Plurality, would have to be evil; then all the things generated by these principles would have to partake of some evil.

This may have contributed to Speusippus' adoption of what later will be called the *Principle of Alien Causality*.

142. Ross (1924), Vol. 2, p. 486 ad loc.: "τῶν νῦν τισίν refers, as Λ 7. 1072b31 shows, to the Pythagoreans and Speusippus." The passage appears as fr. 34fL = 58IP = 44T.

143. Krämer (1963), pp. 213–214 wants to see in this, specifically in the 'coming forward' (see προελθούσης in a35) of the nature of the beings, an anticipation of the Neoplatonic procession (πρόοδος) of hypostases out of the One: as if the passage were saying "when the procession of the beings out of the One has got on a little further." On my reading (which is not by any means uniquely determined by the text), it is just a question of when we first get beings: as we shall see, that is when we get numbers.

144. = 34eL, 57IP (1092a9–17), 43T.

145. Not just by Tarán, on whom see below, but by Ross (1924), Vol. 2, p. 489 *ad* 1092a13–15.

146. Lang (1911) p. 69, prints 34eL as if the clause did not come from Speusippus.

147. Tarán (1981), p. 338: "That the clause ὥστε μηδὲ ὄν τι εἶναι τὸ ἓν αὐτό is merely an inference of Aristotle, which need not represent Speusippus' own opinion at all, ought to be clear from the grammar. For this clause is of *intended*, not of actual result. Had εἶναι been an infinitive in indirect statement depending on φήσιν, the negative would have been οὐδέ, not μηδέ." But, first, the rule about the negative in indirect discourse, as is well known, has exceptions (LSJ s.v. μή B5c provides examples with φημί, as does Kühner-Gerth ii 194). Anyway, it does not matter: even if, grammatically speaking, it is Aristotle who is here drawing the conclusion, nothing in the grammar indicates that Speusippus did not draw it.

Tarán's statement (ibid.) that "it is only because they have neglected the syntax of this clause" that scholars have thought Speusippus' one was not a being is a gross exaggeration. Merlan (one of the scholars here slandered), for example, knows perfectly well that the sentence in Aristotle leaves open the possibility that it is Aristotle's own conclusion (see Merlan [1960a], p. 104, which Tarán, curiously, cites explicitly for its neglect of the rigors of Greek grammar). See also Dillon (1984), pp. 326–327 (although there are some things here I should not accept), Burnyeat (1987), p. 238, n. 63.

148. "To be is not the substance of anything; for being is not a kind" (τὸ δ' εἶναι οὐκ οὐσία οὐδενί· οὐ γὰρ γένος τὸ ὄν, *Posterior Analytics* B 7. 92b13–14). This follows from Aristotle's frequently expressed view that "being is said in many ways" (τὸ ὂν λέγεται πολλαχῶς, *Metaphysics* Z 1. 1028a10, etc.: cf. references in Bonitz [1870] 220b38ff.); the connection is explicit in *Eudemian Ethics* A 8. 1217b25–35, and cf. *Metaphysics* I 2. 1054a13–18. A somewhat different argument is provided for the claim in *Metaphysics* B 3. 998b22–28; cf. *Topics* Δ 1. 121a14–19.

149. In an argument at *Metaphysics* Z 6. 1031b4, 9–10, Aristotle ignores the special status he accords to the predicate *being*, but there he is arguing ad hominem (not therefore fallaciously; see Dancy [1975a], pp. 14–17). He cannot be so arguing here; see next paragraph.

150. Tarán (1981), pp. 33–34, 42, 338, Dillon (1984), p. 326; Dillon even thinks that τι is "a touch of sarcasm".

151. Indeed, one of the things Aristotle himself says about non-being is that it *is* non-being, and that this makes it an object of belief (Γ 2. 1003b10, *De interpretatione* 11. 21a32–33).

152. His Actualism is, if I am right, a highly nuanced one; see Dancy (1983), esp. pp. 426–428 (65–67 of the 1986 reprint).

153. On Plato, *Republic* vi 509b2–10, see later.

154. *De communi mathematica scientia liber*. I quote from the edition of Festa (1975); the text may also be found in fr. 72IP and in Tarán (1981) on pp. 90–92.

155. The most famous cases are:

(1) the excerpts from an anonymous writer influenced by and responding to the Sophists of the fifth and fourth centuries B.C. in Iamblichus' *Protrepticus* (printed as DK 89, ii 400–404); see Guthrie (1965), pp. 314–315; Kerferd (1981), pp. 54–55 for brief descriptions, Cole (1961) for more extended discussion; and

(2) Excerpts from Aristotle's lost *Protrepticus* in the same book (the texts are printed as parts of Aristotle, *Protrepticus* frs. 4–15 in Walzer [1934] and Ross [1955a]); see Gadamer (1928) (pp. 167–171 in the 1985 reprint); Düring (1961), pp. 24–29; against the skepticism of Rabinowitz (1957); Berti (1962), pp. 454–458; and Guthrie (1981), pp. 75–78.

There are other cases; see, e.g., Merlan (1960a), p. 148 on excerpts from the *Epinomis* in *Universal Math* vi.

156. Merlan (1960a) Ch. 5.

157. Ibid., p. 120: "Some, perhaps most of it may be a literal quotation from Speusippus."

158. Tarán (1981), p. 107: "The preceding arguments conclusively prove, I trust, that *DCMS* IV cannot go back to Speusippus and also that this text cannot be used as a source for the reconstruction of his thought."

159. See Dillon (1984), Tarrant (1985).

160. Some of the discrepancies Tarán thinks he sees between *Universal Math* and Speusippus have been discussed earlier:

1. According to *Universal Math*, the numbers are derived from the One and Plurality (15.16–17); according to Tarán this is non-Speusippean. See pp. 79–85, and notice that there is no necessity in *Universal Math* iv that the derivation involve anything but causality or ontological priority: 14.23–15.5, 18.17 (perhaps part of Iamblichus' introduction and concluding summary, but showing at least that Iamblichus did not think a temporal process was in question).

2. *Universal Math* has beauty present in mathematical objects (18.5), which Tarán thinks is non-Speusippean (but see n. 140).

Some others will be dealt with in later notes; see, e.g., n. 200 on ὑφεστάναι.

161. ἐν ἀρχῇ; the translation 'principle' is here very odd, but the context dictates it (see appendix).

162. The parallel is noted in Merlan (1960a), pp. 118–119; Krämer (1963) 213; and Tarán (1981), p. 104 (who maintains that it is insignificant: see n. 163).

163. Tarán denies that this is Speusippean: "the Aristotelian testimony shows that Speusippus did not distinguish between beauty and goodness in this sense" (Tarán [1981], p. 105). In fact, the Aristotelian testimony shows nothing of the kind: in discussing Speusippus, Aristotle simply lumps beauty and goodness together as not present in the principles but coming in later, and there is no conflict whatever between this and the preceding quoted text. (See also Dillon [1984], p. 327.)

164. 18.2–3 οὐδέπω ὑπάρχει οὔτε καλὰ οὔτε ἀγαθά: either the author of this passage is using ὑπάρχειν in the way that the Stoics did (see earlier, p. 72), or, more likely, 'ὑπάρχειν,' like 'εἶναι' (see 15.8 and below) can be used of the One in a predicative construction without that conflicting with the One's non-existence.

165. 18.11 προηγουμένως: see LSJ s.v.

166. But Aristotle does not always go this way: cf *Eudemian Ethics* A 8. 1218b4–6 makes it sound as if a variety of goodness can appear among unchanging things, and, in quite a different way, so does *Metaphysics* Λ 7. 1072b1–13. (Here again, I am indebted to Dan Devereux.)

167. The Greek here is a trifle difficult; see note 251.

168. Among those who accept Speusippus' Meinongianism this is a major question; see, e.g., Dodds (1928), p. 140, Merlan (1960a), pp. 104–106, Moreau (1956), p. 1166, Merlan (1960a), pp. 132–133 (partly responding to Moreau), Isnardi Parente (1971a), pp. 123ff., Isnardi Parente (1975).

169. = 48.2–7T; in 62IP. This text is used quite uncritically, it seems to me, by Merlan (1960a), pp. 132–133; see Burkert (1972), pp. 63–64; Tarán (1981), pp. 351–354.

170. = 35aL, 64IP, 45aT, 64IP.

171. The occurrence of ὑπεράνω here does not by itself seem to me much cause for worry (*pace* Isnardi Parente [1971a], pp. 127–128). As with ὑφεστάναι (see n. 200), if Speusippus is at the root of this passage, either the word did not occur in Speusippus, but came to some Neoplatonist's mind in trying to paraphrase Speusippus, or it did occur in Speusippus.

172. E.g., recently, Krämer (1969), pp. 11ff.

173. For a collection of ancient references, see Whittaker (1969), pp. 91–97.

174. On this passage, see Dodds (1928), pp. 136ff., Rist (1962), pp. 389–391, 397–401; Merlan (1967), pp. 91–95, Whittaker (1969), pp. 96–97. (Dodds argues that it means "Moderatus shows that the first one *in Plato's Parmenides* is above being"; this is generally accepted.)

175. Whittaker (1969), pp. 91–92.

176. See Henry and Schwyzer (1964–1982), Vol. 3, p. 357.

177. See also 9.3.52, etc.

178. I find myself here and later at least partly in agreement with White (1979), pp. 180–181.

179. Indeed, Socrates has just been made to say this in 508e3–4 if Adam (1902), Vol. 2, p. 61 is right about the text (he proposes to read γιγνωσκομένην instead of γιγνωσκομένης), and I think he is.

180. And the only other occurrence of the word or phrase in Plato I know of (*Republic* ix 587c1), although it is in a more obscure context, also does not seem to leave room for the idea 'beyond.'

181. This and the following references come from Jackson (1882), p. 137, n. 2, where they are used for a somewhat different purpose.

182. There is a curious passage (called to my attention by Dan Devereux) in Simplicius' commentary on the *De caelo* (Heiberg [1893], p. 485.19–22; Ross [1955a], p. 57, Ross [1952], p. 58): "That Aristotle too thinks there is something above mind and substance is plain from his saying clearly, toward the end of his book *On Prayer*, that god is either mind or something on the far side of mind" (ὅτι γὰρ ἐννοεῖ τι καὶ ὑπὲρ τὸν νοῦν καὶ τὴν οὐσίαν ὁ 'Αριστοτέλης, δῆλός ἐστι πρὸς τοῖς πέρασι τοῦ Περὶ εὐχῆς βιβλίου σαφῶς εἰπών, ὅτι ὁ θεὸς ἢ νοῦς ἐστιν ἢ καὶ ἐπέκεινά τι τοῦ νοῦ). Replace *substance* with *being* again; then Simplicius ascribes to Aristotle the belief that there is something above being.

I imagine what happened was this. Aristotle said in *On Prayer* something like what he also says in *Eudemian Ethics* H 14. 1248a27–29, that the principle or starting point of λόγος is something better than λόγος, a god; Simplicius records this in the citation at the end of his sentence. But this, to Simplicius the Neoplatonist, meant that that something was better than Being: for the Neoplatonists, Mind and Being were the same, the second hypostasis of Plotinus.

Rist (1985) has a more radical suggestion, according to which *On Prayer* never existed, and Simplicius' 'quotation' derives ultimately from the *Eudemian Ethics*. For present purposes it does not matter.

183. There is a sort of appendix tacked on to the end, 155e–157b.

184. The theory in question here is a reconstruction based on *Metaphysics* M 6–8. See Wedberg (1955), pp. 80–84; Annas (1976), pp. 13–21 (a crucial line is missing at the bottom of p. 17: perhaps 'make up 2 but cannot be combined with other units to'), her notes on M 6–8, and Annas (1975).

The classic discussion of the theory is Cook Wilson (1904), esp. 248a–255a, but this is responsible for a widely held dogma to the effect that Plato's formal numbers were numerical properties and not collections of units: see Ross (1924), Vol. 2, p. 427; Ross (1951), pp. 180–182, Cherniss (1945), pp. 33–37; Findlay (1974), pp. 444–445; Tarán (1981), pp. 13–14, n. 65. (For dissent, see Mueller [1986], pp. 111–115, Burnyeat [1987], pp. 234–238.) The dogma derives from an interpretation of the theory of forms in the dialogues according to which the forms are properties; so if there are forms for numbers, these too must be properties. This is, I think, an erroneous interpretation of the dialogues, and apart from them, there is not the slightest evidence in favor of the dogma. Indeed, Cherniss (p. 37) and Tarán (pp. 15–16) have to add the curious twist that no one among Aristotle, Speusippus, or Xenocrates understood Plato's theory; so in principle there can be no evidence for the dogma apart from the dialogues.

Tarán, in addition, takes from Kneale and Kneale (1962), p. 392, the idea that Speusippus' fluctuation between singular and plural in referring to the number ten, in the fragment from *Pythagorean Numbers* (see the plurals τὰ δέκα, etc., in [Iamblichus], *Theologoumena arithmeticae* 83.6 [4L.18, 28T.15] et passim as opposed to the singulars ὁ δέκα, etc. in 83.16 [4L.27, 28T.22–23] et passim) shows that "he failed to grasp the notion that numbers are not aggregates of units" (Tarán [1981], p. 16, n. 78). But then Plato's constant use of the plural (e.g., *Cratylus* 432a10, *Phaedo* 96e2, 101b4, 105a7, *Laws* v 737e6–7) ought to show that he, too, had failed to grasp this.

On the Greek conception of numbers, see Klein (1934), pp. 53–64 (in Klein [1968], pp. 46–60) and Fowler (1987), pp. 14–16.

185. Annas ([1975], p. 149, with n. 9; [1976], p. 19) adds *Metaphysics* Z 2. 1028b18–21 (quoted earlier, p. 78) to the list, but this is a mistake: 1028b19 is not confined to the mathematicals.

186. Apart from the texts about to be quoted, see *Metaphysics* Λ 1. 1069a36 = 42a4L = 31.5–6T, in 73IP; M 1. 1076a21–22 = 42b.3–4L = 32.4–5, in 74IP; M 6. 1080b14–16 = 42c.4–5 = 33.3–5T, in 75IP; M 8. 1083a28 = 42d.9L = 34.7–8T, in 76IP; N 2. 1090a7–10 = 43.3–6L = 36.5–7T, (quoted later); N 3. 1090a25–26 = 43.13–14L = 36.19–20T (these last two are in 80IP).

187. = 42eL, 77IP, 35.2–5T.

188. = 42d1–5L = 34.1–4T, in 76IP.

189. = 33eL, 52IP, 30T.

190. Tarán (1981), p. 305: "This fragment specifically states that Speusippus' first οὐσία is mathematical number." But it does not state that the One is an οὐσία, or a number.

191. The only dissenting voice is that of [Alexander], *Metaphysics*, Hayduck (1891), p. 721.11, who thinks Aristotle is talking about "the Pythagoreans, or even Plato" (οἱ Πυθαγόρειοι, φησίν, ἢ καὶ Πλάτων). Tarán (1981), p. 304, n. 91, says "he understands little or nothing of Speusippus," and this seems right. If [Alexander] is in fact the twelfth-century commentator Michael of Ephesus, as seems likely (see Hayduck [1891], p. v, 440 apparatus *ad* 1–2), it is not very surprising that he has lost contact with Speusippus.

192. Theophrastus' *Metaphysics* III 6b5–6 (= 51L, 87IP, 59T) lumps "Speusippus and those around him" (οἱ περὶ Σπεύσιππον) together with various unnamed others and contrasts them with Xenocrates; "for the latter places all [things] about the universe, alike perceptibles, intelligibles, mathematicals, and even divine [things] as" well (6b7–9 οὗτος γὰρ ἅπαντά πως περιτίθησιν περὶ τὸν κόσμον, ὁμοίως αἰσθητὰ καὶ νοητὰ καὶ μαθηματικὰ καὶ ἔτι δὴ τὰ θεῖα), whereas the former "stop once having gone up to a certain point" (6a23–24 μέχρι τινὸς ἐλθόντες καταπαύονται). Ross and Fobes (1929), p. 56 *ad* 5 take this as an "echo" of Aristotle's 'episodic' criticism, but it rather sounds as if Theophrastus is saying only that Speusippus and the others did not go all the way to the bottom of the universe in their derivations: "once having generated numbers, planes, and bodies [i.e., presumably, geometrical solids] they leave aside just about [all] the others" (6a25–27 τοὺς γὰρ ἀριθμοὺς γεννήσαντες καὶ τὰ ἐπίπεδα καὶ τὰ σώματα σχεδὸν τἆλλα παραλείπουσιν). So Isnardi Parente (1971b), p. 61; Isnardi Parente (1980), p. 324; Tarán (1981), p. 382. Still, Theophrastus does echo the 'episodic' criticism in *Metaphysics* I (so also Tarán [1981], p. 321, n. 122): in 4a9–13 he describes a view according to which there is no 'community' (κοινωνία) between the intelligible entities and those of nature, and in 4a13–14 he characterizes the universe on this view as 'episodic' (ἐπεισοδιῶδες), so perhaps for Theophrastus the two criticisms go together.

If 4a13–14 is an echo of the 'episodic' criticism of Speusippus, the chances are that the view criticized in 4a18–b5, according to which the only intelligible entities are the mathematical ones (a18–19) and number is first and most dominant (b4–5) is Speusippus' view and not also Xenocrates' (as Ross and Fobes [1929], p. 42, suggest). (Dan Devereux first called my attention to the correspondence between this passage and what we hear of Speusippus.)

193. 1090b5–13 = 44L, 50T; b5–7 = 81IP.

194. = 50L, 86IP, 37T.

195. But not the only one; cf., e.g.,

(1) The argument at *Metaphysics* A 9. 990b22–991a8 = M 4. 1079a19–b3 (there is nothing in A to correspond to b3–11); on this, Owen (1968), p. 122 = Owen (1986), pp. 235–236; Vlastos (1973b); Annas (1977).

(2) The argument alluded to at *Metaphysics* A 9. 990b15–17 = M 4. 1079a11–13 and preserved by Alexander from *On Ideas*, Hayduck (1891), 82.11–83.17, 83.22–30 (in fr. 3, Ross [1955a], pp. 124–125, Ross [1952], pp. 127–128; omitted in Rose [1886]); on this, see Owen (1957); Leszl (1975), pp. 185–237; Barford (1976); Rowe (1979).

196. The literature on this argument is now enormous. The interpretation that follows is my own, but owes obvious debts to Vlastos (1954), Strang (1963), and Cohen (1971).

197. 84.21–85.12 is part of fr. 4 in Ross (1952), p. 129; Ross (1955a), p. 126; 84.21–85.5, 85.9–12 are part of Rose (1886) fr. 188, p. 151.

198. 84.22 τινων πλειόνων: Barnes and Lawrence (1984), p. 2438, translate "of several particulars," but that would restrict the assumption to particulars and block the extension to forms from the outset.

199. 84.25 τῶν καθ' ἕκαστα: see n. 198, and notice that this is not the same phrase as the one in question there. Here the more general premise, which is not restricted to particulars, is applied to particulars.

200. 84.28 κατ' ἰδίαν ὑφεστώς: see p. 72.

Tarán (1981), pp. 102–103, bases another argument against the Speusippean origin of *Universal Math* iv on the occurrence of ὑφίσταται at 18.4. He takes over from Dörrie the idea that ὑφίστασθαι = 'exist,' 'subsist' is late; Dörrie (1955b) had used this to argue that the end of *Universal Math* iv (Festa [1975], p. 18.1–12) was not from Speusippus, although the rest was (see p. 277 of Dörrie [1976]). Tarán argues that the passage cannot be separated from the rest of the chapter, and thus the occurrence of ὑφίσταται shows that the whole chapter cannot be from Speusippus.

Dillon (1984), p. 330, trying to save the chapter for Speusippus (with which endeavor I am in sympathy: see pp. 89 ff.), says "the use of ὑφίσταται to mean 'subsist' . . . [does not] seem to me impossibly un-Speusippean." But even if the ultimate source for the chapter is Speusippus, we need not suppose it a verbatim extract. Still, Dillon is correct to point out the presence of the word in the requisite sense in Epicurus (but he provides no references at all for this), so perhaps this usage does go back as far as the Academy. On balance, I am inclined to think it does.

In any case, there is plainly no argument against the Speusippean origin of *Universal Math* iv to be based on the occurrence of ὑφίσταται in 18.4. If we suppose that Alexander in 83.25 and 84.28 is paraphrasing Aristotle, that shows how easily ὑφίστασθαι could creep into paraphrases among later commentators; the same would of course be true of Iamblichus. If we suppose that the vocabulary of 83.25 and 84.28 goes back to Aristotle, then the word could easily be Academic; and Iamblichus could be quoting Speusippus.

201. In 85.1, Harlfinger (1975) prints παρά τε τὸν καθ' ἕκαστα ('apart from the [man] among the particulars'), from a manuscript not reported in Hayduck (1891). Perhaps this is right; it does not matter for the argument, as far as I can tell.

202. The latter two labels go back to Vlastos (1954), pp. 324, 325 (= Allen [1965], pp. 236, 237), where the two subclauses are stated as independent assumptions. The advantage of putting them as subclauses is that we avoid the outright contradiction that results from:

(SP*) The form F is itself F.
(NI*) If anything is F, it is not the same as the F.

This contradiction exercised Vlastos (1954), pp. 325ff. (= Allen [1965], pp. 237ff.), because it seemed to render the regress superfluous. It also confused Cherniss, who seems to have supposed that an argument with contradictory premises had to be invalid (Cherniss [1957], p. 255 = Allen [1965], p. 368, Cherniss [1977], p. 328): he fails to consider that it is a reductio ad absurdum argument that he is dealing with.

But the preceding formulation involves no contradiction and develops into a regress nicely. (See Cohen [1971], p. 467, for a rather more complicated way of doing this that is, I think, equivalent to the above).

Code (1985), p. 106, would no doubt protest against my use of the label *Self-Predication* here, and it is true that nothing in the argument requires anything to be predicated of *itself*. But the label seems to me useful as long as it does not mislead.

203. Unless Philippson (1936) is right in supposing that *On Ideas* preceded it, which I doubt (see n. 82 of the first study). But neither chronology for the two publications entails anything about who invented the argument.

204. Vlastos (1954), pp. 320–329 = Allen (1965), pp. 232–241. Curiously, Vlastos denied that Aristotle had anticipated him; see Vlastos (1954), p. 339, n. 36 = Allen (1965), n. 3 on pp. 250–251, and later, for somewhat different reasons, denied it again (Vlastos [1969b], p. 300, n. 35 = Vlastos [1973a], pp. 350–351, n. 36). I think he was wrong both times; see Fine (1982a), p. 167, n. 16.

205. So, e.g., Taylor (1915–16), pp. 44–45 in Taylor (1934a); Cherniss (1932), pp. 135–136 (pp. 294–295 in Cherniss [1977]); Vlastos (1954), p. 319 (= Allen [1965], p. 232); Owen (1953), pp. 83–84 (= Allen [1965], p. 320; Owen [1986], p. 70); Cherniss (1957), pp. 252ff. (= Allen [1965], p. 364ff.; Cherniss [1977], pp. 325ff.), Teloh and Louzecky (1972), pp. 89–92, etc.

206. An assumption sometimes challenged; e.g., Annas (1981), pp. 217, 235–236; Wieland (1982), pp. 125–150, esp. pp. 148–150. Wieland, it seems to me, has gone too far.

207. It is the plurality that is bothersome to the theory; the infinity of that plurality is merely frosting on the cake. See also Mates (1979), p. 212; Curd (1986); Miller (1986), pp. 47–48.

208. Owen (1965b), pp. 133–139 (= Strawson [1968] 156–163, Barnes et al. [1975], pp. 21–26; Owen [1986], pp. 207–211). This has been widely challenged: see Kung (1981), pp. 227–232; Fine (1982b); Code (1985), pp. 101–110; and Lewis (1985), pp. 134–136. I am still inclined to think there is something in it, but that would take us far afield.

209. See Dancy (1975b), pp. 349–351, 361–372.

210. Nothing that I know of in Aristotle explains why this regress is acceptable whereas other regresses of movers are not. The ones that are not are, in a sense, spatial, whereas this one is temporal, and Aristotle does not treat space and time on a par with each other. But, of course, more needs to be said than that. For the echoes of this problem in Thomas Aquinas, the most illuminating discussion is Brown (1966), and this may shed some light on Aristotle.

211. = 4.11–17L, 28.10–14; in 122IP (on Isnardi Parente [1980], p. 114). The passage is also to be found, with an English translation, in Thomas (1939), pp. 76–77.

212. 83.2 τελεστικωτάτην; 'most initiative' Thomas (1939), p. 77. There is a deliberate play on two senses of τελεστικός: 'capable of completing' and 'connected with mystic rites' (see LSJ *s.v.*). Speusippus is about to show that the number 10 is a 'complete' or 'perfect' number, in a special sense (see later).

213. 83.5 παντελέστατον: alternatively, 'all-perfect.'

214. There is much disagreement as to whether this reference to Philolaus comes from Speusippus: see, e.g., E. Frank (1923), pp. 140–141 (Speusippus referred to Philolaus, but in fact was making it up); Burkert (1972), p. 246 with n. 40 ("It is unlikely, considering the way it is phrased,

that this reference to Philolaus comes from Speusippus himself"); Tarán (1981), pp. 260–261 (the fact that the words are not Speusippus' own does not show that Speusippus did not refer to Philolaus); Huffman (1988), p. 1 (the reference "is in all probability of neo-Pythagorean origin," but Huffman is in error in citing Tarán in support of this). Tarán's view is clearly right.

215. This is not among the more hotly contested fragments; see Burkert (1972), pp. 264–265. The term μορφαί also appears here, and Barnes (1979), Vol. 2, p. 88 (= Barnes [1982], p. 390) takes these to be the numbers themselves.

216. There is some question about the genuineness of this; see Burkert (1972) 379–380, n. 46. But the correspondence Burkert notes between 432.7–8 does not seem to me as suspicious as it does to him. The fragment speaks of two primary forms of being (τὰ τῶ ὄντος πρώτιστα δύο εἴδεα); these are number (ἀριθμός) and magnitude (μέγεθος) according to DK (i 432 in translation, and iii 142b9–10), plurality (πλῆθος) and magnitude (μέγεθος) according to Burkert (following Nicomachus, *Introductio arithmeticae* ii 5).

217. This one is rejected outright by Burkert (1972), pp. 220–221, n. 14, partly because of "the telltale εἰδέων πραγματεία." But I cannot see what the word εἴδη here means; DK i 438 translates "Formen [*Prinzipien*? s. 44B5]"; it is not at all clear that Platonic forms are in question.

218. Iamblichus says (*in Nicomachi arithmeticam introductionem* 10.20–22, repeated in substance by Syrianus, *in Met.* 123.7–9 and 142.21–23, coupled in all three places with a saying attributed to Philolaus): "The disciples around Hippasus [i.e., Hippasus and the Pythagoreans who sided with him] said number [was the] first paradigm of cosmos-making, and again [that number was] the discriminating instrument of [the] cosmos-fashioning god" (οἱ δὲ περὶ Ἵππασον ἀκουσματικοὶ ἀριθμὸν εἶπον παράδειγμα πρῶτον κοσμοποιίας, καὶ πάλιν κριτικὸν κοσμουργοῦ θεοῦ ὄργανον). (This passage is printed in DK 18.11, i 109.27–29.) In the absence of any parallel for this vocabulary this early, Iamblichus is not to be trusted. See also Burkert (1972), pp. 248–249 with 249 n. 50.

219. Annas (1976), p. 186: "Aristotle is not necessarily claiming that Speusippus said nothing on the subject, merely that he has no independent rationale for his theory." See also Mueller (1987), p. 254. I find it hard to read the passage this way.

220. See Annas (1976), p. 11; she also lists, on the other side, *Laws* vii 818c3–6 (the translation of Taylor (1934b), p. 205, reprinted in Hamilton and Cairns (1961), p. 1388, should be altered here: for "could not tell three from two" read "could not tell one, two, and three apart") and *Sophist* 238b2–3.

221. See Heath (1921), Vol. 1, p. 69; Heath (1926), Vol. 2, pp. 279–280; Mueller (1981), p. 58 with n. 1 and 2, p. 113.

222. Cherniss (1944), p. 303, n. 202; and Tarán (1981), pp. 19–20, 276–277, 277–278, 279–280 have correctly pointed this out.

223. = 4.22–25L, 28.18–21T; on Isnardi Parente (1980), p. 114.

224. 4.25–32L, 28.21–27T; Isnardi Parente (1980), pp. 114–115.

225. 4.32–37L, 28.27–31T; Isnardi Parente (1980), p. 115.

226. See Heath (1921), Vol. 1, p. 318; at the end of [Iamblichus'] extract, Thomas (1939), p. 83, n. b, writes: "The abrupt end suggests that the passage went on in this strain for some time; but the historian of mathematics need not feel much disappointment." This is perhaps a bit extreme.

227. It is not the sense given to the notion of a 'perfect number' by Euclid vii def. 23 (vii 22 in Heath [1926]), according to which a perfect number is the sum of its proper divisors: 6, 28, and 496 are the first three, and 10 is not a perfect number in this sense at all. See also Heath (1926), Vol. 2, pp. 293–294 on the notion of a perfect number (but he does not mention the present passage). Plato, *Republic* viii 546b4 mentions a perfect number, but (*pace* LSJ *s.v.* τέλειος, I.5b, p. 1770a) he need not mean what Euclid does: see Adam (1902), Vol. 2, pp. 289–290.

According to Burkert (1972), p. 431: "there is no trace, before Aristotle, of 'perfect' numbers in the sense of Euclid. For the Pythagoreans, as Aristotle knew them, the number 10 is τέλειον, and neither 6 nor 28 plays any role." This makes it sound as if there might be a trace *in* Aristotle of the Euclidean notion of a perfect number, but Burkert cites none. On p. 435 he says: "it is probable on other grounds that the Euclidean idea of a 'perfect number' was first developed in the Academy (above, nn. 27–28)." But there is nothing in the text or in those notes (on p. 431) that makes it even plausible.

228. E. Frank (1923), p. 247, opts for the latter. It may be that an early conception of number had the number sequence beginning with 3; see Heath (1921), Vol. 1, pp. 70–71, on the definition of *even* in Nicomachus I vii 4 (Hoche [1866], pp. 13.20–14.2).

229. This is a strange conception of prime numbers and, in particular, is not that of Euclid vii defs. 12 and 14 (11 and 13 in Heath [1926], Vol. 2, p. 278). (*Pace* Tarán [1981], p. 278, who says: "Speusippus' conception of composite number is the same as that of Euclid, *Elem.*, VII, Def. 14". According to that definition, if 1 is a prime number, every number is composite.)

230. Which is also quite strange, because, if 1 is a submultiple, 2 is a multiple, as is every other number in the sequence. See Thomas (1939), p. 79, n. c.

231. So, unlike Mueller (1987), p. 254, I am disinclined to accept the suggestion in Annas (1976), p. 186, that "one can suspect that perhaps Speusippus did not claim to derive *units* from one and plurality, only *numbers*." But Mueller (1986), pp. 115–116 is clearly right that there is a plurality of instances of each mathematical object (*pace* Tarán [1981], p. 23, n. 120).

232. And, if this is right, it counts in some measure against the interesting conjecture in Mueller (1987), pp. 254–255: "For Speusippus . . . starting from the one is just starting from the units which make up numbers. If this interpretation is correct, Speusippus' one would be more like a material than a formal principle, and multiplicity would be something like a set-forming operation which brings units together to form numbers." (Cf. Mueller [1986], p. 120.)

233. Rabinowitz (1957), p. 88; cf. Merlan (1960a), pp. 130–131.

234. 36T, 80IP, first half; 1090a2–4, 7–16, 25–31, 35-b5 = 43L.

235. 1090a11–12 οὐθενὸς γὰρ οὔτε φησὶν ὁ λέγων αὐτὸν εἶναι: Jaeger (1957) supplies ⟨αἴτιον⟩ after αὐτόν; Ross (1924), Vol. 2, p. 480 *ad* 11 says "οὐθενός depends on αἴτιον, which can be supplied from αἴτιος l. 13."

236. See here Tarrant (1974), although much of this is extremely speculative, even by the standards customary in dealing with Speusippus.

237. But it can be made to look, formally speaking, quite close to the claim that is implausible. (PAC) could be formalized as

$$(x)[(y)(Fy \rightarrow C[x,Fy]) \rightarrow \neg Fx],$$

which looks alarmingly close to

$$(x)(y)[Fy \rightarrow (C[x,Fy] \rightarrow \neg Fx)],$$

which is false. It might clarify matters to write the latter, false, principle as

$$(x)[(\exists y)(Fy \; \& \; C[x,Fy]) \rightarrow \neg Fx].$$

238. Formally: suppose there is something x that causes everything that is F to be F, and that nothing can cause itself to be F:

(1)	$(y)(Fy \rightarrow C[x,Fy])$	P
(2)	$(x)\neg C[x,Fx]$	P

then we can deduce:

(3)	$Fx \rightarrow C[x,Fx]$	(1) X UI
(4)	$\neg C[x,Fx]$	(2) X UI
(5)	$\neg Fx$	(4), (3)

239. *Nicomachean Ethics* B 6. 1106a33–b5.

240. Once more, under the proviso that nothing can cause itself to be. Some defenders of the ontological argument for the existence of God may construe it as establishing that God is the cause of his own existence, e.g., perhaps, Spinoza.

241. Merlan (1960a), pp. 96–140.

242. I have altered the punctuation at one point, mentioned in the notes to the translation.

243. I do not know whether it has ever been translated into English before. Isnardi Parente (1980), pp. 160–162, 168–169 has it in Italian.

244. The previous chapter discussed principles common to all the mathematical sciences.

245. 14.25–26 συναναιρεῖ μὲν γὰρ οὐ συναναιρεῖται δέ: Aristotelian terminology: cf. *Topics* Z 4. 141b28, Δ 2. 123a15, *Metaphysics* K 1. 1059b30–31, *Categories* 7. 7b38, Ammonius *in Categorias* 74.6, 19 (LSJ). The science of numbers, we shall learn (cf. 17.25–29), is prior to that of geometrical magnitudes (hereafter, *geometricals*); according to the present claim, that would mean that the 'abolition' of numbers would require that of geometricals along with them, but not conversely.

246. 14.26 συνεπιφέρει μὲν οὐ συνεπιφέρεται δέ: Aristotelian terminology again: cf. *Topics* Z 6. 144b17, H 2. 157b23, *Prior Analytics* A 46. 52b7 (LSJ). But this is carelessly written: it should, I imagine, read "and they are coimported without coimporting": geometricals carry numbers with them, but numbers do not carry geometricals; where there are magnitudes there are numbers, but not conversely.

Steven Strange comments: "I'm inclined to attribute the carelessness here to a scribe, not to the divine Iamblichus, and to transpose the offending words." I suspect he is right.

247. The fact that geometricals depend for their existence on numbers makes numbers outrank geometricals; the fact that geometricals carry numbers with them shows that they are more complex than numbers.

248. 14.18–15.5 is taken by Merlan (1960a), p. 98, as "obviously a kind of introduction"; he does not ascribe this to Speusippus.

249. 15.7–10: see pp. 90–91, 97, 98 ff. earlier.

250. *Plurality*, πλῆθος, is the term Speusippus apparently used for his second principle: see Ross (1924), Vol. 1, p. lviii, Vol. 2, p. 455 *ad* 9; Annas (1976), p. 74; Tarán (1981), pp. 324–325. The passages on which this claim is based are *Metaphysics* N 4. 1091b30–35, 1091a29-b1, Λ 7. 1072b30–34, N 1. 1087b4–9, M 9. 1085b4–12, and the commentaries of [Alexander] and

Syrianus on 1091b30 (Hayduck [1891], 823.12, and Kroll (1902), 184.22, respectively).

251. 15.11–12 ἣν καὶ διαίρεσιν οἷόν τ' εἶναι καθ' αὑτὸ παρέχεσθαι. The gender makes the attachment of καθ' αὑτό difficult; Festa: "καθ' αὑτὴν conieceram." But I imagine it is attracted to the neuter οἷον.

252. 15.13–14 προσηκόντως εἰς δύναμιν παραδεικνύντες: alternatively, "making a comparison as appropriately as possible."

253. 15.17 πιθανῆς ἀνάγκης: πιθανός more commonly means 'persuasive', but if the author is trying to tie into the persuasion of necessity by reason in Plato, *Timaeus* 47e–48a (a suggestion of Strange's), it should bear the passive sense here (which LSJ find in Aristophanes and Plato himself).

254. I.e., the principle of plurality.

255. 15.19 μέγεθος: as often, this word is hard to translate; sometimes the sense required is 'largeness': cf. the argument of 15.24–29.

For (alleged) paraphrases of 15.17–20, see Merlan (1960a), p. 98; Rabinowitz (1957), pp. 85–86; Dillon (1984), p. 14; Tarán (1981), pp. 94–95. No one is prepared to offer a translation.

256. In 15.23–25, apparently Tarán (1981), p. 96 with n. 431, takes καθ' ἑαυτό with κακὸν κτλ.: "it is by itself neither evil nor ugly," he paraphrases. I cannot see how he gets this from the Greek. But it is true that there is something a little devious here.

At first sight, the supposition that is to be shown wrong is that the principle of plurality (hereafter, just *Plurality*) is bad (or ugly). What we know of Plurality is that what it is, by virtue of itself, is the cause of division and magnitude (largeness: see n. 255). But the arguments that follow are against a supposition to the effect that Plurality is *all* bad or ugly; that it is in *no way* admirable or praiseworthy. Perhaps, the supposition actually has the form: things are bad just inasmuch as they are plural; plurality is what badness *is*; Plurality is bad, just because it pluralizes. And perhaps this is forced, the author thinks, even by the bare supposition that Plurality is bad: because the One and Plurality are the first principles in the universe, there is nothing to appeal to by way of explaining the truth of 'Plurality is bad' except Plurality itself (certainly we cannot nominate the One for that office); so 'Plurality is bad' commits you to 'Plurality is bad just because it pluralizes'.

257. 15.27–28 μεγαλοπρεποῦς: an illustration of the interweaving of the large with a quality (so Merlan [1960a], p. 99); see next note.

258. Here Merlan (1960a), pp. 112–113, cites *Nicomachean Ethics* Δ 2. 1122a21–23: "in these [*sc.* heavy expenses] [magnificence] exceeds liberality in largeness. For just as the name itself suggests, it is heavy expenditure

fitting in its largeness." (ἐν τούτοις δ' ὑπερέχει τῆς ἐλευθηριότητος μεγέθει. καθάπερ γὰρ τοὔνομα αὐτὸ ὑποσημαίνει, ἐν μεγέθει πρέπουσα δαπάνη ἐστίν). Merlan thinks Aristotle here speaks of magnificence as liberality *plus* largeness, and that the author of *Universal Math* iv might have meant to say this. He says: "it may be that *Isc* [*Universal Math* iv] expressed itself elliptically: as if somebody wanted to write 'the great coupled with a certain quality becomes the reason of the difference between magnificence and liberality' but omitted the words 'the difference between.'" I agree with Tarán (1981), p. 96, n. 432, that "this interpretation . . . cannot be got out from the text," but so does Merlan. At any rate, the author is saying that magnificence can be treated as largeness connected with a certain quality, so largeness (= magnitude under a different translation: see n. 255) cannot be all bad.

259. 16.3–4 καλῶν τινων ἐν τοῖς ἀριθμοῖς: or just 'certain beautiful [ones] among the numbers'; i.e., certain beautiful numbers, such as, no doubt, the number 10. (Strange finds this alternative translation quite implausible.)

260. The One is to be praised as the source of beautiful things such as the number 10, or as the source of the beautiful features of the number 10 (which does not make the One beautiful); Plurality, which 'receives' this, cannot then be all bad; so it cannot be *the* bad. See the next note.

261. See n. 256; here is where it is most clear that the author has gone from the supposition (for the purposes of a reductio) that Plurality is bad (or ugly) in 15.18–19 to the claim that it is *the* bad (or the ugly). For he is now saying that if Plurality is receptive of the One, it is receptive of something praiseworthy, and so cannot itself be *altogether* blameworthy, and that this shows the supposition wrong.

262. Dillon (1984), p. 14: causing plurality "is a value-free activity"; Tarán (1981), p. 96, "and the implication is that it is not good or beautiful either." But the implication, if it is there, is not one the author makes explicit at this point. He makes the point later, 18.1–12, but it is not clear that the arguments for it are the present ones.

263. 16.12 ἐν ἀρχῇ: what this means is "in [the] beginning," and ordinarily it would be so translated; but the author intends us to hear the connection between this phrase and the term ἀρχή immediately preceding (16.10), 'principle.'

264. εἰκότως: 'reasonably' is the more normal translation, but it can be misleading. Tarán (1981), p. 98, n. 439, apparently construes the text to mean that the numbers are 'reasonably indefinite,' and explains this as referring to the fact that they are only indefinite in one direction.

265. Adopting the punctuation and construction of 16.17 Tarán (1981), p. 98, n. 439 says he got from Cherniss.

266. 16.18 παραλαβοῦσα: there is no object expressed in the Greek.

267. The 'first receptacle,' which is Plurality, or magnitude, once it has 'received' the One, 'stamps out' the 'form'—here 'species' would do—of numbers; that is, the One and Plurality generate the numbers. The numbers are, as you might expect, unlimited; that is, given their derivation from Plurality or magnitude, which has in itself no limits (this is explicit in the next line, 16.19). But they are definite in form, either in that each number is of a definite structure (so Tarán), or in that the whole structure is definite.

268. 16.20 ὡς τὸ εἰκὸς: a stylistic variant for εἰκότως in 16.17.

269. 16.21–22: this could refer either to the idea of one or to the unlimited matter and receptacle. Given the sequel (17.5), it looks more like the latter.

270. The syntax of 16.20–22 (the apodosis of the conditional) is difficult. Dillon (1984), p. 15, translates: "it would be unreasonable not to expect that, since the form of the One that imposes itself upon it is totally uniform, we should get a uniform class of things resulting"; but this is, of course, more paraphrase than translation.

271. Or 'a different cause, for magnitude': see text and Merlan's translation, quoted later n. 276. Tarrant's version (n. 276) seems not to account for the aorist.

272. 17.16 διάστασιν τόπων: Merlan (see n. 276) paraphrases this as "spatial interval"; Tarán (1981), p. 100, follows him. This sounds right.

273. 17.17 πρῶτον: that is, it is here that they first appear, but *first* could be read as saying that position and spatial intervals appear first and then place. This sounds odd. This construal follows Merlan (n. 276), including the supplement anticipating ἐνταῦθα φανῆναι in 17.18.

274. 17.17 κατὰ τὰ αὐτά: or 'in the same ways': see Tarrant's translation, quoted in n. 276.

275. 17.18–19 παρὰ τὸ τὴν . . . διαφορὰν . . . παραδιδόναι; following Tarán (1981), p. 100, n. 445, rather than Merlan, who prints παρὰ τὸν . . . διαφορὰν κτλ., and translates as in n. 276.

276. 17.13–19: Merlan (1960a), p. 130, translates: "After another cause [viz. that] of magnitude has been posited, it remains to posit—just as in numbers the monad conformable to the One, so in lines—the point. Only here [scil. in the realm of geometricals] will appear position and spatial interval in

the case of lines, planes, and solids; but also space conformable to them, [so as], in accordance with the difference of the receptacle, to confer something peculiar to the genus stemming from it."

Contrast here Tarrant (1974), p. 134: "The remaining alternative is to postulate some other cause of magnitude (sc. for geometricals); and, just as the monad is used for the One in numbers, to postulate the point in lines, and position and distance; and (around spaces) lines, areas, and solids first of all, with space too then appearing according to the same principles until the difference in the receptacle bestows its own particular characteristic upon the 'kind' which comes from it."

277. 17.20 συμμεμολυσμένον: see Merlan (1960a), pp. 120–121; see especially Aristotle, *Meteorology* Δ 3. 381a12–22: what is 'scalded' (μεμολυσμένον: this translation is no good) is something that has too much cold in it, or in the medium in which it is 'scalded,' to have what is indeterminate in it 'concocted'; the result is that it is harder and has less moisture in it that something boiled. The alternative, preferred by Tarrant (1974), p. 134, n. 17, and Tarán (1981), p. 100, n. 447, is 'tainted.'

278. 17.21 ἐκ ταύτης: the nearest noun phrase to which this can refer is 17.18–19 τὴν τῆς ὑποδοχῆς διαφοράν.

279. Tarrant (1974), p. 134, gives a translation of 17.20–22 with a very different upshot: "And if one were to make the claim and criticism that the elements of continuity and interfusion arising from this nature were more pronounced and more unwieldy one would not, perhaps, be in error." He has omitted 'than numbers.' The alternative sense 'to give as cause' for αἰτιᾶσθαι is surely better here: the reason the geometricals are continuous rather than discrete, like numbers, is that they come of a different receptacle.

280. 17.22–25: it seems to me likely that something has got mangled here. The author is saying that he includes in the second kind all of lines, planes, and solids, which connects more directly with the sentence at 17.13–19. 17.20–22 is an interruption.

281. 17.28 ὁ λόγος: Tarán (1981), p. 101 'the argument'; Tarrant (1974), p. 135, 'reason'.

282. The One and Plurality: 15.15–16.

283. 18.4 ὑφίσταται: see n. 200. Here the word only means 'exist.'

284. 18.6–7 τῆς γεωμετρικῆς οὐσίας.

285. Merlan (1960a), p. 98, dismisses 18.13–23 along with 14.18–15.5 (see n. 248) as non-Speusippean.

Bibliography

Ackrill, J. L. 1963. *Aristotle's* Categories *and* De Interpretatione, translated with notes. Oxford: Clarendon Press.

Adam, James. 1902. *The Republic of Plato*, 2 vols. Cambridge: Cambridge University Press; reprinted 1963.

Alexander, see Bruns (1887) (*De anima)* and (1892) (*De mixtione*); Hayduck (1891) (*in Met.*); Wallies (1891) (*in Top.*); Wendland (1901) (*in De sensu*).

Allan, D. J. 1936. *Aristotelis De caelo libri quattuor*. Oxford: Clarendon Press (corrected edition, 1955).

______. 1960. "Aristotle and the *Parmenides*." In Düring and Owen (1960), pp. 133–144.

Allen, R. E., ed. 1965. *Studies in Plato's Metaphysics*. London: Routledge & Kegan Paul; New York: The Humanities Press.

______. 1969. "Individual Properties in Aristotle's *Categories*." *Phronesis* 14: 31–39.

______. 1970. *Plato's* Euthyphro *and the Earlier Theory of Forms*. London: Routledge & Kegan Paul; New York: Humanities Press.

______. 1971. "Plato's Earlier Theory of Forms." In G. Vlastos, ed., *The Philosophy of Socrates: A Collection of Critical Essays*, pp. 319–334. Garden City, N.Y.: Doubleday Anchor Books.

______. 1973. "Substance and Predication in Aristotle's *Categories*." In E. N. Lee, A. P. D. Mourelatos, and R. Rorty, eds., *Exegesis and Argument: Studies in Greek Philosophy Presented to Gregory Vlastos*, pp. 362–373 (*Phronesis* Supp. Vol. 1). Assen: Van Gorcum; New York: Humanities Press.

______. 1983. *Plato's* Parmenides: *Translation and Analysis*. Minneapolis: University of Minnesota Press; Oxford: Blackwell.

Annas, Julia. 1974. "Individuals in Aristotle's *Categories*: Two Queries." *Phronesis* 19: 146–152.

______. 1975. "On the Intermediates." *Archiv für Geschichte der Philosophie* 57: 146–166.

______. 1976. *Aristotle's* Metaphysics, *Books M and N*. Oxford: Clarendon Press.

______. 1977. "Aristotle on Substance, Accident and Plato's Forms." *Phronesis* 22: 146–160.

______. 1981. *An Introduction to Plato's* Republic. Oxford: Clarendon Press.

______. 1982. "Aristotle on Inefficient Causes." *Philosophical Quarterly* 32: 3ll–326.

Anonymous, see Westerink (1962).

Anton, John P., and George L. Kustas, eds. 1971. *Essays in Ancient Greek Philosophy*. Albany: State University of New York Press.

______, and Anthony Preus, eds. 1983. *Essays in Ancient Greek Philosophy*, Vol. 2. Albany: State University of New York Press.

Apostle, Hippocrates G. 1966. *Aristotle's* Metaphysics, trans., nn. Bloomington, Ind., London: Indiana University Press.

______. 1969. *Aristotle's* Physics. Bloomington, Ind., London: Indiana University Press.

Archer-Hind, R. D. 1894. *The* Phaedo *of Plato*, 2d ed. London: Macmillan (1st ed., 1883). Reprinted New York: Arno Press, 1973.

Archimedes, see Heiberg and Stamatis (1972).

Arrighetti, Graziano, ed. 1973. *Epicuro: Opere*. Turin: Giulio Einaudi, 1960; rev. ed., 1973.

Asclepius, see Hayduck (1888).

Asmis, Elizabeth. 1984. *Epicurus' Scientific Method*. Ithaca, N.Y., London: Cornell University Press.

Austin, Scott. 1986. *Parmenides: Being, Bounds, and Logic*. New Haven, Conn., London: Yale University Press.

Bailey, Cyril. 1928. *The Greek Atomists and Epicurus: A Study*. Oxford: Clarendon Press, 1928. Reprinted New York: Russell and Russell, 1964.

______. 1947. *Titi Lucreti Cari De rerum natura libri sex, Edited with Pro-*

legomena, Critical Apparatus, Translation, and Commentary, 3 vols. Oxford: Clarendon Press.

Barford, R. 1976. "A Proof from the *Peri Ideon* Revisited." *Phronesis* 21: 198–219.

Barnes, Jonathan. 1976. "Aristotle, Menaechmus, and Circular Proof." *Classical Quarterly* 26: 278–292.

______. 1979 and 1982. *The Presocratic Philosophers*, 2 vols. London, Henley, and Boston: Routledge & Kegan Paul, 1979. Reprinted in one vol., London, New York: Routledge & Kegan Paul, 1982.

______, ed. 1984. *The Complete Works of Aristotle: The Revised Oxford Translation*, 2 vols. Princeton, N.J.: Princeton University Press.

______. 1985. "Editor's Notes." *Phronesis* 30: 99–110.

______, and Gavin Lawrence. 1984. "Fragments." In Barnes (1984), Vol. 2, pp. 2384–2465.

______, M. Schofield, and R. Sorabji, eds. 1975. *Articles on Aristotle*. Vol. 1. *Science*. London: Duckworth.

Becker, Oskar. 1936. "Eudoxos-Studien V: Die eudoxische Lehre von den Ideen und den Farben." *Quellen und Studien zur Geschichte der Mathematik, Astronomie und Physik*, B 3.3: 389–410.

Bekker, Immanuel, ed. 1831. *Aristotelis Opera*, 2 vols. Berlin: G. Reimer; 2d ed., ed. O. Gigon, Berlin: Walter de Gruyter, 1960.

Berti, Enrico. 1962. *La filosofia del primo Aristotele*. Padua: CEDAM.

Bicknell, P. J. 1967. "Parmenides' Refutation of Motion and an Implication." *Phronesis* 12: 1–5.

Bluck, R. S. 1955. *Plato's* Phaedo. London: Routledge & Kegan Paul. Reprinted New York: Liberal Arts Press, 1959.

______. 1975. *Plato's* Sophist: *A Commentary*, ed. Gordon C. Neal. Manchester: Manchester University Press.

Bogaard, P. A. 1979. "Heaps or Wholes: Aristotle's Explanation of Compound Bodies." *Isis* 70: 11–29.

Bogen, James, and James E. McGuire, eds. 1985. *How Things Are: Studies in Predication and the History of Philosophy and Science*. Dordrecht: D. Reidel.

Bolzan, J. E. 1976. "Chemical Combination According to Aristotle." *Ambix* 23: 134–144.

Bonitz, Hermann. 1849. *Aristotelis Metaphysica*, Vol. 2: *Commentaria*. Bonn: Marcus. Reprinted Hildesheim: Georg Olms, 1960.

______. 1870. *Index Aristotelicus*. In Vol. 5 of *Aristotelis Opera*, ed. I. Bekker. Berlin: G. Reimer. Reprinted Graz: Akademische Druck- und Verlagsanstalt, 1955.

Bowen, Alan C. 1982. "The Foundations of Early Pythagorean Harmonic Science: Archytas, Fragment I." *Ancient Philosophy* 2: 79–104.

______. 1983. "Menaechmus *versus* the Platonists: Two Theories of Science in the Early Academy." *Ancient Philosophy* 3: 12–29.

Brakas, George. 1988. *Aristotle's Concept of the Universal. Studien und Materialien zur Geschichte der Philosophie* 26. Hildesheim, Zürich, New York: Georg Olms.

Brandis, C. A., ed. 1836. *Scholia Aristotelis*. Immanuel Bekker, ed., *Aristotelis opera edidit Academia regia borussica*, Vol. 4. Berlin: G. Reimer.

Brandwood, Leonard. 1976. *A Word Index to Plato*. *Compendia*, Vol. 8. Leeds: W. Maney & Son.

Bréhier, Émile. 1962. *La théorie des incorporels dans l'ancien stoïcisme*, 3d ed. Paris: J. Vrin.

Brentlinger, John. 1972. "Incomplete Predicates and the Two-World Theory of the *Phaedo*." *Phronesis* 17: 61–79.

Brown, Patterson. 1966. "Infinite Causal Regression." *Philosophical Review* 75: 510–525. Reprinted in A. Kenny, ed., *Aquinas: A Collection of Critical Essays*, pp. 214–236. Garden City, N.Y.: Anchor Books, 1969.

Brumbaugh, Robert S. 1961. *Plato on the One: The Hypotheses in the* Parmenides. New Haven, Conn.: Yale University Press.

Bruns, Ivo, ed. 1887. *Alexandri Aphrodisiensis Praeter commentaria scripta minora: De anima liber cum mantissa*. *Supplementum aristotelicum* 2.1. Berlin: G. Reimer.

______, ed. 1892. *Alexandri Aphrodisiensis Praeter commentaria scripta minora: Quaestiones, De fato, De mixtione*. *Supplementum aristotelicum* 2.2. Berlin: G. Reimer.

Burger, Ronna. 1984. *The* Phaedo: *A Platonic Labyrinth*. New Haven, Conn., London: Yale University Press.

Burkert, Walter. 1972. *Lore and Science in Ancient Pythagoreanism*, trans. E. L. Minar, Jr. Cambridge, Mass.: Harvard University Press.

Burnet, John. 1900–07. *Platonis opera*, 5 vols. Oxford: Clarendon Press. Vol. 1, 1900; Vol. 2, 1901; Vol. 3, 1903; Vol. 4, 1902; Vol. 5, 1907; often reprinted.

______. 1911. *Plato's* Phaedo. Oxford: Clarendon Press. Reprinted 1924, etc.

Burnyeat, M. F. 1987. "Platonism and Mathematics: A Prelude to Discussion." In Graeser (1987), pp. 213–240.

Cargile, James. 1979. *Paradoxes: A Study in Form and Predication*. Cambridge, London: Cambridge University Press.

Carteron, Henri. 1926, 1931. *Aristote:* Physique, 2 vols. Paris: Société d'Édition "Les Belles Lettres" (Budé). Vol. 1, 1926; Vol. 2, 1931; 3d ed., 1961.

Charlton, W. 1970. *Aristotle's* Physics *Books I and II*. Oxford: Clarendon Press.

Cherniss, Harold. 1932. "Parmenides and the *Parmenides* of Plato." *American Journal of Philology* 53: 122–138. Reprinted in Cherniss (1977), pp. 281–297.

______. 1935. *Aristotle's Criticism of Presocratic Philosophy*. Baltimore: Johns Hopkins Press. Reprinted New York: Octagon Books, 1964.

______. 1944. *Aristotle's Criticism of Plato and the Academy*, Vol. 1. Baltimore: Johns Hopkins Press. Reprinted New York: Russell & Russell, 1962.

______. 1945. *The Riddle of the Early Academy*. Berkeley, Los Angeles: University of California Press. Reprinted New York: Russell & Russell, 1962.

______. 1950–51. "Plato as Mathematician." *Review of Metaphysics* 4: 395–425. Reprinted in Cherniss (1977), pp. 222–252.

______. 1957. "The Relation of the *Timaeus* to Plato's Later Dialogues." *American Journal of Philology* 78: 225–266. Reprinted in Allen (1965), pp. 339–378, Cherniss (1977), pp. 298–339.

______. 1976. *Plutarch's* Moralia, xiii 1. Loeb Classical Library. Cambridge, Mass.: Harvard University Press; London: William Heinemann.

______. 1977. *Selected Papers*, ed. L. Tarán. Leiden: E. J. Brill; New York: Humanities Press.

Chisholm, R. M., ed. 1960. *Realism and the Background of Phenomenology*. Glencoe, Ill.: The Free Press.

Cleve, Felix M. 1949. *The Philosophy of Anaxagoras: An Attempt at Reconstruction*. New York: King's Crown Press, Columbia University.

Code, Alan. 1985. "On the Origins of Some Aristotelian Theses about Predication." In Bogen and McGuire (1985), pp. 101–131, 323–326.

Cohen, S. Marc. 1971. "The Logic of the Third Man." *Philosophical Review* 80: 448–475.

Cole, A. T. 1961. "The *Anonymus Iamblichi* and his Place in Greek Political Theory." *Harvard Studies in Classical Philology* 65: 127–163.

Cook Wilson, J. 1904. "On the Platonist Doctrine of the ἀσύμβλητοι ἀριθμοί." *Classical Review* 18: 247–260. Reprinted in J. Cook Wilson, *On the Interpretation of Plato's* Timaeus*; On the Platonist Doctrine of the* ἀσύμβλητοι ἀριθμοι. New York, London: Garland Publishing Co.

Cornford, F. M. 1930. "Anaxagoras' Theory of Matter." *Classical Quarterly* 24: 14–30, 83–95.

______. 1935. *Plato's Theory of Knowledge: The* Theaetetus *and* Sophist *of Plato*, trans. with running comm. London: Kegan Paul, Trench & Trubner. Reprinted New York: Library of Liberal Arts, 1957.

______. 1939. *Plato and Parmenides: Parmenides'* Way of Truth *and Plato's* Parmenides. London: Routledge & Kegan Paul. Reprinted New York: Liberal Arts Press, 1957.

Cousin, Victor, ed. 1864. *Procli philosophi platonici Opera inedita*, Vol. 3. *Procli Commentarium in Platonis Parmenidem*. Paris. Reprinted Hildesheim: Georg Olms, 1961.

Cresswell, M. J. 1987. "Aristotle's *Phaedo*." *Australasian Journal of Philosophy* 65: 131–155.

Curd, Patricia Kenig. 1986. "*Parmenides* 131c–132b: Unity and Participation." *History of Philosophy Quarterly* 3: 125–136.

Dancy, R. M. 1975a. *Sense and Contradiction: A Study in Aristotle*. Dordrecht, Boston: D. Reidel.

______. 1975b. "On Some of Aristotle's First Thoughts about Substances." *Philosophical Review* 84: 338–373.

______. 1978. "On Some of Aristotle's Second Thoughts about Substances: Matter." *Philosophical Review* 87: 372–413.

______. 1981. "Aristotle and the Priority of Actuality." In S. Knuuttila, ed., *Reforging the Great Chain of Being: Studies of the History of Modal Theories*, pp. 73–115. Dordrecht: D. Reidel.

———. 1983. "Aristotle and Existence." *Synthese* 54: 409–442. Reprinted in Knuuttila and Hintikka (1986), pp. 49–80.

———. 1984. "The One, The Many, and the Forms: *Philebus* 15b1–8." *Ancient Philosophy* 4: 160–193.

Davies, J. Llewelyn. 1897. "Plato's Later Theory of Ideas." *Journal of Philology* 25: 4–25.

De Falco, V., ed. 1975. *[Iamblichi] Theologoumena arithmeticae* [1922]; corrected edition by U. Klein. Stuttgart: B. G. Teubner.

DG, see Diels (1879).

Diehl, E., ed. 1903. *Procli Diadochi in Platonis Timaeum commentaria*. Stuttgart: B. G. Teubner. Reprinted Amsterdam: A. M. Hakkert, 1965.

Diels, Hermann. 1879. *Doxographi Graeci collegit recensuit prolegomenis indicibusque instruxit*. Berlin: Walter de Gruyter, 1965 (photoreprint of edition of 1879).

———, ed. 1882, 1895. *Simplicii in Aristotelis Physicorum commentaria*. *Commentaria in Aristotelem graeca* 9–10. Berlin: Reimer.

DK: Diels, Hermann. *Die Fragmente der Vorsokratiker*, ed. Walther Kranz, 3 vols. 9th ed. Berlin: Weidmann, 1952.

Dillon, John. 1984. "Speusippus in Iamblichus." *Phronesis* 29: 325–332.

DL: Diogenes Laertius, see Long (1964); Hicks (1925).

Dodds, E. R. 1928. "The *Parmenides* of Plato and the Origin of the Neoplatonic 'One'." *Classical Review* 22: 129–142.

———. 1959. *Plato:* Gorgias: *A Revised Text with Introduction and Commentary*. Oxford: Clarendon Press.

Dörrie, Heinrich. 1955a. "Ὑπόστασις: Wort- und Bedeutungsgeschichte." *Nachrichten der Akademie der Wissenschaften*, phil.-hist. Klasse, No. 3: 35–92. Reprinted in Dörrie (1976), pp. 12–69.

———. 1955b. Review of Merlan (1960a). *Philosophische Rundschau* 3: 14–25. Reprinted in Dörrie (1976), pp. 275–285.

———. 1976. *Platonica minora*. *Studia et testimonia antiqua* 8. Munich: W. Fink.

Düring, Ingemar. 1957. *Aristotle in the Ancient Biographical Tradition*. *Studia graeca et latina Gothoburgensia* 5. Göteborg: Elanders.

———. 1960. "Aristotle on Ultimate Principles from 'Nature and Reality': *Protrepticus* Fr. 13." In Düring and Owen (1960), pp. 33–55.

______. 1961. *Aristotle's* Protrepticus*: An Attempt at Reconstruction. Studia Graeca et latina Gothoburgensia* 12. Stockholm: Almqvist & Wiksell.

______. 1966. *Aristoteles: Darstellung und Interpretation seines Denkens.* Heidelberg: Carl Winter.

______, and G. E. L. Owen, eds. 1960. *Aristotle and Plato in the Mid-Fourth Century. Symposium Aristotelicum* 1. *Studia Graeca et Latina Gothoburgensia* XI. Göteborg: Elanders Boktryckeri Aktiebolag.

Ebbesen, Sten. 1986. "The Chimera's Diary." In Knuuttila and Hintikka (1986), pp. 115–143.

Einarson, Benedict, and Phillip H. De Lacey. 1967. *Plutarch's Moralia*, Vol. 14. *1086C–1147A*. Loeb Classical Library. London: William Heinemann; Cambridge, Mass.: Harvard University Press.

Festa, N., ed. 1975. *Iamblichi De communi mathematica scientia liber* [1881], corrected edition by U. Klein. Stuttgart: B. G. Teubner.

Field, G. C. 1930. *Plato and his Contemporaries*. London: Methuen & Co.; 3d ed., 1967.

Findlay, J. N. 1974. *Plato: The Written and Unwritten Doctrines*. London: Routledge & Kegan Paul; New York: Humanities Press.

Fine, Gail. 1982a. "Aristotle and the More Accurate Arguments." In M. Schofield and M. C. Nussbaum, eds., *Language and Logos: Studies in Ancient Greek Philosophy Presented to G. E. L. Owen*, pp. 155–177. Cambridge: Cambridge University Press.

______. 1982b. "Owen, Aristotle, and the Third Man." *Phronesis* 27: 13–33.

______. 1984. "Separation." *Oxford Studies in Ancient Philosophy* 2: 31–87.

______. 1986. "Immanence." *Oxford Studies in Ancient Philosophy* 4: 71–97.

Fowler, D. H. 1987. *The Mathematics of Plato's Academy: A New Reconstruction*. Oxford: Clarendon Press.

Frank, Daniel H. 1984. *The Arguments "From the Sciences" in Aristotle's* Peri Ideon. *American University Studies*, Series V, Philosophy, Vol. 2. New York: Peter Lang.

Frank, Erich. 1923. *Plato und die sogenannten Pythagoreer: Ein Kapitel aus der Geschichte des griechischen Geistes*. Halle: Max Niemeyer.

______. 1955. "Die Begründung der mathematischen Naturwissenschaft durch Eudoxus." In Frank, *Wissen, Wollen, Glauben: gesammelte*

Aufsatze zur Philosophiegeschichte und Existentialphilosophie, ed. L. Edelstein, pp. 134–157. Zürich, Stuttgart: Artemis.

Fränkel, Hermann. 1960. *Wege und Formen frühgriechischen Denkens: literarische und philosophiegeschichtliche Studien*, 2d ed. Munich: C. H. Beck.

Frede, Dorothea. 1978. "The Final Proof of Immortality in Plato's *Phaedo* 102a–107a." *Phronesis* 23: 27–41.

Frede, Michael. 1978. "Individuen bei Aristoteles." *Antike und Abendland* 24: 16–39; trans. W. Mann, "Individuals in Aristotle," in Frede, *Essays in Ancient Philosophy*, pp. 49–71, 367. Minneapolis: University of Minnesota Press, 1987.

Frede, Michael, and Günther Patzig. 1988. *Aristoteles 'Metaphysik Z': Text, Übersetzung und Kommentar*, 2 vols. Munich: C. H. Beck.

Friedländer, Paul. 1958. *Plato* i: *An Introduction*, trans. H. Meyerhoff. New York: Pantheon. 2d ed., Princeton, N.J.: Princeton University Press, 1969.

Friedlein, G., ed. 1873. *Procli Diadochi in primum Euclidis Elementorum librum commentarii*. Leipzig: B. G. Teubner. Reprinted Hildesheim: Georg Olms, 1967.

Fujisawa, Norio. 1974. "Ἔχειν, Μετέχειν, and Idioms of 'Paradeigmatism' in Plato's Theory of Forms." *Phronesis* 19: 30–58.

Furley, David J. 1967. *Two Studies in the Greek Atomists*. Princeton, N.J.: Princeton University Press.

______. 1973. "Notes on Parmenides." In E. N. Lee, A. P. D. Mourelatos, and R. M. Rorty, eds., *Exegesis and Argument: Studies in Greek Philosophy Presented to Gregory Vlastos* (*Phronesis*, Supp. Vol. 1), pp. 1–15. Assen: Van Gorcum; New York: Humanities Press.

______. 1976. "Anaxagoras in Response to Parmenides." In R. A. Shiner and J. King-Farlow, eds., *New Essays on Plato and the Pre-Socratics* (*Canadian Journal of Philosophy*, Supp. Vol. 2), pp. 61–85. Guelph: Canadian Association for Publishing in Philosophy. Reprinted in Anton and Preus (1983), pp. 70–92.

______. 1987. *The Greek Cosmologists*, Vol. 1. *The Formation of the Atomic Theory and its Earliest Critics*. Cambridge, London: Cambridge University Press.

______, and R. E. Allen, eds. 1970, 1975. *Studies in Presocratic Philosophy*,

2 vols. London: Routledge & Kegan Paul; Atlantic Highlands, N.J.: Humanities Press.

Furth, Montgomery. 1971. "Elements of Eleatic Ontology." *Journal of the History of Philosophy* 6: 11–132. Reprinted in Mourelatos (1974), pp. 241–270.

______. 1988. *Substance, Form and Psyche: An Aristotelian Metaphysics*. Cambridge: Cambridge University Press.

Gadamer, Hans-Georg. 1928. "Der aristotelische 'Protreptikos' und die entwicklungsgeschichtliche Betrachtung der aristotelischen Ethik." *Hermes* 63: 138–164. Reprinted in Gadamer, *Gesammelte Werke*, Vol. 5. *Griechische Philosophie* i, pp. 164–186. Tübingen: J. C. B. Mohr (Paul Siebeck), 1985.

Gaiser, Konrad. 1963. *Platons Ungeschriebene Lehre: Studien zur systematischen und geschichtlichen Begründung der Wissenschaften in der Platonischen Schule*. Stuttgart: Ernst Klett (reprinted, with an afterword, 1968).

______. 1965. "Platons Farbenlehre." In H. Flashar and K. Gaiser, eds., *Synusia: Festgabe für W. Schadewalt*, pp. 173–222. Pfullingen: Neske Verlag.

Gallop, David. 1975. *Plato:* Phaedo. Oxford: Clarendon Press.

______. 1984. *Parmenides of Elea: Fragments*. Toronto, Buffalo, London: University of Toronto Press.

Gifford, Edwin Hamilton. 1905. *The* Euthydemus *of Plato*. Oxford: Clarendon Press. Reprinted New York: Arno Press, 1973.

Gigon, Olof. 1958. "Interpretationen zu den antiken Aristoteles-Viten." *Museum Helveticum* 15: 147–193.

______. 1962. *Vita Aristotelis marciana*. Berlin: Walter de Gruyter.

______. 1987. *Aristotelis Opera*, Vol. 3: *Librorum deperditorum fragmenta*. Berlin, New York: Walter de Gruyter.

Glucker, John. 1978. *Antiochus and the Late Academy*. *Hypomnemata* 56. Göttingen: Vandenhoeck & Ruprecht.

Goldschmidt, Victor. 1972. " Ὑπάρχειν et ὑφιστάναι dans la philosophie stoïcienne." *Revue des études grecques* 85: 331–344.

Goodwin, William Watson. 1965. *Syntax of the Moods and Tenses of the Greek Verb*. London: Macmillan; New York: St. Martin's Press (reprint of an edition of 1889).

Gould, Josiah B. 1970. *The Philosophy of Chrysippus*. Albany: State University of New York Press; Leiden: E. J. Brill.

Graeser, Andreas, ed. 1987. *Mathematics and Metaphysics in Aristotle/Mathematik und Metaphysik bei Aristoteles: Akten des X. Symposium Aristotelicum, Sigriswil, 6.–12. September 1984*. Bern, Stuttgart: Verlag Paul Haupt.

Grube, G. M. A. 1931. "Note on *Phaedo* 104d1–3." *Classical Philology* 26: 197–199.

Guthrie, W. K. C. 1962–81. *A History of Greek Philosophy*, 6 vols. Cambridge: Cambridge University Press. Vol. 2, *The Presocratic Tradition from Parmenides to Democritus*, 1965. Vol. 4, *Plato, The Man and his Dialogues: Earlier Period*, 1975. Vol. 5, *The Later Plato and the Academy*, 1978. Vol. 6, *Aristotle: An Encounter*, 1981.

Hackforth, R. 1955. *Plato's* Phaedo. Cambridge: Cambridge University Press.

Hadot, Pierre. 1969. "Zur Vorgeschichte des Begriffs 'Existenz': Ὑπάρχειν bei den Stoikern." *Archiv für Begriffsgeschichte* 13: 115–127.

Hahm, David E. 1977. *The Origins of Stoic Cosmology*. Columbus: Ohio State University Press.

Hammond, N. G. L., and H. H. Scullard, eds. 1970. *The Oxford Classical Dictionary*. Oxford: Clarendon Press.

Hardie, R. P., and R. K. Gaye. 1930. *Aristotle:* Physica. In W. D. Ross, ed., *The Works of Aristotle*, Vol. 2. Oxford: Clarendon Press.

Harlfinger, Dieter. 1975. "Edizione critica del testo del 'De ideis' di Aristotele." In Leszl (1975), pp. 15–39.

Hayduck, M. 1888. *Asclepii in Aristotelis Metaphysicorum libros A–Z commentaria. Commentaria in Aristotelem graeca* 6,2. Berlin: G. Reimer.

———, ed. 1891. *Alexandri Aphrodisiensis in Aristotelis Metaphysica commentaria. Commentaria in Aristotelem graeca* 1. Berlin: G. Reimer.

Heath, Thomas. 1921. *A History of Greek Mathematics*, 2 vols. Oxford: Clarendon Press.

———. 1926. *The Thirteen Books of Euclid's* Elements, 3 vols., 2d ed. Cambridge: Cambridge University Press (1st ed., 1908). Reprinted New York: Dover Press, 1956.

Heiberg, J. L., ed. 1893. *Simplicii in Aristotelis De caelo commentaria. Commentaria in Aristotelem graeca* 7. Berlin: G. Reimer.

______, and E. S. Stamatis, eds. 1969–77. *Euclides Elementa*, 4 vols., and *Scholia*, 1 vol. in 2 parts. Leipzig: B. G. Teubner.

______, and ______, eds. 1972. *Archimedis Opera omnia cum commentariis Eutocii*. Stuttgart: B. G. Teubner.

Heinaman, Robert. 1981. "Non-substantial Individuals in the *Categories*." *Phronesis* 26: 295–307.

Heinze, Richard. 1892. *Xenokrates: Darstellung der Lehre und Sammlung der Fragmente*. Leipzig: B. G. Teubner. Reprinted Hildesheim: Georg Olms, 1965.

Henry, Paul, and Hans-Rudolph Schwyzer, eds. 1964–82. *Plotini Opera*, 3 vols. Oxford: Clarendon Press.

Hicks, R. D. 1907. *Aristotle:* De Anima. Cambridge: Cambridge University Press. Reprinted Amsterdam: Adolf M. Hakkert, 1965.

______. 1925. *Diogenes Laertius: Lives of Eminent Philosophers*, 2 vols. Loeb Classical Library. Cambridge, Mass.: Harvard University Press; London: William Heinemann.

Hoche, Richard. 1886. *Nicomachi Geraseni pythagorei Introductionis arithmeticae libri II*. Leipzig: B. G. Teubner.

Huffman, Carl. 1988. "The Role of Number in Philolaus' Philosophy." *Phronesis* 33: 1–30.

Hussey, Edward. 1983. *Aristotle's* Physics, *Books III and IV*. Oxford: Clarendon Press.

Huxley, G. L. 1963. "Studies in the Greek Astronomers, I: Eudoxian Topics." *Greek, Roman and Byzantine Studies* 4: 83–96.

______. 1970. "Eudoxus of Cnidus." In C. C. Gillispie, ed., *Dictionary of Scientific Biography*, Vol. 4, pp. 465b–467b. New York: Scribner's.

Iamblichus, see Festa (1975).

[Iamblichus], see De Falco (1975).

Irwin, Terence. 1979. *Plato:* Gorgias. Oxford: Clarendon Press.

______. 1988. *Aristotle's First Principles*. Oxford: Clarendon Press.

Isnardi Parente, Margherita. 1971a. "Ancora su Προηγουμένως in Speusippo." *La Parola del Passato* 26 [fasc. 137]: 120–128.

______. 1971b. "Théophraste, *Metaphysica* 6a23 ss." *Phronesis* 16: 49–64.

______. 1975. "Proodos in Speusippo?" *Athenaeum* 53: 88–110.

———. 1979. *Studia sull'Accademia platonica antica*. *Saggi filosofici* 1. Florence: Olschki.

———. 1980. *Speusippo: Frammenti; Edizione, traduzione e commento*. Naples: Bibliopolis.

———. 1981. *Senocrate, Ermodoro: Frammenti; Edizione, traduzione e commento*. Naples: Bibliopolis.

Jackson, Henry. 1882. "On Plato's *Republic* VI 509D sqq." *Journal of Philology* 10: 132–150.

Jacoby, F. 1902. *Apollodors Chronik*. *Philologische Untersuchungen* 16. Berlin.

Jaeger, Werner. 1948. *Aristotle: Fundamentals of the History of His Development*, trans. R. Robinson, 2d ed. Oxford: Clarendon Press.

———. 1957. *Aristotelis Metaphysica*. Oxford: Clarendon Press.

Joachim, H. H. 1903. "Aristotle's Conception of Chemical Combination." *Journal of Philology* 29: 72–86.

———. 1922. *Aristotle* On Coming-to-be and Passing-Away. Oxford: Clarendon Press.

Jones, Barrington. 1972. "Individuals in Aristotle's *Categories*." *Phronesis* 17: 107–123.

Kahn, Charles. 1985. "The Beautiful and the Genuine: A Discussion of Paul Woodruff, *Plato, Hippias Major*." *Oxford Studies in Ancient Philosophy* 3: 261–287.

———. 1988. "On the Relative Date of the *Gorgias* and the *Protagoras*." *Oxford Studies in Ancient Philosophy* 6: 69–102.

Karpp, Heinrich. 1933. *Untersuchungen zur Philosophie des Eudoxos von Knidos*. Würzburg-Anmühle: Verlag Konrad Triltsch.

Kerferd, G. B. 1969. "Anaxagoras and the Concept of Matter before Aristotle." *Bulletin of the John Rylands Library* 52: 129–143. Reprinted in Mourelatos (1974), pp. 489–503.

———. 1981. *The Sophistic Movement*. Cambridge, London: Cambridge University Press.

Keyt, David. 1963. "The Fallacies in *Phaedo* 102a–107b." *Phronesis* 8: 167–172.

Kirk, G. S., and J. E. Raven. 1957. *The Presocratic Philosophers: A Critical History with a Selection of Texts*. Cambridge: Cambridge University

Press; corrected reprints 1960, 1962, 1963; 2d ed., Kirk, Raven, and Schofield (1983).

______, ______, and M. Schofield. 1983. *The Presocratic Philosophers: A Critical History with a Selection of Texts*, 2d ed. Cambridge, London: Cambridge University Press.

______, and Michael C. Stokes. 1960. "Parmenides' Refutation of Motion." *Phronesis* 5: 1–4.

Klein, Jacob. 1934–36. "Die griechische Logistik und die Entstehung der Algebra." *Quellen und Studien zur Geschichte der Mathematik, Astronomie und Physik*, Abt. B: *Studien* 3.1 (1934): 18–105, 3.2 (1936): 122–235. Translation, see Klein (1968).

______. 1968. *Greek Mathematical Thought and the Origin of Algebra*, trans. Eva Brann. Cambridge, Mass., London: The M.I.T. Press.

Klibansky, R., and C. Labowsky, eds. 1953. *Plato Latinus*, Vol. 3. *Parmenides usque ad finem primae hypothesis nec non Procli commentarium in Parmenidem pars ultima adhuc inedita interprete Guillelmo de Moerbeka*. London: Warburg Institute.

Kneale, William, and Martha Kneale. 1962. *The Development of Logic*. Oxford: Clarendon Press (corrected reprint, 1975).

Knorr, Wilbur R. 1975. *The Evolution of the Euclidean Elements: A Study of the Theory of Incommensurable Magnitudes and Its Significance for Early Greek Geometry*. Dordrecht: D. Reidel.

______. 1978. "Archimedes and the Pre-Euclidean Proportion Theory." *Archives internationales d'histoire des sciences* 28: 183–244.

______. 1983. "Construction as Existence Proof in Ancient Geometry." *Ancient Philosophy* 3: 125–148.

______. 1986. *The Ancient Tradition of Geometrical Problems*. Boston, Basel, Stuttgart: Birkhäuser.

Knuuttila, S., and J. Hintikka, eds. 1986. *The Logic of Being: Historical Studies*. Dordrecht, Boston: D. Reidel.

Krämer, Hans Joachim. 1964. *Der Ursprung der Geistesmetaphysik: Untersuchungen zur Geschichte des Platonismus zwischen Platon und Plotin*. Amsterdam: P. Schippers.

______. 1969. "'ΕΠΕΚΕΙΝΑ ΤΗΣ ΟΥΣΙΑΣ: Zu Platon, Politeia 509 B." *Archiv für Geschichte der Philosophie* 51: 1–30.

Kroll, G., ed. 1902. *Syriani in Metaphysica commentaria. Commentaria in Aristotelem graeca* 6,1. Berlin: Reimer.

Kühner-Gerth: Kühner, Raphael, and Bernhard Gerth, *Ausführliche Grammatik der griechischen Sprache*, Part 2: *Satzlehre*, 2 vols. Hannover, Leipzig: Hahn. Vol. 1, 1898; Vol. 2, 1904; reprinted 1966.

Kung, Joan. 1981. "Aristotle on Thises, Suches and the Third Man." *Phronesis* 26: 207–247.

Lambert, Karel. 1983. *Meinong and the Principle of Independence: Its Place in Meinong's Theory of Objects and Its Significance in Contemporary Philosophical Logic*. Cambridge, London: Cambridge University Press.

Lang, Paul. 1911. *De Speusippi Academici scriptis*. Bonn (dissertation). Reprinted Hildesheim: Georg Olms, 1965.

Lasserre, François. 1966. *Die Fragmente des Eudoxos von Knidos*. Berlin: Walter de Gruyter.

Leszl, Walter. 1975. *Il 'De ideis' di Aristotele e la teoria platonica delle idee. Academia Toscana di Scienze e lettere, 'La Colombaria', Studi* 40. Florence: Leo S. Olschki.

Lewis, Frank A. 1985. "Plato's Third Man Argument and the 'Platonism' of Aristotle." In Bogen and McGuire (1985), pp. 133–174.

Lloyd, A. C. 1976. "The Principle that the Cause is Greater than its Effect." *Phronesis* 21: 146–156.

Lloyd, G. E. R. 1966. *Polarity and Analogy: Two Types of Argumentation in Early Greek Thought*. Cambridge: Cambridge University Press.

Long, A. A. 1971a. "Language and Thought in Stoicism." In Long (1971b), pp. 75–113.

———, ed. 1971b. *Problems in Stoicism*. London: Athlone Press of the University of London.

———. 1974. *Hellenistic Philosophy: Stoics, Epicureans, Sceptics*. New York: Charles Scribner's Sons.

———, and D. N. Sedley. 1987. *The Hellenistic Philosophers*, 2 vols. Cambridge: Cambridge University Press.

Long, H. S. ed. 1964. *Diogenis Laertii Vitae philosophorum*, 2 vols. Oxford: Clarendon Press.

Malcolm, John. 1968. "On the Place of the *Hippias Major* in the Development of Plato's Thought." *Archiv für Geschichte der Philosophie* 50: 189–195.

Mates, Benson. 1979. "Identity and Predication in Plato." *Phronesis* 24: 211–229.

Mathewson, R. 1958. "Aristotle and Anaxagoras: An Examination of F. M. Cornford's Interpretation." *Classical Quarterly* 8: 67–81.

Matthen, Mohan. 1984. "Forms and Participants in Plato's *Phaedo*." *Nous* 18: 281–297.

Matthews, G. B., and S. M. Cohen. 1967–68. "The One and the Many." *Review of Metaphysics* 21: 630–655.

Meinong, Alexius. 1904. "Über Gegenstandstheorie." Reprinted in Meinong (1971), pp. 483–530.

______. 1971. *Gesamtausgabe* ii: *Abhandlungen zur Erkenntnistheorie und Gegenstandstheorie*, ed. R. Haller. Graz: Akademische Druck- und Verlagsanstalt.

Merlan, Philip. 1960a. *From Platonism to Neoplatonism*. The Hague: Martinus Nijhoff, 1954; 2d ed., 1960; 3d ed., 1968 (pagination the same as in 1960 edition).

______. 1960b. "The Life of Eudoxus." Appendix to *Studies in Epicurus and Aristotle*, pp. 98–104. *Klassisch-philologische Studien* 22. Wiesbaden: Harrassowitz.

______. 1967. "Greek Philosophy from Plato to Plotinus." In A. H. Armstrong, ed., *The Cambridge History of Later Greek and Early Medieval Philosophy*, pp. 11–132. Cambridge: Cambridge University Press.

Miller, Mitchell H., Jr. 1986. *Plato's* Parmenides*: The Conversion of the Soul*. Princeton, N.J.: Princeton University Press.

Minio-Paluello, L. 1956. *Aristotelis Categoriae et liber de interpretatione*, 2d ed. Oxford: Clarendon Press.

Mohr, Richard. 1984. "Forms in Plato's *Euthydemus*." *Hermes* 112: 296–300.

______. 1985. *The Platonic Cosmology*. *Philosophia Antiqua* 42. Leiden: E. J. Brill.

Moorhouse, A. C. 1962. "ΔEN in Classical Greek." *Classical Quarterly* 12: 235–238.

Morani, Moreno. 1987. *Nemesii Emesini De natura hominis*. Leipzig: B. G. Teubner.

Moreau, Joseph. 1956. Review of Merlan (1960a) (1st ed.). *Revue Belge de Philologie et d'Histoire* 34: 1164–1167.

Morrow, G. R. 1970. *Proclus: A Commentary on the First Book of Euclid's* Elements. Princeton, N.J.: Princeton University Press.

Mourelatos, Alexander P. D. 1970. *The Route of Parmenides: A Study of Word, Image, and Argument in the Fragments*. New Haven, Conn., London: Yale University Press.

______, ed. 1974. *The Pre-Socratics: A Collection of Critical Essays*. Garden City, N.Y.: Doubleday Anchor.

______. 1976. "Determinacy and Indeterminacy, Being and Non-Being in the Fragments of Parmenides." In R. A. Shiner and J. King-Farlow, eds., *New Essays on Plato and the Pre-Socratics*, pp. 45–60. *Canadian Journal of Philosophy*, Supp. Vol. 2. Guelph, Ontario: Canadian Association for Publishing in Philosophy.

______. 1979. "'Nothing' as 'Not-Being': Some Literary Contexts that Bear on Plato." In G. W. Bowersock, W. Burkert, and M. C. J. Putnam, eds., *Arktouros: Studies Presented to Bernard M. W. Knox*, pp. 319–329. Berlin, New York: Walter de Gruyter.

Mueller, Ian. 1980. *Coping with Mathematics (The Greek Way)*. Chicago: Morris Fishbein Center for the Study of the History of Science and Medicine, Publication no. 2.

______. 1981. *Philosophy of Mathematics and Deductive Structure in Euclid's* Elements. Cambridge, Mass., London: The M.I.T. Press.

______. 1986. "On Some Academic Theories of Mathematical Objects." *Journal of Hellenic Studies* 106: 111–120.

______. 1987. "Aristotle's Approach to the Problem of Principles in *Metaphysics* M and N." In Graeser (1987), pp. 241–259.

Nehamas, Alexander. 1972–73. "Predication and Forms of Opposites in the *Phaedo*." *Review of Metaphysics* 26: 461–491.

Nemesius, see Morani (1987).

Nicomachus, see Hoche (1886).

Niebel, Eckhard. 1959. *Untersuchungen über die Bedeutung der geometrische Konstruktion in der Antike*. *Kantstudien* Ergänzungshefte 76. Cologne: Kölner Universitäts-Verlag.

O'Brien, Dennis. 1967, 1968. "The Last Argument of Plato's *Phaedo*." *Classical Quarterly* 17 (1967): 198–231, 18 (1968): 95–106.

Owen, G. E. L. 1953. "The Place of the *Timaeus* in Plato's Dialogues." *Classical Quarterly* 3: 79–95. Reprinted in Allen (1965), pp. 313–338; Owen (1986), pp. 65–84.

______. 1957. "A Proof in the ΠΕΡΙ ΙΔΕΩΝ," *Journal of Hellenic Studies* 77: 103–111. Reprinted in Allen (1965), pp. 293–312; Owen (1986), pp. 165–179.

______. 1960. "Eleatic Questions." *Classical Quarterly* 10: 84–102. Reprinted in Furley and Allen (1975), pp. 48–81, Owen (1986), pp. 3–26.

______. 1965a. "Inherence." *Phronesis* 10: 97–105; R. Nickel, "Inhärenz," trans. in F.-P. Hager, ed., *Logik und Erkenntnistheorie des Aristoteles*, pp. 296–307. Darmstadt: Wissenschaftliche Buchgesellschaft, 1972. Reprinted in Owen (1986), pp. 252–258.

______. 1965b. "The Platonism of Aristotle." *Proceedings of the British Academy* 51: 125–150. Reprinted in Strawson (1968), pp. 147–174; Barnes et al. (1975), pp. 14–34; Owen (1986), pp. 200–220.

______. 1968. "Dialectic and Eristic in the Treatment of the Forms." In Owen, ed., *Aristotle on Dialectic: The* Topics. *Proceedings of the Third Symposium Aristotelicum*, pp. 103–125. Oxford: Clarendon Press. Reprinted in Owen (1986), pp. 221–238.

______. 1970. "Plato on Not-Being." In Vlastos (1970), pp. 223–267. Reprinted in Owen (1986), pp. 104–137.

______. 1986. *Logic, Science, and Dialectic: Collected Papers in Greek Philosophy*, ed. M. Nussbaum. London: Duckworth; Ithaca, N.Y.: Cornell University Press.

Parsons, Terence. 1980. *Nonexistent Objects*. New Haven, Conn.: Yale University Press.

Partington, H. R. 1961. *History of Chemistry*, Vol. 1, Part 1, Ch. 4, "Aristotle," pp. 69–122. London: Macmillan.

Peck, A. L. 1931. "Anaxagoras: Predication as a Problem in Physics." *Classical Quarterly* 25: 27–37, 112–120.

Philippson, Robert. 1925. "Akademische Verhandlungen über die Lustlehre." *Hermes* 60: 444–481.

______. 1936. "Il ΠΕΡΙ ΙΔΕΩΝ di Aristotele." *Rivista di filologia e di istruzione classica* 64: 113–125.

Philoponus, see Vitelli (1887–88), Vitelli (1897).

Plotinus, see Henry and Schwyzer (1964–82).

Plutarch, see Einarson and De Lacey (1967), Cherniss (1976).

Prauss, Gerold. 1966. *Platon und der logische Eleatismus*. Berlin: Walter de Gruyter.

Proclus, see Diehl (1903) (*in Tim.*); Friedlein (1873) (*in Eucl.*); Cousin (1864) (*in Prm.*).

Pseudo-Alexander, see Hayduck (1891).

Rabinowitz, W. Gerson. 1957. *Aristotle's* Protrepticus *and the Sources of Its Reconstruction. University of California Publications in Classical Philology* 16.1. Berkeley, Los Angeles: University of California Press.

Reesor, Margaret E. 1954. "The Stoic Concept of Quality." *American Journal of Philology* 75: 40–58.

______. 1957. "The Stoic Categories." *American Journal of Philology* 78: 63–82.

Reeve, C. D. C. 1981. "Anaxagorean Panspermism." *Ancient Philosophy* 1: 89–108.

Reynolds, L. D. 1965. *L. Annaei Senecae ad Lucilium epistulae morales*, 2 vols. Oxford: Clarendon Press.

Rist, John M. 1962. "The Neoplatonic One and Plato's *Parmenides*." *Transactions of the American Philological Association* 93: 389–401.

______. 1969. *Stoic Philosophy*. Cambridge: Cambridge University Press.

______. 1971. "Categories and Their Uses." In Long (1971b), pp. 38–57 (= Rist [1969], pp. 152–172).

______. 1985. "The End of Aristotle's *On Prayer*." *American Journal of Philology* 106: 110–113.

______. 1989. *The Mind of Aristotle: A Study in Philosophical Growth. Phoenix* Supp. Vol. 25. Toronto, Buffalo, London: University of Toronto Press.

Robinson, John Mansley. 1968. *An Introduction to Early Greek Philosophy: The Chief Fragments and Ancient Testimony, with Connecting Commentary*. Boston, New York: Houghton Mifflin Co.

Rose, V., ed. 1886. *Aristotelis qui ferebantur librorum fragmenta*. Stuttgart: B. G. Teubner, 1886; reprinted 1967.

Ross, W. D. 1924. *Aristotle's* Metaphysics*: A Revised Text with Introduction and Commentary*, 2 vols. Oxford: Clarendon Press (corrected reprint, 1953).

______. 1928. *The Works of Aristotle Translated into English*. Vol. 8. *Metaphysica*. Oxford: Clarendon Press, 1908; 2d ed., 1928.

______. 1936. *Aristotle's* Physics*: A Revised Text with Introduction and Commentary*. Oxford: Clarendon Press (corrected reprint, 1955).

______. 1951. *Plato's Theory of Ideas*. Oxford: Clarendon Press; corrected 2d ed., 1953.

______. 1952. *The Works of Aristotle Translated into English*. Vol. 12. *Select Fragments*. Oxford: Clarendon Press.

______, ed. 1955a. *Aristotelis Fragmenta selecta*. Oxford: Clarendon Press; reprinted 1958.

______. 1955b. *Aristotle: Parva Naturalia*. Oxford: Clarendon Press.

______, and F. H. Fobes. 1929. *Theophrastus: Metaphysics*. Oxford: Clarendon Press. Reprinted Hildesheim: Georg Olms, 1967.

Routley, Richard. 1980.*Exploring Meinong's Jungle and Beyond: An Investigation of Noneism and the Theory of Items* (Interim edition). Canberra, Australia: Australian National University.

Rowe, C. J. 1979. "The Proof from Relatives in the *Peri Ideon*: Further Reconsideration." *Phronesis* 24: 270–281.

Runciman, W. G. 1959. "Plato's *Parmenides*." *Harvard Studies in Classical Philology* 64: 89–119. Reprinted in Allen (1965), pp. 149–184 (cited from this reprint).

______. 1962. *Plato's Later Epistemology*. Cambridge: Cambridge University Press.

Ryle, Gilbert. 1966. *Plato's Progress*. Cambridge: Cambridge University Press.

Sachs, Eva. 1914. *De Theaeteto Atheniensi mathematico*. Berlin: Inaugural diss. (O. Francke).

Sandbach, F. H. 1930. "Ἔννοια and Πρόληψις in the Stoic Theory of Knowledge." *Classical Quarterly* 24: 44–51. Reprinted in Long (1971b), pp. 22–37.

Schiller, Jerome. 1967. "*Phaedo* 104–105: Is The Soul a Form?" *Phronesis* 12: 50–58.

Schofield, Malcolm. 1973. "Eudoxus in the *Parmenides*", *Museum Helveticum* 30: 1–19.

______. 1975. "Doxographica Anaxagorea." *Hermes* 103: 1–24.

______. 1980a. *An Essay on Anaxagoras*. Cambridge: Cambridge University Press.

______. 1980b. "Perception, Argument, and God." In Schofield, Burnyeat, and Barnes (1980), pp. 283–308.

______, Myles Burnyeat, and Jonathan Barnes, eds. 1980. *Doubt and Dogmatism: Studies in Hellenistic Epistemology*. Oxford: Clarendon Press.

Sedley, David. 1982. "Two Conceptions of Vacuum." *Phronesis* 27: 175–193.

Seneca, see Reynolds (1965).

Shorey, Paul. 1903. *The Unity of Plato's Thought*. Chicago: University of Chicago Press; reprinted 1960.

______. 1930, 1935. *Plato* v–vi: *The Republic*, 2 vols. Loeb Classical Library. London: William Heinemann; Cambridge, Mass.: Harvard University Press (rev. ed. of Vol. 1, 1937).

Simplicius, see Diels (1882, 1895) (*in Phys.*); Heiberg (1893) (*in De caelo*).

Sorabji, Richard. 1972. "Aristotle, Mathematics, and Color." *Classical Quarterly* 22: 293–308.

______. 1983. *Time, Creation and the Continuum: Theories in Antiquity and the Early Middle Ages*. London: Duckworth.

Sprague, Rosamond Kent. 1962. *Plato's Use of Fallacy: A Study of the* Euthydemus *and Some Other Dialogues*. London: Routledge & Kegan Paul.

______. 1965. *Plato:* Euthydemus. Indianapolis: Bobbs-Merrill.

______. 1967. "Parmenides' Sail and Dionysodorus' Ox." *Phronesis* 12: 91–98.

______. 1973. *Plato:* Laches *and* Charmides. Indianapolis: Bobbs-Merrill.

Stallbaum, G. 1885. *Platonis Opera omnia* i 2: *Phaedo*, ed. 3. Gotha: Hennings.

Stenzl, Julius. 1929. "Speusippos." *Paulys Real-encyclopädie der classischen Altertumswissenschaft*, ed. G. Wissowa, W. Kroll, et al. Stuttgart: J. B. Metzler, 1893ff.: 2nd series, Vol. 6, coll. 1636–1669.

Stocks, J. L. 1930. *De caelo*. In W. D. Ross, ed., *The Works of Aristotle*, Vol. 2. Oxford: Clarendon Press.

Strang, Colin. 1963. "Plato and the Third Man." *Proceedings of the Aristotelian Society, Supplementary Volume* 37: 147–164. Reprinted in Vlastos (1970–71), Vol. 1, pp. 184–200.

Strawson, P. F., ed. 1968. *Studies in the Philosophy of Thought and Action*. London: Oxford University Press.

SVF, see von Arnim (1903–24).

Syrianus, see Kroll (1902).

Tarán, Leonardo. 1971. "The Creation Myth in Plato's *Timaeus*." In Anton and Kustas (1971), pp. 372–407.

———. 1979. "Aristotle, *Metaphysics* Z 2, 1028 B 13–19." *Mnemosyne* Series 4, Vol. 32: 167–170.

———. 1981. *Speusippus of Athens: A Critical Study with a Collection of the Related Texts and Commentary*. *Philosophia Antiqua* 39. Leiden: E. J. Brill.

Tarrant, Dorothy. 1928. *The* Hippias Major *Attributed to Plato*. Cambridge: Cambridge University Press.

Tarrant, H. A. S. 1974. "Speusippus' Ontological Classification." *Phronesis* 19: 130–145.

———. 1985. Review of Tarán (1981). *Classical Philology* 80: 78–83.

Taylor, A. E. 1915–16. "Parmenides, Zeno and Socrates." *Proceedings of the Aristotelian Society* 16: 243–289. Reprinted in Taylor (1934a), pp. 28–90.

———. 1934a. *Philosophical Studies*. London: Macmillan & Co.

———. 1934b. *Plato: The* Laws. London: J. M. Dent & Sons. Reprinted as *Everyman's Library* 275. London: J. M. Dent & Sons; New York: E. P. Dutton & Co., 1960; also in E. Hamilton and H. Cairns, eds., *The Collected Dialogues of Plato, Including the Letters*, pp. 1226–1513. New York: Pantheon Books, 1961.

———. 1961. *Plato: The* Sophist *and the* Statesman, ed. R. Klibansky and E. Anscombe. London: Thomas Nelson & Sons.

Teloh, Henry, and David James Louzecky. 1972. "Plato's Third Man Argument." *Phronesis* 17: 80–94.

Theophrastus, see Ross and Fobes (1929).

Thomas, Ivor. 1939. *Selections Illustrating the History of Greek Mathematics*, Vol. 1. *From Thales to Euclid*. Loeb Classical Library. Cambridge, Mass.: Harvard University Press; London: William Heinemann.

Todd, Robert B. 1976. *Alexander of Aphrodisias on Stoic Physics: A Study of the* De mixtione *with Preliminary Essays, Text, Translation, and Commentary*. *Philosophia Antiqua* 28. Leiden: E. J. Brill.

Ueberweg/Praechter: *Friedrich Ueberwegs Grundriss der Geschichte der Philosophie*, 1. Theil. *Die Philosophie des Altertums*, ed. Karl Praechter. Berlin: S. Mittler & Sohn, 1926. Reprinted Basel, Stuttgart: Benno Schwabe & Co., 1960.

Usener, Hermann. 1887. *Epicurea*. Leipzig: B. G. Teubner. Reprinted Dubuque, Iowa: Wm. C. Brown Reprint Library, n.d.

Verdenius, W. J. 1958. "Notes on Plato's *Phaedo.*" *Mnemosyne* Series 4, Vol. 11: 193–243.

Vitelli, H., ed. 1887–88. *Ioannis Philoponi in Aristotelis Physicorum commentaria. Commentaria in Aristotelem graeca* 16–17. Berlin: G. Reimer.

______, ed. 1897. *Ioannis Philoponi in Aristotelis libros De generatione et corruptione commentaria. Commentaria in Aristotelem graeca* 14,2. Berlin: G. Reimer.

Vlastos, Gregory. 1939. "The Disorderly Motion in the *Timaeus.*" *Classical Quarterly* 33: 71–83. Reprinted, with additions, in Allen (1965), pp. 379–399.

______. 1950. "The Physical Theory of Anaxagoras." *Philosophical Review* 59: 31–57. Reprinted in Mourelatos (1974), pp. 459–488, Furley and Allen (1975), pp. 323–353.

______. 1954. "The Third Man Argument in the *Parmenides.*" *Philosophical Review* 63: 319–349. Reprinted in Allen (1965), pp. 231–263.

______. 1956. "Postscript to the Third Man: A Reply to Mr. Geach." *Philosophical Review* 65: 83–94. Reprinted in Allen (1965), pp. 279–291.

______. 1965. "Creation in the *Timaeus*: Is It a Fiction? (1964)." In Allen (1965), pp. 401–419.

______. 1969a. "Reasons and Causes in the *Phaedo.*" *Philosophical Review* 78: 291–325. Reprinted in Vlastos (1970), pp. 132–166; Vlastos (1973a), pp. 76–110.

______. 1969b. "Plato's 'Third Man' Argument (*Parm.* 132A1-B2): Text and Logic." *Philosophical Quarterly* 19: 289–301. Reprinted in Vlastos (1973a), pp. 342–365 (revised).

______, ed. 1970, 1971. *Plato: A Collection of Critical Essays*. Garden City, N.Y.: Doubleday Anchor Books. Vol. 1, *Metaphysics and Epistemology*, 1970; Vol. 2, *Ethics, Politics, and Philosophy of Art and Religion*, 1971. Both vols. reprinted Notre Dame, Ind.: University of Notre Dame Press, 1978.

______. 1973a. *Platonic Studies*. Princeton, N.J.: Princeton University Press; 2d ed., 1981.

______. 1973b. "The 'Two-Level Paradoxes' in Aristotle." In Vlastos (1973a), pp. 323–334.

______. 1987. "'Separation' in Plato." In *Oxford Studies in Ancient Philosophy* 5: 187–196.

von Arnim, Hans. 1903–24. *Stoicorum veterum fragmenta*, 4 vols. Leipzig: B. G. Teubner. Vols. 2 and 3, 1903; Vol. 1, 1905, Vol. 4, 1924. Reprinted Wm. C. Brown Reprint Library, n.d.

______. 1914. *Platons Jugenddialoge und die Entstehungszeit der Phaidros*. Leipzig: Teubner. Reprinted New York: Arno Press, 1976.

von Fritz, Kurt. 1926–27. "Die Ideenlehre des Eudoxos von Knidos und ihr Verhältnis zur platonischen Ideenlehre." *Philologus* 82: 1–26. Reprinted in von Fritz, *Schriften zur griechischen Logik*, Vol. 1, pp. 147–169. Stuttgart: Frommann, 1978.

______. 1935. Review of Karpp (1933). *Gnomon* 11: 407–416.

Wagner, Hans. 1967. *Aristoteles: Physikvorlesung*. Vol. 11 of *Aristoteles Werke in deutscher Übersetzung*, ed. E. Grumach and H. Flashar. Berlin: Akademie-Verlag; Darmstadt: Wissenschaftliche Buchgesellschaft; 2d ed., 1972.

Wallies, M., ed. 1891. *Alexandri Aphrodisiensis in Aristotelis Topicorum libros octo commentaria. Commentaria in Aristotelem graeca* 2.2. Berlin: G. Reimer.

Walzer, Richard, ed. 1934. *Aristotelis Dialogorum fragmenta in usum scholarum*. Florence: G. Sansoni. Reprinted Hildesheim: Georg Olms, 1963.

Watson, Gerard. 1966. *The Stoic Theory of Knowledge*. Belfast: The Queen's University.

Wedberg, Anders. 1955. *Plato's Philosophy of Mathematics*. Stockholm: Almqvist & Wiksell.

Wedin, Michael V. 1980. "'Said of' and 'Predicated of' in the *Categories*." *Philosophy Research Archives* 5: 419–432.

Weinberg, Steven. 1977. *The First Three Minutes: A Modern View of the Origin of the Universe*. New York: Basic Books.

Wendland, Paul, ed. 1901. *Alexandri in librum De sensu commentarium. Commentaria in Aristotelem greaca* 3.1. Berlin: G. Reimer.

West, M. L. 1966. *Hesiod: Theogony, Edited with Prolegomena and Commentary*. Oxford: Clarendon Press.

Westerink, L. G. 1962. *Anonymous Prolegomena to Platonic Philosophy: Introduction, Text, Translation and Indices*. Amsterdam: North-Holland Publishing Co.

White, Nicholas P. 1979. *A Companion to Plato's* Republic. Indianapolis, Cambridge: Hackett.

Whittaker, John. 1969. " Ἐπέκεινα νοῦ καὶ οὐσίας." *Vigiliae Christianae* 23: 91–104.

Wieland, Wolfgang. 1982. *Platon und die Formen des Wissens*. Göttingen: Vandenhoeck & Ruprecht.

Williams, C. J. F. 1982. *Aristotle's* De Generatione et Corruptione. Oxford: Clarendon Press.

Wilpert, Paul. 1949. *Zwei aristotelische Frühschriften über die Ideenlehre*. Regensburg: Verlag Jose Habbel.

Wilson, see Cook Wilson.

Woodruff, Paul. 1978. "Socrates and Ontology: The Evidence of the *Hippias Major*." *Phronesis* 23: 101–117.

______. 1982. *Plato:* Hippias Major. Indianapolis: Hackett Publishing Co.; Oxford: Blackwell.

Zeuthen, H. G. 1896. "Die geometrische Construction als 'Existenzbeweis' in der antiken Geometrie." *Mathematische Annalen* 47: 222–228.

Index Locorum

Principal discussions are indicated by **bold** *type.*

General Index